CORPORATIONS, ENTREPRENEURS, POLICY MAKERS

BY WAY OF
ADVICE

GROWTH STRATEGIES FOR
THE MARKET DRIVEN WORLD

CORPORATIONS, ENTREPRENEURS, POLICY MAKERS

BY WAY OF ADVICE

GROWTH STRATEGIES FOR THE MARKET DRIVEN WORLD

MARCEL CÔTÉ
A VIEW FROM THE GARDEN

MOSAIC PRESS
Oakville - New York - London

CANADIAN CATALOGUING IN PUBLICATION DATA

Côté, Marcel, 1942-
     By way of advice : growth strategies for the market driven world

Includes bibliographical references and index.
ISBN 0-88962-492-5 (bound)   ISBN 0-88962-493-3 (pbk.)

1. Economic development.   2. Entrepreneurship.
I. Title

HD82.C67 1991   338.9   C91-095083-0

Co-published by MOSAIC PRESS, P.O. Box 1032, Oakville, Ontario, L6J 5E9, Canada. Offices and warehouse at 1252 Speers Road, Units #1 & 2, Oakville, Ontario, L6L 5N9, Canada and THE SCHOOL OF POLICY STUDIES, Queen's University, Kingston, Ontario, Canada.

Copyright Marcel Côté, 1991
Typeset Aztext
Printed and bound in Canada

ISBN 0-88962-492-5 (bound)   ISBN 0-88962-493-3 (pbk.)

MOSAIC PRESS:

In Canada:
     MOSAIC PRESS, 1252 Speers Road, Units #1 & 2, Oakville, Ontario L6L 5N9, Canada. P.O. Box 1032, Oakville, Ontario L6J 5E9

In the United States:
     Distributed to the trade in the United States by: National Book Network Inc., 4720-A, Boston Way, Lanham, M.D., 20706, U.S.A..

In the U.K.:
     John Calder (Publishers) Ltd., 9-15 Neal Street, London, WCZH 9TU, England

FOREWORD

Marcel Côté has had broad and practical economic experience in both government and the private sector. He also has an excellent scholarly grasp of economic theory and literature, much of it very recent material. Furthermore, he is a man of common sense and an astute, careful observer. Combining these qualities and advantages, he has produced a text that is at once up to date and down to earth.

Nothing could be more useful or needed at present. Simplistic, wishful and erroneous assumptions have been leading both governments and industries astray, yielding frustrations and disappointments to say nothing of wastes of resources and time. Côté's clear, concrete, no-nonsense explanations of such matters as entrepreneurship, technological research, business management venture capital, exchange rates, government interventions, and the dovetailing economic roles of innovations and imitations could do wonders, if they are needed, in replacing preordained failures with likely economic success.

Côté is especially good at sorting out what is ineffectual hype from what is significant substance. He separates weak artificialities from strong necessities: for example, contrasting attempts at promoting business incubation which do little more than go through motions, against the conditions and circumstances that actually do promote plentiful business incubation.

A stable economy, paradoxically, is a turbulent economy. An inert or stick-in-the-mud economy, again paradoxically, is highly unstable. Côté explains such paradoxes lucidly in practical terms. Along the way, he demystifies theory. But --another paradox-- the less a mystery economic life becomes, the less humdrum it appears too, in much the same sense that the less mystifying our own bodies and their processes become, the more interesting and even miraculous we see them to be. Under Côté's guidance, economic growth is anything but dull, infused as it is with the "ordinary" miracles of men's and women's skills, wills, experiments, luck and intelligence.

Governments have become key players in economic life as Côté points out. He also explains something less well recognized: why and how the social framework of a given place such as a city, town or region, determines in major ways whether that place chills and chokes economic development or affords it fertile climate. It follows that citizens --simply as responsible citizens of democracies-- need to understand what both their governments and local societies are doing to economic life for better or worse.

Beyond usefulness to business people and officials, then, Côté's book is also a civics lesson, arguably more important, if anything, than the narrower political texts customarily considered civics education. Ideally, every responsible and well-educated citizen ought to understand this material. It's too important in all our daily lives to be relegated to experts only. Here is a good way to get a handle on economic growth without need to master whole libraries. Côté has mastered them and, with exemplary good sense, tested against his and others' experience of economic life.

Jane Jacobs

This book is dedicated...

... to Thilda, Wayne, Diane and a million other entrepreneurs, who have planted the seeds of economic growth

... to George, Brian, Robert and the other helmsmen who are asked to grow a garden overnight

... to all those who worry about tomorrow and about the world which will be left to their children

... to the people of Eastern Europe and elsewhere whose challenge is to grow a market economy from the ashes of a barren ideology

So that we all understand a little bit better the process of wealth creation under the forces of entrepreneurship and competitiveness

TABLE OF CONTENTS

IN SEARCH OF
THE REAL ECONOMY

CHAPTER ONE

A TALE OF TWO CITIES

*"Inch by inch, row by row,
m' gonna make my garden grow..."*

Arlo Guthrie

J acobsville rose from humble roots. Its founding in 1928 was barely noticeable. The town was established along a bend in the Northern River, in the middle of one of the richest timber forests of the Northern counties. For scores of years, lumberjacks had come up every year from the South to cut timber and float it down the Northern River after the October rains.

Then in 1927, Jacobs, a rich merchant from the South, obtained the cutting rights for large stands of timber lands in the area and decided to finance a permanent settlement. In May of the next year, his adopted son, known as the "Nephew", made the 150 miles journey up the river, heading the first group of settlers. A record harvest was felled during the summer, allowing for the repayments of most of the funds advanced by Jacobs. By October, several buildings had already been put up to house the families of the settlers during their first winter in Jacobsville, as the place was already known.

In 1929, more families moved to Jacobsville, triggering a construction boom that created a new side street dotted with freshly-built houses. Although cutting wood to be "exported" down south was the main economic activity of Jacobsville, the town already supported the embryo of a local economy.

In the next winter, the trail to the South was widened to a winter road for horse-drawn sleighs, reducing travel time from four days to about forty hours. A year later, the Nephew drove a truck to Jacobsville on the winter road in less than eight hours.

In 1933, five years after its founding, Jacobsville was a village of 1700 inhabitants. The Nephew, the duly elected mayor, still ran the general store, but concentrated on buying and reselling lumber in partnership with his uncle. On the side, he also became the major local financier, lending to new settlers and to those who were starting small businesses. He was only 27 years old.

Fuelled by demand for the area's timber, the local economy did not even feel the Great Depression which was near its peak in the rest of the country. The local economy had expanded tremendously since the opening of the workers' camp five years earlier. Almost as many people worked in the town as in the forest. The Nephew's father-in-law built a small sawmill to provide cut lumber for the local construction industry. One of his first employees, Martin, soon left to build a second sawmill to sell cut lumber down South.

The trail between Jacobsville and the South had been transformed into an all-season road. The owner of the second general store, who was also the postmaster, set up a regular "taxi" service to the South. Local truck owners also offered transportation services to the South. A young lawyer from the South started spending two days a week in Jacobsville.

A year later, Martin doubled the capacity of his sawmill and added a planing mill. He expanded again the following year and his work force stood at 65. In the summer of 1935, two of the largest forestry operators announced plans for a third sawmill. Several smaller businesses also opened up in that period, a second hotel, two bank branches, the first garage and several new stores.

The population of Jacobsville reached four thousand in 1935. The lawyer decided to move in, as did a doctor and a dentist. A small hospital was built. Responding to complaints, the government improved the road to the South and built two new bridges. Driving time between Jacobsville and the Southern towns was reduced to four hours.

Machine shops sprang up to service forestry operators and local contractors. One of them, owned by Adam, started to manufacture a loading attachment that turned out to be very popular with forestry operators. In 1939, Adam tasted sweet success when he shipped his first loader to the South. The shipment to the South of a piece of equipment manufactured in Jacobsville established a milestone for Jacobsville's economy. It represented the first diversification of Jacobsville's economic base out of the forestry industry.

In 1939, the mining industry appeared, adding to the diversification. A big, rich copper deposit was discovered seventeen miles east of Jacobsville, and it attracted a whole new crowd of mine prospectors and promoters. Jacobsville grew rapidly in the following years, as three mines started operations and the railroad arrived in town.

Jacobsville is a composite of various boom towns that sprung up in Northern Canada when I was growing up. They made economic growth appear easy: all you needed was entrepreneurship and natural resources. Then Main Street explodes, large firms appear, etc. But these towns' glory faded rapidly. Their challenge was to get a second wind, most didn't. Unlike most, Jacobsville kept on growing. It had the right ingredients for sustained growth: a dynamic entrepreneurial tradition and an economic base that adapted to remain competitive. Here's how it did it.

5

By the time Jacobsville celebrated its fifteenth anniversary, it boasted a population of 14,000. The edges of the forest were receding, and many newcomers built their houses outside the city limits, where land was cheaper and taxes non-existent. Several farmers had established themselves, selling their milk to the local dairy. Two new villages had sprung up, one by the mines, the other west of Jacobsville. The lawyer now found himself mayor. A printer published a weekly newspaper and helped his brother open up the town's second dairy. Three bakeries, several restaurants, and more hotels per capita than anywhere else in the country, helped serve the needs of residents and visitors.

Martin, who had started his sawmill barely ten years previously, now called himself an "industrialist", a term that other owners of manufacturing businesses also began to use to introduce themselves. Martin employed over three hundred people and had opened a second sawmill in West Jacobsville. But he was not the only dynamic industrialist. Adam, the manufacturer of forestry equipment, diversified into the fabrication of custom mining equipment for the local mines. One of the local trucking firms specializing in the transportation of dynamite, which required special trucks, landed several contracts down South and it employed over 75 people.

In 1953 when the 31,000 residents of the Jacobsville area celebrated the city's twenty-fifth anniversary, the Nephew was no longer the richest man in Jacobsville. Martin had made a bundle and spent some of it building a large house on the bluff overlooking the river. Adam's sons were also doing very well. Local gossips also had it that two brothers who discovered a copper deposit on one of their mining properties made several million dollars in one day, when their company went public in 1945.

The next twenty-five years affected Jacobsville as much as its first quarter century did, as the town grew into a city. The forest gradually receded and farmland spread. Martin's mill closed in the late fifties, making way for the town's first shopping centre. Although new mills opened in villages closer to the forest, the "lumber people" slowly ceased to be the kings in town as new industries grew in importance.

For a while, people thought that Jacobsville would become the copper capital of the world. A big smelter opened, and even in the late seventies, when the mines had lost some of their competitive lustre, the smelter still employed over 1200 people. But no other major finds occurred in the area.

6

Two of the original mines closed in the early sixties, but not before they contributed significantly to the development of ADAMCO, a company that became the pride of Jacobsville.

When Adam died suddenly in 1945, on his fiftieth birthday, his two sons took over the business. Initially, they expanded into the mining business, switching gradually from custom equipment to standard excavating equipment, and then to crushing equipment. The brothers always maintained that the encouragement of local mining companies in their first few years as manufacturers had been the major factor in their successful expansion, because their purchases provided the brothers with cash-flows and the opportunity to perfect their products. Then, the brothers diversified into heavy machinery. Their next big move was in 1950, when they acquired a mining equipment manufacturing company. With two operations, they set out to become the major manufacturer of heavy stationary equipment.

By the time Jacobsville celebrated its fiftieth anniversary in 1978, ADAMCO employed 8000 people world-wide, and over 3500 in the Jacobsville area. Locals got used to hearing the ADAMCO plane overhead. Each brother built a huge house on the family estate located five miles north of Jacobsville, on a hill overlooking the river and the countryside.

In its first fifty years, Jacobsville's population had grown to 150,000. Its economic base was diversified. The region was famous for the dynamism of its businesses. "Come grow with us" was the official slogan of the Chamber of Commerce. People kept coming, finding or creating jobs and giving Jacobsville one of the youngest populations in the country, and making its hotelkeepers and night club owners happy.

New firms kept cropping up. Some failed, but people were used to it and there were enough successes to compensate. The old generation of builders, such as the Nephew, Martin and the sons of Adam, was still around, but it was their sons and daughters who became the new movers and shakers. As well, a young generation of entrepreneurs, many of them newcomers, started to build their businesses, dreaming of the day they would buy one of the houses on the bluff overlooking the river.

In less than 100 years, Los Angeles grew from a few isolated hamlets to a dynamic city-region of more than 10 million people. But Jacobsville is a more typical example of the vigorous cities of the industrial world. It thrives on the two basic engines of economic growth. First, luxuriant entrepreneurship perpetuates itself and continually adds to the city's economic base. Second, large companies that emerge within a genera- tion and others that are drawn continually improve their competitivity and expand their reach. These two engines allow a dynamic local business community to thrive, feeding the needs of the growing eco- nomic base.

Such miracles of economic growth appear easy to replicate. How- ever, this is not the case. The Jacobsvilles are the exceptions. Entrepre- neurship does not thrive everywhere. Mature companies do not always flourish. There is arid soil and harsh climates, where growth is stifled and, despite the best efforts, the economy fails to blossom.

Smithburg, a milltown 100 miles northwest of Jacobsville, was founded in 1948 by the General Pulp and Paper Company ("General Paper") in the centre of one of the richest stands of timber in the country. Here, in a virgin forest, it built the biggest pulp and paper mill ever designed at the time.

From the outset, General Paper planned Smithburg as a model town. It engaged a first-rate town planning expert and one of the country's leading architectural firms. Smithburg had to be, and was at the time, not only a source of pride for General Paper, but also a trend-setting development, a model city of the future.

When the mill opened in 1951, a paved road and a railroad had already been completed, linking Smithburg to the South. Huge celebrations were organized to salute Smithburg's official inauguration. Officials from the government, the financial community, and General Paper came for the ceremonies. Architects and planners all over the world read about Smithburg in trade magazines and professional journals. General Paper took pride in pointing out that an efficient use of the terrain, mass-production building methods and an attention to the choice of materials had significantly reduced the overall cost of the project, without sacrific- ing quality. Furthermore, the clean, modern and well-designed mill met the same standard of quality and appearance.

Residents were proud of their new town. Beautiful houses, wide paved streets, concrete sidewalks edged with trees, and a wide variety of good quality single family houses, duplexes and apartment buildings reflected the social commitment of General Paper. The town centre, Mainstreet as it was called, comprised a stylish grouping of several interconnected buildings, which housed various stores and services, along with the local office of General Paper and city hall.

General Paper employed 1,000 workers, 500 at the mill and another 500 in the forestry operations. The town planners correctly estimated that another 1500 persons would work in Smithburg's local economy.

In 1958, ten years after the first workers arrived, Smithburg was a charming city of 9000 inhabitants, with its own hospital, an arena, a beautiful four-story city hall, three churches, and four hotels. General Paper paid good salaries, higher than anywhere else in the north and was heavily involved in community activities.

No one at the time doubted that the future belonged to Smithburg. Indeed this is why Jacobsville's business elite joined with Smithburg civic authorities to push for the completion of the road between the two towns. The road finally opened a few years later.

But Smithburg did not grow much more. In fact, it slowly withered. For Smithburg was a sterile city from day one, regardless of its beauty. When it celebrated its thirtieth anniversary in 1978, its population stood at 7000. General Paper then employed only 650 persons, despite two expansions (which unfortunately had spoiled the appearance of the plant.) Two other paper mills and three large sawmills had started up in the area, but neither had any significant impact on Smithburg's economy.

Smithburg did not age gracefully either. Although the natural beauty of the site didn't change much, the company-built houses looked weather-beaten. Mainstreet had a tumble-down look. Brush growing on vacant lots testified to the absence of any recent construction, and a few storefronts were boarded up. The mayor, a mid-level General Paper manager, tried to balance a city budget that depended too much upon General Paper's contribution.

Besides the paper and sawmills, Smithburg supported few manufacturing enterprises, all quite small: a concrete products plant, a printer and a few machine shops. The town's second largest private employer was a trucking firm founded in Smithburg, but which had diversified geographically, leaving only eighty-five of its two hundred employees in Smithburg.

In the mid eighties, unemployment in Smithburg hovered around 10%. The mills were not hiring. Jobs in the forest also became scarce. Sons and daughters who went away to university did not come back. Indeed, several hundred people commuted to work in Jacobsville every day, a 90-minute drive each way. People began joking that there were now more Smithburg citizens in Jacobsville than in Smithburg.

For most readers, Smithburg is a distant reality, something not to be concerned about. But Smithburg stands for all the ills that we fear in a modern economy: outdated technology, obsolete facilities, high unemployment and an uncertain future. We are all concerned about economic growth, job opportunities, increased standard of living, Japanese competition, "will I be able to afford the good life when I retire", etc. Smithburg represents the failure of our system. An economy can't always rejuvenate itself on command. Whether we live in Smithburg or elsewhere, this inability to control our economic future is a major source of worry.

The crisis that shook Smithburg in 1983 pitted Smithburg against the rest of the world. It started when the government tried to increase stumpage fees in response to other countries' complaints of unfair subsidization of lumber exports. General Paper's activities in Smithburg were already unprofitable and the stumpage tax was the last straw. To forestall a major closure, a multi-million dollar subsidy was proposed to modernize the mill. But the modernized mill requested additional timber concessions, which raised the ire of the other forestry operators. After several months of negotiations, a new allocation was agreed upon, which left everybody unhappy but General Paper. Conservationists were especially appalled by the agreement, which they condemned as over-harvesting and slowly depleting the area's forests.

Smithburg's victory didn't last long. A few years later, the new owners of General Paper shut down the mill. High interest rates and a rising exchange rate caused record losses. Some saw the shut-down as a bargaining ploy of the new owners to get additional government assistance. The 8000 Smithburg residents sided with the company and the Chamber of Commerce started a campaign. Some residents threatened to disrupt the annual deer hunting season if the government did not give them what "was due to them".

When residents did set up a roadblock in the fall of 1987, Smithburg became a national symbol of failed industrial policies. Politicians flocked to Smithburg (passing through Jacobsville without noticing anything helpful) to get their pictures taken in the midst of angry residents, with the guns, the hunters, the police and the closed mill. Within a few weeks, a National Commission of Inquiry was formed to investigate the state of traditional industries and to report to the government on policies to prevent additional Smithburgs.

The economy is like a garden. But some gardens are luxuriant while others barely sustain themselves. Some soil is more fertile and some climates are more accommodating. Unfortunately, there is no magic formula to ensure luxuriant growth. A gardener needs a good understanding of how nature works, of the soil and climate, and then, patience and dedication.

This book is about economic growth. Readers are invited on a tour of this peculiar garden, to discover conditions conducive to economic growth and others that stifle it. We will investigate the mechanisms which ensure healthy growth. First, sustained entrepreneurship which seeds new productive organizations and rejuvenates the mix of economic activities. Second, the continuous adaptation, under competitive pressures, of existing organizations, and in particular the mature corporations which are analogous to the large trees that dominates a garden.

We will discover how and why entrepreneurship flourishes. We will visit the world of large companies, where CEOs worry about "sharks" and "the Japanese". We will visit Boston, Switzerland, Denmark and Atlantic Canada. We will stop in successful Jacobsvilles and in ossified Smithburgs in order to discover the conditions under which, in the real world, the engines of growth perform better.

By the time we finish our journey, we will understand better the working of the economy and the complex interactions that govern its rhythms of growth. But before starting our journey, let us observe the curious rituals of the high priests of our economy, those that I call the raindancers.

CHAPTER TWO

THE DANCES OF THE RAINMAKERS

... suddenly the President addressed him:

"and you, Mr. Gardiner? What do you think about the bad season on the Street?"

... "In a garden", he said, "growth has its season. There are spring and summer, but there are also fall and winter. And then spring and summer again. As long as the roots are not severed, all is well and all will be well."

He raised his eyes. (....) The President seemed quite pleased."

Jerzy Kosinski, "Being There"

New York, Plaza Hotel, Sunday, September 22, 1985, 4 p.m. Six men facing the journalists, six of the most powerful men in the world, reporting the results of a hastily convened meeting in New York, where the fate of the world economy was debated.

At the podium stood the Secretary of the Treasury of the United States. Next to him stood the Chairman of the United States Federal Reserve Board. Behind them were the Ministers of Finance of France, Japan, West Germany and Great Britain. Together, they are referred to as the Group of Five countries, or simply G-5, the most powerful economies of the industrial world.

The press conference hit the front pages in all major capitals of the world. The G-5 Ministers had agreed for the first time to coordinate their monetary and fiscal policies and to let the dollar fall further in relative value. Japan and West Germany would stimulate their economies, while the United States was to reduce its budgetary deficit. On the following day, President Ronald Reagan held a nationally-televised press conference to present the official U.S. response.

International money markets reacted immediately. In the week following the Plaza meeting, the dollar fell rapidly against major currencies. Officials in government offices and central banks congratulated themselves. The New York Times, Le Monde and other authoritative newspapers wrote ponderous editorials. Business Week published a cover story.

The Plaza Hotel meeting is now enshrined in history, a milestone in the history of international cooperation between the major economic powers.[1] The leaders of the seven large industrial countries (Canada and Italy joining to make them the G-7) were already meeting regularly every summer for an annual Economic Summit, one of the biggest media events ever designed. Throughout the year, frequent meetings of G-7 Finance Ministers are held, and they also arouse tremendous interest.

What happened to the dollar after the Plaza Hotel meeting? Not much. The U.S. dollar had been falling against the other major currencies since early 1985, after having risen for several years. It just continued to fall after the Plaza Hotel meeting. Indeed, not even the crash of the major stock markets in October 1987 had a major influence on the broad movements in the values of major currencies.

DO THESE MEETINGS DO ANYTHING?

All these high-level get-togethers contribute to a certain stability in financial markets, at least in the short-term, by charting a course. They also provide the leaders of the G-7 countries with arguments to promote unpopular fiscal and monetary measures at home. But their impact on the economic growth of the industrial countries is dubious at best. They are meetings of rainmakers and their dance is widely reported. But the rain does not necessarily respond to their leaps and pirouettes.[2]

FIGURE 2.1
THE VALUE OF THE U.S. DOLLAR IN THE EIGHTIES

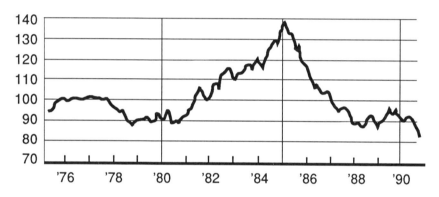

What do they do at these get-togethers? They trade stories, that is, their respective views of where they think the world economy is going. They coax each other to open up their markets to imports. They talk about ever-pressing Third World problems. But their main concern is checking global imbalances, preventing inflationary and deflationary pressures from spreading from one country to another. Generally, the countries in "surplus" situations carefully goad countries in "deficit" situations to put their economic houses in order.

They talk about the strength of the dollar, the rise of the yen, the stability of the European Currency Unit (ECU). There is always material for discussion on exchange rates, as they determine the relative prices of each country's exports. But as the aftermath of the Plaza Hotel meeting showed, controlling the relative value of exchange rates is an art that central banks have not yet mastered.

These meetings also address the fundamental economic anxieties of our time, and in that sense, as rituals, they are very useful. For the twentieth century will most likely be remembered as the period when the state of the economy became the dominant anxiety of modern civilizations. A thousand years ago, plagues, famine, roaming bandits and barbarians might have headed the list of worries. Three hundred years ago, peasants might have worried about the following year's weather. Contemporary man worries about the economy.

THE ANXIETIES OF OUR TIME

Our anxieties take three basic forms. *First, will the present economic situation last?* Will the "good times" continue? Will inflation rekindle? Will interest rates jump again? Will I have a job next year? Business persons particularly worry about short term economic conditions as they must plan for the year ahead and commit resources to particular areas. As usual, economists come out with contradictory predictions. Nobody really knows what will happen next year, whether a recession will precipitate a crisis. Economic forecasters have a terrible record. Who is to be believed? Exchange rates fluctuate uncontrollably. Deficits rise out of control, in government budgets, in the balance of payments. Is the economic structure as shaky as it sometimes appears?

Second, is the prosperous high-income post-industrial society which we have known for several decades something that will last forever? Is there any truth in the dour predictions that foresee economic misery becoming the norm in a few decades as our natural resources are depleted, and environmental disasters shake the economic foundations of our societies? Will my children find a job 20 years from now? Will the Japanese take over our economy? Will the government be able to pay my social security when I retire 30 years from now? Will our country continue to get richer? Will we ever solve the economic problems of the poor? Will economic growth last in the face of increasing world wide competition? Is our economy slowly going down the drain, on a path similar to that of Great Britain after the Second World War? Again, nobody knows for sure. Lots of theories, but no sure answers.

Third, will the economic problems of the rest of the world ever be solved? China, India, Bangladesh, Haiti, the slums of Mexico and the

16

barrios of Rio de Janeiro, the hungry children of Africa, the debt crisis, the United Nations running out of money, the insufficiency of international aid: all these pictures of poverty and dire economic need on the nightly news. And things do not seem to be improving. Will the world eventually explode? Will the poor people of the world tolerate forever our flaunting of riches?

With all these uncertainties, we are glad that these people meet at the Plaza to solve our economic problems. What is less known is how little of substance the policy makers discuss at these meetings, how uncertain they are about what they should do, how restrictive are the political constraints that they face, how contradictory is the advice they receive. Indeed, they must be happy to meet behind closed doors and compare notes about how difficult their jobs are.

They are not powerless. National governments control their Central Bank, which has an important leeway in setting domestic interest rates and exchange rates. Governments also have some leeway with fiscal policy, dealing with government revenues and expenditures and budgetary deficits, although political constraints are such that real action can be undertaken on the fiscal front only in periods of political stability or during a recession.

Governments can also take trade actions, imposing quotas, raising tariffs, demanding restraints; but these measures are defensive, of limited impact and less and less popular. Finally, government can undertake a whole gamut of economic reforms such as tax reform. Unfortunately, nobody really knows the true impact on economic growth of such measures. Moreover, the implementation of these reforms takes time. Politicians work within a two to four-year framework. Ideological politicians are a rare breed. Most politicians don't see themselves as responsible for the long term. When a trade-off is demanded between the short and the long-term, they usually heed the electorate's wishes, which are short-term.

SHIPS SAILING TUMULTUOUS SEAS

The contemporary view of modern industrial economies can be stated metaphorically. Imagine large ships navigating through dangerous waters in the dark of the night, surrounded by icebergs threatening on all sides. Position lights are dim, obstacles are numerous, danger is everywhere. Good helmsmen are vital. Not only do collisions have to be avoided, but

17

the helmsmen must also bring their ships to port. The challenge is analogous to that of steering modern economies on a sustained growth path, the universal panacea that solves most of the politicians' problems.

Central bankers and Ministers of Finance have become the helmsmen of modern economies. Recessions continually threaten. Crises abound: balance of payments, budgetary deficits, creeping or skyrocketing inflation, stubborn unemployment, etc. The industrial world's helmsmen have to get together frequently to adjust their policies and to prevent the world economic system from crashing. Moreover, they have to chart their course together to stay in formation and avoid collisions.

This metaphor describes fairly well the contemporary anxieties towards the working of industrial economies, their stability and their growth. But does it really apply? Is that the real world? Isn't someone trying to scare us? Maybe these Ministers of Finance and central bankers are less important than we assume they are in keeping the economy on a growth path. Maybe these meetings of helmsmen are only public relations affairs, to convince us that governments are in control.

Governments have not always held responsibility for the economy. The pre-industrial world's economic health depended on the weather and nature's bounty. Agriculture was the mainstay of the economy. The size of the harvest was an Act of God. Rulers could only spoil nature's gifts by waging wars and raising taxes. Good governments kept the peace, built roads and taxed little.

This simple world started to change in the eighteenth century. Manufactured goods became more important, as did trade. Sharp fluctuations in the level of economic activity began to appear. Recessions and crises in financial markets became regular features. Governments attempted to smooth their impact, mainly through interventions by central banks. Democracies emerged at the same time, and people started to rely on governments to keep the economic system working properly and to keep the economy growing.

The Great Depression of the 1930s consecrated the idea of government responsibility for the economy. At the time, few people understood what went on. It started with the crash of the New York stock market in October 1929. A periodic recession set in at the same time. Increases in unemployment were observed in 1930 in most industrial countries. The recession turned out to be deep and long-lasting. The situation deteriorated further in 1931 and 1932. Bankruptcies multiplied. Bank failures became commonplace. Governments were blamed for the economic mess. Marches and demonstrations multiplied in capital cities.

Within a period of a few years, what had started as a typical recession in the United States had spread to all industrialized countries. As economies collapsed in 1930-1933, unemployment swelled to over 20 per cent. At a time when there was only one breadwinner in most families, there was no unemployment insurance, no social security and only embryonic public welfare programs. The hardships that fell on the people of the industrialized countries are hardly conceivable today. Poverty and hunger hit the middle class, and the middle class turned towards its politicians, demanding strong remedial action.

Two names emerge from that period: John Maynard Keynes and Franklin Delano Roosevelt. Keynes supplied the theoretical foundations justifying government intervention, and in particular, government deficits. Up to then, a balanced budget had been the paragon of sound economic management. In *The General Theory of Employment, Interest and Money*, published in 1936, Keynes set forth his thesis that in periods of recession, governments should stimulate the demand side of the economy by increasing expenditures and running a deficit, compensating for the depressed state of private investments. Regulating aggregate demand in order to avoid recession became the dominant canon of economic policy making.

There are no indications that Roosevelt read Keynes, or that he was more than vaguely familiar with his theories. Indeed, in 1932, Roosevelt ran as a defender of balanced budgets. But he was an activist president. As soon as he took office in early 1933, he meddled with the economy. He straightened out the mess in the U.S. banking system, which had collapsed as the money supply shrank. He set up numerous agencies and organizations to put people back to work. He slowly increased government expenditures, although in retrospect, the deficits in the thirties were relatively small. For instance, in 1936, a bad year, the U.S. government deficit was still less than 0.5 per cent of the GNP, not much of a stimulus.

It took the Second World War and its demand for rearmament to provide a strong enough stimulus to fully reinflate the American economy. The War not only settled the score with Nazism, it taught a basic economic lesson to all governments, a lesson which ensured that the Great Depression will never recur. Sufficiently strong government intervention will prevent the economy from deflating in a time of falling private demand.

In the decades following the Second World War, governments enlarged their central role in the economy. Roosevelt was the leader to emulate and Keynes was the chief theoretician. In Europe and Japan, governments became the prime architects of economic reconstruction. In Canada and in the United States, the federal governments, under the advice of Keynesian economists, set out to smooth the business cycle out of the economy. Economics had not only arrived, it had became a major tool of government.

A subtle shift also occurred within the field of economics. Macroeconomics, looking at the economy from the perspective of the country and of government, became the dominant branch, displacing micro-economics. Macroeconomics is concerned primarily with the management of aggregate demand. Policy, and thus power, involved macroeconomics. Paul Samuelson, a young economist at the time, but already famous among his peers, wrote his highly-influential college textbook, *Economics*. Its strong emphasis on macroeconomics, and especially Keynesian economics, set the pace for how economics was taught for the next 30 years. Professors stood in front of their blackboards and showed their students how governments could manage aggregate demand and fine-tune the economy with the proper mix of fiscal and monetary policies.

During the same period, the other major branch of economics, microeconomics, which is concerned with the behaviour of individual consumers and firms, and which deals with such things as supply and demand, evolved far away from policy, into a highly abstract compendium of mathematical theories. Microeconomics became not only dull, but also removed from reality.

By the seventies, governments had become the central economic players in all industrial democracies. Economic problems were mostly defined in political terms, to be solved by governments. Politicians and their key economic advisers set the agenda. What was important to them became important to the economy. Over the years, it led to the ritual of the Plaza Hotel meeting, high-powered Summits where government officials from major countries huddle, make big commitments and announce them in a highly dramatic tone. The world takes notice and rejoices. The media love it. Rain dance rituals, for the 1990s. Happily, the rain sometimes shows up.

But often it doesn't show up, and people are starting to ask why. The field of economics is now in turmoil. Sceptics abound, especially among economists. Keynesian theories are rejected by a growing number of influential economists. This "breakdown of the concensus", as it has been called, reveals a profound disarray among economists about the inner workings of the economy.[3]

Politicians have also run out of new ideas to latch onto. Aware of the void, the average citizen worries more and more about the future. Too many things seem to happen in ways that conventional economics has not foreseen. Doubts have spread about future economic growth. Doomsday books top the bestseller lists as more and more people fear that tomorrow will not be as prosperous as today. Economists, with their contradictory statements, are becoming the butt of economic jokes.

SHOULD WE BE ANXIOUS?

Worries. Anxieties. But really, should we be so concerned? Are things going that badly? Aren't we worried mainly because we feel that there is something suspicious in the rituals of the rain dancers? For when we look closely at the performance of the economy, the results are not that negative.

Will the economy stay in good shape for the coming years? Most of the time, the economy performs well. Inflation in most industrial countries is under control, although the media tend to announce the arrival of a major crisis whenever there is a blip upward. Interest rates, always too high if one is a borrower, always too low if one is a saver, remain nevertheless fairly stable. New jobs continue to be created. All industrial countries now can afford to offer a basic social security net to provide for the minimum needs, whatever happens to an individual.

The frequency and length of recessions are good indicators of this healthy shape. As the figure on the next page indicates for the American economy, recessions are now short and infrequent. Most of the time, most people who want to work are working. Immense progress has been made. Recessions are less frequent and are now twice as short as they were 75 years ago.[4] The business cycle slowly tapers off.

21

FIGURE 2.2
U.S. RECESSIONS IN THE TWENTIETH CENTURY

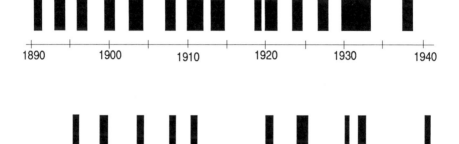

Source: National Bureau of Economic Research

Will economic growth of the advanced economies continue its long-term march, allowing everyone a prosperous retirement? We have to look at the past to get a measure of the long term. Sustained growth is a basic characteristic of industrial economies. Over the long run, output per person expands at a regular pace. Table 2.1 illustrates the phenomena for over a century for the major industrial countries.

What is obvious is sustained economic growth, despite two world wars, which not only shifted production to war material, but also destroyed the productive capacities of European countries and of Japan. Sustained economic growth despite the Great Depression, when for a while, the advanced economies went into a tailspin. Sustained economic growth despite the worries of the seventies and of the eighties, the oil crisis, the debt crisis, the productivity crisis.

What about the misery of the Third World? Only a proper perspective can allow us to understand what is going on in Third World economies. Most of these economies took off less than 50 years ago. Before World War II, these countries had essentially agrarian economies, based on self-sufficient (and generally very poor) peasants, a situation similar to the industrialized countries before their industrialization.

TABLE 2.1
ECONOMIC GROWTH IN THE TWENTIETH CENTURY

	Real average annual growth per capita			
	1870 1913	1913 1950	1950 1973	1973 1987
UNITED STATES	2.0%	1.6%	2.2%	2.4%
CANADA	2.6%	1.9%	2.2%	2.2%
FRANCE	1.4%	1.1%	4.1%	1.7%
GREAT BRITAIN	1.0%	0.8%	2.5%	1.5%
GERMANY	1.6%	0.7%	4.9%	2.0%
JAPAN	1.5%	0.9%	8.0%	2.8%

Source: Maddison, 1989

The development of most advanced economies took more than a 100 years. In the eighteenth and nineteenth centuries, annual growth rates were 1 to 2 per cent. Only in this century did we witness sustained growth of 2 to 4 per cent. Most Third World countries are currently developing much faster. Average rates of 4 per cent to 7 per cent sustained over whole decades are common. Indeed, they are leaping from a pre-industrial stage to an industrial stage at rates never witnessed in the past.

From an historical perspective, Third World countries are progressing very well. Their late start explains more than anything else the huge gap between their level of economic development and that of the most advanced economies. Indeed, that gap was much bigger 50 years ago, and nearly unimaginable 100 years ago. The gap is closing slowly, although it is still substantial. Fortunately, Third World countries benefit from the advances and lessons of the industrialized countries in building their economies. They should reach the stage of our advanced economies in less than 100 years. But for a while, the Third World will lag behind. We just have to get use to the lag and hope that it will diminish rapidly.

Eastern Europe could fare much better. It is lagging significantly in economic terms behind Western Europe. But it has a well educated experienced work-force, socialized to working in large organizations. Its democratic structures are young, but relatively robust. Property rights appear to be enforceable. How long will it take them to rebuid a market economy on the ruins of their old communist structures? Ten years? Twenty years? (It took about fifteen years to rebuild the German and Japanese economies, devastated by the Second World War.) How quickly will Eastern Europeans respond to the opportunities of a market economy, after sixty years during which individual initiatives and entrepeneurship were stifled? How quickly will they be able to build the financial infrastructures and the physical infrastructures which are essential to a modern economy? How many years will it take for their labour force to acquire the discipline and the motivation which are so important to achieve competitive productivity? Will they do better than the Japanese and the Germans of fifty years ago? I bet they will.

THE ELUSIVENESS OF GROWTH

Does this mean that all these worries are only a question of perception? Indeed, there are problems of perception. The economy is more robust than commonly assumed. Growth is sustained and over time, its cumulative impact is tremendous, something which is not always realized. And Third World countries will be reaching in 100 years what took 200 years for the advanced economies, despite all the gloom brought by the current problems of many of them, especially in Africa.

But real problems exist. All industrialized countries find themselves in a similar predicament: economic growth has become the universal panacea to economic and social ills. More growth is needed. Thus, economic growth dominates the political agenda. Not wild growth, but growth which would allow citizens to live better, governments to be fairer; growth that would provide a surplus that would permit more attention to be paid to improving the environment, to protecting the past, to enriching the future.

But managed growth is elusive. Economists are not much help with their embarrassing lack of consensus on the proper policies. Politicians also help little, with their preoccupations with the visible and the short-term. Moreover, as shrewd rainmakers, policy makers know that their options are constrained. Any false move can make the economy worse or adversely affect some groups. On many important factors such as exchange rates, they also know that they have little real control. So they tend to plan at the margin, resulting in more noise than rain.

Most of their attention is focused on the short-term. If this helps long-term growth, that is for the better. Indeed, there is no reason why sound short-term management of the economy should not enhance long-term growth. But concentrating on the short run is a highly unsatisfactory solution. Who would drive a car by looking only 10 feet beyond the hood?

The challenges of managed economic growth are more than short-term. The inability of governments to rekindle the economy of the Smithburgs of this world provides a good illustration of the problems of short-termism. Every industrialized country contains backward regions that chronically lag behind. These regions demand their fair share, a highly justified demand in a democracy. The formula to stimulate their economy, which typically lags behind by 30 per cent to 40 per cent on the basis of average income per capita, has yet to be found.

Northern Germany, Hokkaido Island in Japan, Atlantic Canada, Southern Italy, the Appalachia, Northern England are such regions. They extract a terrible tribute from their richer but guilt-ridden neighbours, particularly through their influence on government policies. Protectionism, universal welfare programs and state intervention find strong support in these regions where many have given up on the private economy. For instance, in Canada, not only is unemployment insurance overly generous, responding to the demands of poorer regions, but there is even a government-sponsored make-work program that offers 13-week jobs to allow a person to qualify for the maximum benefits under the unemployment insurance program!

Yet alongside the Smithburgs of this world lie the Jacobsvilles. And the advanced economies are covered with Jacobsvilles, regions with healthy economies that perpetuate and grow. Jacobsville is a fictitious city, but the Jacobsvilles, which can grow from an initial village to a region with several hundred thousand residents in less than a hundred years, are very common. Quite a few cities in North America, Europe and Japan have shown much more sustained dynamism. Los Angeles went from a few lightly populated Franciscan missions to a dynamic and vigorous metropolitan economy with a population of more than 10 million people, all within a century.

What drives the economic growth of the Jacobsvilles? The rain dancers who fiddle at the margin with exchange rates, interest rates, tariffs and government deficits? Not really. What made Jacobsville's economy grow? Entrepreneurs and competitive corporations. The entrepreneurs were always looking for opportunities, developing new products and building organizations. They were successful mainly because they were driven, but also because the diversifying Jacobsville economy generated opportunities, because markets were expanding, because technological changes opened new vistas, etc. Competitive corporations adapted to changing needs and market conditions, especially those that exported. They avoided the fate of the General Paper mill.

The engines of growth are not to be found in macroeconomics and its rain dances. Microeconomic processes make the economy grow and grow. In downtown Jacobsville, the economy does not appear as a big ship sailing dangerous waters, with icebergs threatening in the dark. Indeed such a metaphor does not have much foundation in the day-to-day economic workings of the Jacobsvilles, the real engines of growth of the industrialized world.

Nevertheless, politicians focus on the short-term and on the next election. Monetary authorities make a good show in their attempt to manage exchange rates and interest rates. Economists are churning data, in an eternal search for the stable correlations that sustain theories. Columnists and analysts thrive on the crises and near crises that are regularly trumpeted in the media. Yesterday, it was the Third World debt crisis, today, it is the coming stock market crash, tomorrow, it will be the fall of the dollar. One day, it will be the rise of the dollar. Crises and near-misses are regular occurrences.

Yet, industrial economies keep on growing, in the wild, thanks to the Jacobsvilles. The annual growth percentages are not high, 2 per cent, 3 per cent, and even 4 per cent in the good years that make up for the recession years when everything stalls. But given our insatiable needs, this growth in the wild is insufficient growth. If it could only be domesticated! If only we could rely on something other than the dances of the rainmakers.

No ship has yet appeared that appeals to the economists more than the "sinking wreck" that gave us the flawed policies of the past.[5] Our infatuation with the management of the economy by governments has led us astray. It is time to put aside the paradigm of the ship barely floating on high seas.[6]

A paradigm defines an analytical approach to a problem. We propose to replace the paradigm of the ships plying through tumultuous waters with that of a garden, where growth occurs naturally, with or without rain dances, with or without good gardeners. But it is a garden that, if well taken care of, will yield bounty so rich that the Jacobsville miracle will fade by comparison.

THE ECONOMY AS A GARDEN

Imagine a garden, with trees of all shapes and sizes, but also plants, flowers, bushes and weeds of all sorts. The big trees, relatively few in number, stand out clearly. They represent large businesses. The more numerous bushes, plants and small trees stand for the more numerous smaller businesses.

The large trees represent a great part of the biomass of the forest. They also provide a canopy which allows the smaller bushes and plants the amount of light and humidity needed for growth. But these plants and bushes also provide the large trees with soil cover, and retain humidity. The whole ecosystem is interdependent.

As the seasons go by, the perennial come and go. Some trees die young, others live to be centenarians. Some winters are harsher and decimate the large trees. Some summers are too hot and dry and plants take a beating. Good years follow bad ones, but the overall richness of the garden depends very much on the general climate of the area.

A healthy garden is in a quasi-steady state situation. Mature trees do not grow anymore. From year to year, they add little to the biomass. Age and natural disasters, lightning, high winds and heavy snow, take their toll. Old trees pass. But new trees replace them, maintaining the overall presence of large trees.

Growth in the garden occurs mainly through the contribution of a limited number of rapidly-growing young trees, and from bushes that benefit from a change in the tree cover following the death of old trees. Moreover, the biomass churns as plants and leaves come and go - not changing much the overall level of the biomass, but changing its composition daily.

Similar patterns can be seen in the economy. Old businesses tend to pass. From time to time, firms make it into the big league and then become familiar fixtures in the economic garden. New businesses continually sprout and some of these firms grow rapidly. Like the leaves and plants in the garden, small companies come and go, changing the composition of the economy. Finally, there are good years and bad years, and the bad years take a heavy toll, as many firms wither away.

The astute observer will discover, among the plants, the tiny seedlings which will become the saplings of tomorrow and much later, the large trees that our children will admire. To understand how the garden grows, we must find these seedlings and learn how they root. In an economy, they are the entrepreneurs that will build the large firms of tomorrow.

We must also find how small trees grow into large trees, which soil conditions and weather conditions favour more rapid growth, how adversely their growth rate is affected by the elements. We must finally find out how mature trees stay healthy, how they grow old without losing branches, how they spread their seeds.

There is no central management of growth in the garden. Growth is widely dispersed among plants, bushes and trees. The garden's fertility will depend on numerous factors: quality of soil, types of plants and trees, layout, drainage, amount of sunshine and rain, proper level of soil nutrients, absence of insects, etc. There is seldom a crisis in a garden. Changes occur slowly.

Left to itself, a garden will still grow, year after year. No gardener is needed. The yield will fall, but plants will reproduce. Still, a good gardener can make the difference between a so-so garden and a luxuriant one by assisting nature and influencing growth rates and patterns. During dry periods, proper watering helps. So does protecting plant roots throughout a harsh winter. The gardener adds fertilizer when the soil is not rich enough and weeds regularly. Thinning gives growing room to more vigorous plants. The gardener carefully considers the layout of the plants, as some combinations reduce the need for pesticides.

On the other hand, poor gardening practices can hurt the garden. But nature usually manages to have its way.

It's the same for an economy. Politicians can spoil the economy, but seldom do they succeed in wrecking it completely. Monetary and fiscal actions are analogous to watering the garden. Only when it does not rain enough does watering become important. Moreover, too much watering can spoil the garden. But good gardening involves much more than watering. Too much attention is paid to short-term tactics such as monetary and fiscal policies, which have a narrow impact. Many other factors are important in the growth of economies.

British economist Alfred Marshall used the analogy of the garden, or more specifically, that of a forest, about 70 years ago. His analogy is even more valid in today's troubled times. A healthy economy, just like a luxuriant garden, is an ecosystem full of interdependencies, both internal and external. The small matters as much as the big. A continual churning of firms and activities slowly helps the system evolve, never wholly rejecting the past, but continually accepting new activities and new technologies.

The major objective of economic policy is balanced growth. This calls for a multiplication of the Jacobsvilles and a weaning of the Smithburgs out of their predicament. Such an objective demands a fundamental shift in our approach to economic growth, away from the high-profile but ineffectual Plaza Hotel roadshows, and toward the gardening practices that yield fast growing regions such as Jacobsville.

The growth of Jacobsville's economy is based on the success of the ventures seeded by the recent generations of entrepreneurs and on the maintenance of conditions that led in the past to entrepreneurial effervescence. Let us explore the complex garden of an economy and discover the processes that feed its growth. Only when we fully understand them will we be able to develop gardening practices that will be more effective than rain dances.

ENTREPRENEURS

CHAPTER THREE

SEEDING ECONOMIC GROWTH

And thus spoke the Eternal:
"Forget the past
Because I will do something new"

Isaiah, Psalm 43

T hilda came to Canada from Lebanon as the young bride of Edouard Thabet. The Thabets live in St-Georges de Beauce, a thriving industrial town with a population of 25,000 located 70 miles south of Quebec City, and operate a vending machine business. Although she raised a family of four, Thilda has always been a full partner in the family business, taking care of purchasing and preparing the food. She managed a sandwich kitchen in the basement of their house, making more than a thousand sandwiches a week.

Thilda had always wanted a business of her own. A few years ago, she decided to open a restaurant in a new downtown shopping centre in St-Georges. Her restaurant borrowed a concept popular in Montreal, that of an upscale restaurant serving French provincial crepes. Thilda hired a young chef from France. The rest of La Crêperie's staff were locals, except for one young woman, Clairette, from a distant village, who boarded with in-laws living in St-Georges. The in-laws became regular clients, spending their weekly board income at La Crêperie, and becoming a regular source of banter and teasing during slow hours.

With the most upscale fast-food restaurant in St-Georges and a good downtown location, Thilda wanted to capitalize on the rising affluence of the area. Most other restaurateurs scoffed at her venture, but Thilda and her friends attributed their scepticism to the normal reaction of competitors about to lose some business.

Unfortunately, the restaurant never hit the break-even point, and a year later, Thilda gave up on her crepe idea, released her chef, and changed to a more conventional formula emphasizing beer and snacks. When the break-even point was reached, she sold out. Under new ownership, the restaurant is now a highly profitable hang-out for young adults.

Thilda's fling in the restaurant business is pretty well forgotten in St-Georges. A would-be entrepreneur tried, had mixed results, and quit, like thousands of others. Only her former chef, now the owner of a prosperous restaurant, will remember Thilda because she gave him his first job in Canada.

Despite its short life, La Crêperie portrays the essential elements of the most important growth mechanism, the seeding of a new activity. It is a typical entrepreneurial venture, although it ended in withdrawal: despite frustrated dreams, it still seeded a new activity.

THROUGH THE MEANDERS OF A COMPLEX PHENOMENON

Economic growth is based on two mechanisms, the implantation by entrepreneurs of new activities into the economy and the expansion of existing activities by established businesses. The most fundamental one, the major source of rejuvenation of an economy, is the implantation of new activities, which we discuss in the following pages.

A successful implantation requires a lot of experimentation, for the seedlings often die. But some take root and grow into saplings, making the garden a bit bigger and a bit more diversified. Thilda's short-lived adventure as a restaurateur provides a good starting point to highlight six key features of this process.

First, entrepreneurial growth is rooted into an on-going local economic system, where people already produce goods and services and sell them, using the money earned to buy a wide array of products and services. Some of the goods and services produced locally are shipped elsewhere, and some of the ones purchased locally come from outside the community. New activities are continually implanted into existing systems of exchange, providing something new to the marketplace.

Second, the implantation is done by an experimenter - an entrepreneur - who believes that a market exists for a particular product. Whether the conviction is based on a hunch or on a detailed market study, one peculiarity of the dream does not change: it is rarely shared with the same conviction by anybody else. An entrepreneur takes the "plunge", to demonstrate the soundness of his or her idea. At ringside stand the supporters and the doubters. Only time will tell whether the experiment will work, whether a need exists, whether the entrepreneur has the right product and whether he or she can manage the venture. In a healthy economy, the stream of entrepreneurs coming on the market with such dreams is endless.

Third, a new venture in town causes the market to be sliced differently and to expand slightly. Business conditions generally allow the presence of one more player: some slack always exists in the marketplace. Other restaurants absorbed some loss of business. But in defending their market, they also cut their costs and improved their product. Overall, consumers got a better deal and as a result, more meals were sold in St-Georges' restaurants. New arrivals expand the market for a product.

Fourth, any new economic activity also brings a small but real expansion in overall demand. The wages and local purchases of La

Crêperie provided an additional push on local demand. This in turn improved local entrepreneurial opportunities. The in-laws went into the "boarding" business, capitalizing on an unused room which they rented to Clairette. Taxi drivers, hairdressers, barmen and others received additional income, reflecting the expansion of the overall economy following Thilda's entry.

Fifth, seeding a new activity is fraught with difficulty. The failure of Thilda's initial concept implied that the demand for this particular service was insufficient for the new business to be profitable. St-Georges might have been ready for crepes, but maybe not a whole restaurant devoted to them. But will we ever really know why it failed? Perhaps the demand for crepes or the appeal of the formula was too limited. Or perhaps it was Thilda's inexperience as a restaurateur.

Finally, the effects of an entrepreneurial venture often reach beyond the immediate activity. Three other ventures started up in the wake of La Crêperie. The in-laws went into the boarding business. The second restaurant concept, which was successful, attracted new owners who had an entrepreneurial flair of their own. Finally, La Crêperie's French chef turned out to be a good entrepreneur himself. On those counts, can we say that La Crêperie was a failure?

La Crêperie contributed to the economic expansion of St-Georges in many ways, most of them small. In the final analysis, it added a thin layer of activities to the local economy. Such a small contribution is characteristic of most new ventures. But over time, these efforts add up to a significant level of activity. Moreover, once in a while, an entrepreneur hits it big. Two years before Thilda opened La Crêperie in St-Georges, Sant Singh Chatwal, an Indian who emigrated to Canada via Ethiopia, opened a small restaurant in Montreal, Le Pique-Assiette. The proposition was simple: a French- Indian alternative to upscale fast-food restaurants, capitalizing on the vegetarian attributes of Indian food as a healthful alternative to hamburgers. I remember walking by Le Pique-Assiette in 1978, curious about whether this seemingly bizarre concept would catch on. Ten years later, Sant Singh Chatwal lived in a penthouse on Central Park in Manhattan, was driving a Mercedes, and operated over fifty Bombay Palace restaurants, all derived from the original Pique-Assiette.

THE GROWTH PROCESS

Jean-Baptiste Say, a nineteenth century French economist, has given his name to a "law" whose fundamental concept is illustrated in Figure 2.1. Say's Law says that supply creates its own demand. It describes the steady-state condition of an economy in equilibrium. In a market economy under equilibrium conditions, production sustains its own demand.[1] But more importantly, Say's Law makes the point that a complex system of exchange, a "circular flow", is at the core of an economy.

FIGURE 3.1
THE CIRCULAR FLOW

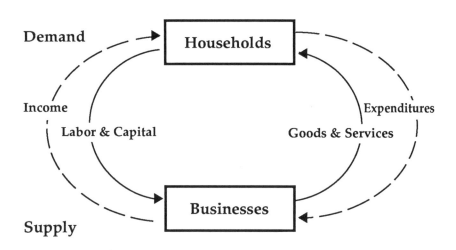

Reduced to its essential elements, a market economy is an integrated system of production and consumption of goods and services. The **consumption** sector, which is the demand side of the economy, is populated by households which derive their income by providing labour and capital. The **production** sector, the supply side of the economy, comprises businesses which produce goods and services.

Money flows in a circular route. Household income buys goods and services supplied by businesses, which use these revenues to pay suppliers of labour and capital — the two ingredients or factors of production. This circular flow of income exchanged for goods and services continues indefinitely, the demand for goods being equal in value to the supply of labour and capital.

In practice, the circular flow is much more complex to allow for investments, governments, a foreign sector, a financial sector, etc. Nevertheless, the basic principle of an exchange economy is depicted by this circular flow anchored around households and producers.

This circular flow captures a static economy, a steady state. But to make it applicable to the real world, a growth dimension must be added. Let us assume that buffers exist at various points along the circular flow in Figure 3.1. These buffers, such as cash balances, inventories, savings and credit, allow for short-term disequilibrium between what is supplied and the income of the buyers. When an entrepreneur attempts to implant a new product, illustratively, he relies initially on some "stored" demand to buy his product while the wages and interest that he pays make their first cycle around. Drawing on these buffers allows an entrepreneur to implant a new activity and create an expansion of the volume of the circular flow, resulting in economic growth.

Initially, the entrepreneur is also helped by the presence of slack in the marketplace. Existing restaurateurs were able to absorb, at least temporarily, a reduction of their own activity while Thilda was carving herself some market share. Slack is as important as buffers to allow an entrepreneur to implant his new activity.

But a new activity can merely displace an existing one. La Crêperie could have replaced a less competitive restaurant, with no overall expansion of economic activity. Does the new venture only pirate customers from other suppliers?

The answer is no. A new activity contributes to a small increase in supply. When Thilda started to sell crepes in St-Georges, she paid wages and interest, which resulted in a small increase in the total demand for goods and services in St-Georges. But the additional demand for crepes was only a fraction of that overall economic demand. Buffers satisfied the surplus demand, until other entrepreneurs, marketing other products, also increased their output. When a new activity successfully implants itself, numerous small adjustments have to be made so that the new supply conditions, slightly enlarged, meet the constraints of the demand side.

Once a new entrant makes it in a sector, the market tightens up as the slack has been used. But a thin layer has been added to the circular flow, essentially because an entrepreneur has introduced a surprise substitute in the marketplace, something "a little better". Because the product is better, there is a slight increase in demand for it. As the production sector responds, it enlarges total revenue and thus affects overall demand, triggering a general response throughout the economy. Every other sector of the economy benefits from a bit more breathing room, a thin layer of slack, a slight increase in demand and thus in their business. This overall expansion of the economy is the additional layer. The "something better" is the glue that bound it to the circular flow. Maybe the next entrepreneur will attack the law business, trying to add a new shingle on Main Street. If it works, another little push will be given to the economy, and again every business will feel it.

This simple mechanism of adding an activity is the photosynthesis of economics and is as important as its counterpart in nature. The mechanism transforms the vision and the will of an entrepreneur into an active element in the complex system of exchanges involving labour, capital and products. Whether the seed sprouts and flourishes depends on many factors: the attractiveness of the product at this early stage, the entrepreneur's reserves of money and credit, and the extent of slack in the sector, which dictates the intensity of the competitive response.

Thilda's contribution could have been bigger. If La Crêperie had been a major innovation, a Bombay Palace-type of thing, then the specific demand for restaurant services would have increased more, and everybody would have had more breathing room. But weakly differentiated entries such as La Crêperie are much more common in the real world.

Established businesses can also seed new activities. From small Mom and Pop operations to large bureaucratic organizations such as IBM and General Motors, existing businesses always introduce new and improved products. As production expands, these additions swell the demand side of the economy and thus add additional layers to the circular flow. Managers as well as entrepreneurs can generate growth. But as we will see later on, they are not as good at it.

TRADING AND GROWTH

New economic activities do not all make the same contribution to economic growth. Some seeds are much more powerful than others. Identifying high potential seeds demands an understanding of the role of trading in the growth process. Indeed, trading, that is selling a product or a service in a market other than the market where it is produced and where its production generates the countervailing income, plays an important role in the process of economic growth.

The productive capacity of a local economy can be divided into two components. A **basic activity** produces tradeable goods or services, and so relies on external demand, as the goods and services are shipped out of the region. The lumber, the machinery, the furniture and the trailer vans exported from Jacobsville were all products of its economic base. Conversely, businesses that produce goods or services for the local market are said to be **local activities**. The local economy encompasses such businesses as retail stores, local professional services such as doctors, and personal services such as hairdressers.

Growth conditions and opportunities are quite different for local activities and for basic ones. Local activities play a less strategic role in the growth process, mainly because local demand is saturated more rapidly and because local activities usually have less growth potential once they are implanted. The saturation of the local marketplace limits the opportunities. There is less slack in the local economy, providing little room for successful business implants. If Thilda's restaurant had closed down, the other local restaurants would have picked up most of its business. The demand for local goods and services depends on the overall level of economic activity in the region, not vice versa.

The economic base is different on two counts. First, growth opportunities are quite different as slack and demand conditions are looser. The fact that a basic product is "tradeable" expands tremendously the size of the potential market. A restaurant addresses only local customers. But a sawmill's timber can be shipped to potential customers in other areas.

Larger markets are also associated with different slack conditions. The market being bigger, established producers can make room more easily for a newcomer whose production typically makes only a marginal contribution to the total supply. Basic activities deal with competitors and clients located mostly in other regions. Slack conditions are looser. Competitors tend to be bigger than the newcomers and can contract production if forced. The markets for basic products are more fluid than local markets, new territories being added at the periphery. Furthermore, most products belong to complex families whose boundaries are somewhat porous: lumber competes with plywood and steel, etc. Such loosely-defined markets make it easier to squeeze new activities into the economic base.

However, new entrants in the basic sector generally need bigger buffers to implant their activities. It is generally tougher to reach the break-even point for basic activities. They face higher barriers to entry because of such things as economies of scale, technical complexities of their products, the larger minimum size of an efficient production facility, and the importance of brand names. In general, basic establishments are larger than local establishments. More slack exists in basic sectors, but the game is much tougher. Opportunities are bigger, but so are the challenges.

The second key feature of basic activities which make them more important to economic growth is the ripple effect they produce in the local economy, known as the **multiplier effect**. The implantation or expansion of a basic activity brings an increase in the local payrolls and in local purchases, increasing local demand and allowing local activities to expand. The expansion of the base sustains a secondary expansion of the local economy, adding a second punch to its growth.

Say that the owner of a sawmill hires more workers. These employees spend their new income partly in the local economy, increasing the volume of local business, and partly on "imported" goods. The local businesses respond by increasing their output, thus generating another wave of expansion. However, that second wave is smaller because not all the mill workers' money was spent in the local economy. Subsequent waves are also always smaller, as some of the money is always spent on outside goods and services. One can visualize this as the ripple produced by a stone thrown in a pool. As it expands, the ripple gets smaller. Nevertheless, the overall effect is larger than the initial impact. Only an increase in the external demand can trigger the multiplier effect.

The multiplier effect roughly doubles the impact of an expansion of the economic base. An increase of $1,000 in the wages paid to mill workers will bring ultimately $2,000 of business in the local economy. Multipliers vary greatly between cities and over time.[2] Civic boosters love them, for they provide an additional kick to any good move in the economic base. Unfortunately, the concept is frequently misused and so economists often denounce it. But the multiplier effect stresses the importance of the economic base, which is our purpose in emphasizing it here.

Figure 3.2 highlights the role of trade in a local economy. Production is divided into the basic sector, with its "tradeable" goods and services sold mostly outside the region ("exports"), and the local sector, producing goods which are only sold within the area. (Here, exports and imports are goods traded with other regions and cities, and not only other countries.)

The basic sector typically employs between 20 per cent and 40 per cent of the labour force, depending on the size of the region; the remaining jobs are in the local sector of the economy.

Whenever products are "exported" or "imported", money is exchanged with outsiders. Over time, the flows of money have to even out. This is a very important point: a region takes in only as much "money" as it ships out. Its balance of payments oscillates around an equilibrium point. Credit can be extended to cover deficits, but there is a limit to everyone's credit.

Trade is only one of the components of the balance of payments, although usually the most important one. Particularly at the regional level, one has to take into account quite a few other transactions and flows in both directions, such as interest payments, taxes and transfer payments. Nevertheless, for our purposes, we can assume that the level of exports determines the level of imports, after allowing for the credit that can be extended to a region.

The dynamics of economic growth rest on the complex interactions among the basic and the local sectors. The reactions of producers to competitors and potential new entrants bring about a continuous shuffling of production, markets and products. This turbulence can sustain rising production if it allows a continuous stream of new entrants and their subsequent expansion. Expanding the local economy can be traced primarily to the expansion of the basic sector. In the long run, new activities in the economic base sustain its growth. There is one avenue which yields the most important opportunities and those that have the highest potential: import substitution. The Jacobsvilles of this world owe their phenomenal growth mostly to import- substitution, the implantation of local activities to compete with goods and services imported from other regions. Import substitution seeds the future exports of a region.

FIGURE 3.2
A SIMPLE MODEL OF A LOCAL ECONOMY

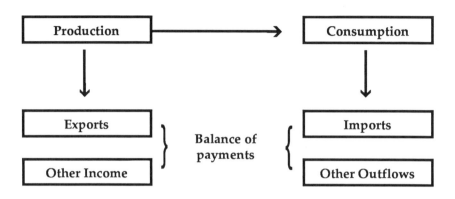

Such a statement may surprise economists, as import-substitution has acquired a bad reputation among them. Wherever import-substitution has been tried, it failed dismally as an economic development strategy. But we are not talking here about such a policy. The natural economic phenomenon of import-substitution is what interests us. A good understanding of the phenomenon tells us why policies that attempt to trigger it artificially generally fail.

MAKING IT IN THE BIG LEAGUE AS THE LOCAL HERO

Ted Turner, the highly successful Atlanta entrepreneur who brought so much change and growth to the North American broadcast industry, started as a local hero offering a homegrown substitute to imported products. Bored with the outdoor sign business that he inherited from his family, Turner bought, in 1969, a money-losing independent television station, WTBS. Not only did WTBS have a poor position on the dial, Channel 28, but it also had to compete with the local affiliates of the national television networks.

Turner's strategy was to position WTBS as a local station, offering local programming, such as Atlanta Braves baseball games, as a substitute to national network programs. To differentiate its product, WTBS capitalized on sports programming, covering events that were too "local" for the network-affiliated stations. Ever attuned to the Atlanta marketplace, the station also repackaged a schedule of low-cost Hollywood movies in a way better suited to local tastes.

Running a low-cost operation allowed WTBS to be profitable with relatively lower ratings than its competitors. Thus, Turner not only discovered a money-making niche in the local market, but he developed a tradeable product that could compete with the networks, not only in Atlanta, but elsewhere. That is the critical feature of the import-substitution mechanism. Turner's next step was to refine the product into a "super-station" and broadcast it into other markets. "If this thing works here, it should also work elsewhere...". WTBS became a national product by making its signal available throughout America on cable television. This success provided Turner with the money to finance additional experiments. In 1980, he launched Cable News Network, CNN, a 24-hour news service for which he is best known today. But it all started with a local product competing against "importations".

IMPORT SUBSTITUTION AND THE DYNAMICS OF REGIONAL GROWTH

Import-substitution is a powerful engine of economic growth for three reasons. First and most important, products "imported" from outside are tradeable, and thus have a higher market potential than "local" products. An economic activity such as La Crêperie was limited in scope, being fundamentally a neighbourhood restaurant. But a local station such as WTBS, successfully competing with the external networks, had the potential of an economic activity national in scope.

Second, import-substitution encourages product innovation. To offer a better alternative than an imported product, the entrepreneur tinkers with the product to modify it or modify its production method. He or she must innovate to differentiate the product or to gain a competitive advantage through lower costs, better service, etc. The new entrant does not have the reputation of its better-known competitors nor is it as sophisticated. Being the local producer is generally not enough.

But a new local producer can tap several advantages that his or her more experienced competitors do not have. First, the labour costs of the entrepreneur are generally lower. Most start-ups benefits from a labour force which has less seniority. Moreover, the start-up is often established in an area where wages are lower. Ted Turner's networks benefitted from lower costs and were able to price their advertising very aggressively. A lower price strategy is typical for new entrants.

A new entrant is also more flexible, less bound by tradition, by predetermined methods and by the efficiency guidelines of accountants and engineers. Thus, they can tailor the jobs more easily to needs and whims of clients. Moreover, the local entrepreneur is physically closer to clients and knows them better. The president is the chief local salesman, a great advantage. Finally, as smaller fry, new entrants can use a rifle approach, using selective price-cutting, without jeopardizing other long-standing relations with established clients.

The innovations that make the new product competitive in the local market often make it a better candidate for future export. Comparing a local activity like La Crêperie and a basic firm such as ADAMCO makes the point. La Crêperie relied mainly on its good location to compete with other restaurants, particularly after the crepes flopped: it did not have to differentiate itself from out-of-town restaurants. The loading attachment developed by Adam for local forestry operations was innovative enough to compete outside the region. So was the programming format of WTBS.

Thirdly, import-substitution fuels its own growth. The level of imports of a region is left unchanged by import-substitution: only the composition of the imports is altered. Thus, the import basket of a region is continually replenished, creating entrepreneurial opportunities for additional import-substitution. If the importation of pink flamingos fails because an entrepreneur now makes them locally, they will be replaced by other imports. The level of imports is determined by the level of exports.

Thus, import-substitution creates new opportunities. Let's go back to Jacobsville. Adam replaced imported machinery with local products and then, as his business grew, started to buy imported trailer vans, until two former employees came to offer him locally-manufactured vans. As the local economy expands, more and more goods and services are imported. The growth of these imports reaches a point where a local entrepreneur sees the opportunity to produce a substitute, as local demand has grown to the point where local production of a substitute can be sustained profitably. Thus, the import-substitution mechanism continually replenishes the opportunities that keep a region growing.

Import-substitution is also a positive-sum game. The gain of one region is not the loss of another one. The import-replacing community gains a new local activity. This is the net gain. In the other regions there is a trade-off, but no change in their overall export levels. Some exporters will lose, generally some old-line established organizations. But there is an off-setting gain somewhere in external markets. Every dollar lost by displaced uncompetitive external organizations is gained by some other external winners, by way of increased exports to our import-replacing region. Import- replacement does not affect the level of imports of an area. It only affects the composition of its import basket; the level stays the same. If broadcast news dies out, Dan Rather will be replaced in Kalamazoo by Club Med, papayas, the Sunday New York Times and Taiwanese tutus.

But then why can't import-substitution be triggered through policies that make imports dear, such as tariffs against imports and subsidies to domestic producers. This is the basic import-substitution strategy that failed miserably wherever it was attempted. The reason is simple. Import-substitution is a powerful mechanism only if it give rise to what we can call "fertile substitutes", that is entrepreneurs that eventually become exporters. To do so, the import-substituters have to face importers head on and become competitive with them. The competition is a filter that allows only the efficient, innovative entrepreneurs to take roots. Protecting or subsidizing the domestic market allows the development of weaklings that will never become exporters. The country gets stuck with inefficient producers and is left worse off than before. Protectionist policies, enacted in futile attempts to trigger import substitution, have generally not succeeded in breeding fertile substituters.

"IT STARTED IN THE GARAGE..."

The seedling of a new activity and its subsequent germination can be best examined with an economic microscope. Why does an entrepreneur decide to tinker with a prototype in his garage? Why does he get the courage to quit his job? How does he make his first sale? How does he convince a supplier to extend credit one more time? All this relates to the specific conditions which surround the birth of the venture, what the entrepreneur wants to sell, how he rates his own chances of success, how others rate them, etc. What makes a seed germinate and bloom into a billion dollar corporation twenty years later has a lot to do with the local conditions that give birth to the start-up.

Import-substitution provides a modest but comfortable cover for high potential activities to be seeded. But it is seldom seen as such. Good Atlanteans thought that Ted Turner was just having fun with the nearly bankrupt third-rate high-frequency TV station he bought in 1969, while he in actuality was developing a breakthrough product. Henry Ford, the most famous entrepreneur of this century, was just one of several hundred machine shop owners in Detroit, when the seeds of the future empire germinated, and it took several years before the world took notice. But the most intriguing import-substituter of recent past are two college drop-outs from Cupertino, California, Steve Jobs and Steve Wozniak. They seeded Apple Corp. when they developed a local substitute to a computer board manufactured in New Mexico.

Apple originated sometime in 1975 in the minds of Steve Jobs and Steve Wozniak, two friends who grew up in the seventies in the Bay area south of San Francisco. Wozniak was the technical genius, working during the day at Hewlett-Packard, and tinkering at night with such things as illegal machines to access long-distance phone lines and computer games. Steve Jobs was the hustler, calling on people, selling, boasting, "Sure, I can do that". Then he would rush to his friend the Woz, who tinkered with micro-processors and wires and usually got it.

The decision to set up Apple can be traced to the return of Steve Jobs, then barely out of his teens, from an extended trip to India. He renewed an old "partnership" with the Woz, which had led the young hustler and the older technological nerd (there was a five-year difference in age) to sell illegal phone machines a few years before. Jobs and Woz hung around the Bay area crowd of hobbyists that were tinkering with home computers. The partners' first product was a computer game, which Jobs sold to Atari. That took only a few weeks. Their next idea was to design a computer for "the people", cheap, small, easy to operate: a personal computer.

In 1976, computers were still huge boxes, costing several thousand dollars and operated by experts. Although the dream of a personal computer was revolutionary, several hundred hobbyists, mainly in the Bay area, were pursuing it. The large manufacturers thought that the hobbyists were decades ahead of their time and that the whole concept of a personal computer was premature and pie-in-the-sky.

There were already a few products on the market. The most popular was the Altair 8800, a $400 kit manufactured in Albuquerque, NM, and introduced in 1975. The Altair had several limitations and Jobs and the Woz set to beat it with their own machine. Within a few months in the spring of 1976, the Woz, moonlighting from his job at Hewlett-Packard, designed what is now known as the Apple I computer, essentially a board to be integrated by hobbyists in a more complete computer kit. Jobs then took it upon himself to sell it in the Bay area as the Apple computer, the

Bay area response to the Altair.

A small manufacturing operation was set up in Steve Jobs' garage. Money was borrowed from friends, Jobs sold his Volkswagen van, a local supplier built boards on credit, product demonstrations were done at local hobbyists meetings, etc., all the stuff of a typical start-up. Over a period of a year, they sold a few hundred boards, mainly in the San Francisco area.

The Apple I board was a typical import-substitute. A locally made product, sold locally from door-to-door by the entrepreneur, it allowed the struggling Apple Corp. to survive in a garage while the Woz was designing Apple's next product and Jobs was lining up money. Moreover, the Apple I yielded much-needed information about the marketplace, which the Woz used in designing the Apple II computer, a revolutionary computer planned as an easy-to-use box for the general public.

In April 1978, one year after they sold their first game to Atari, they unveiled the Apple II. They hit a gusher with the new computer. Within a year, Jobs had recruited some experienced executives and had lined up several million dollars from venture capitalists. By the end of 1980, sales of Apple Corp. were already $320 million.

Established computer makers, particularly IBM which dominated the market, did not discover Apple Corp. until it was well-rooted, just like they did not believe there was a significant market for personal computers. Two drop-outs took on IBM, one of the best managed firms in the world, in what was the frontier of new technology, and they won.

Such a situation is not out of the ordinary. Starting a business to compete directly with established basic producers is risky, but routinely done. Most product managers in large corporations can name local shoe-string operations that somehow compete with them. Local substitution is common, as a local market can always offer some cracks where an intrepid local entrepreneur can implant his substitute, and convince local buyers that he has a better solution. Moreover, the entrepreneur usually starts so small that he is not detected for a while by the established competitors. Thus, he manages to get a good foothold before the larger established competitors take him seriously. IBM did not start to work on its personal computer until 1980, four years after the Woz started tinkering.

MISSING THE GOLDEN GOOSE

Hewlett-Packard should not be too proud either. The Woz had offered them the Apple I design in 1976 and they turned it down, triggering Steve

Jobs determination "to show the bastards that...". One that did not miss them was Alan Markkula, a former executive at Intel, who bought one-third of the company for $91,000 in December 1976, on the strength of the Apple I board and the plans for the Apple II. He brought business acumen and contacts in the industry to the start-up. His word was very important to get additional financing for the start-up.

But it was easy to miss Apple when it was a start-up: two kids with no money tackling the IBMs of this world from a garage in Cupertino. There must have been thousands of dreamers and schemers at the time, knocking on the door of the established computer makers. But Apple was a one-in-a-million start-up, entering the marketplace at the right time, when the personal computer industry was about to explode. But it also started up properly, as an import-substituter, selling a tradeable product on the local market. Of the hundreds of personal computer companies that began operating in that period, one was to make it big, and it is not surprising that it started under proper conditions.

But the economy is so full of start-ups that it was easy to miss. Hewlett-Packard and IBM may have been blind for a few years, but they were not standing still. They had all kinds of projects of their own, and introducing a personal computer in 1976 was not one of their priorities. But established businesses can be just as dynamic as entrepreneurs, and in the process, are also making a significant contribution to growth. They have to — competition does not allow them to remain at a standstill. This leads to the second mechanism that sustains the growth of the economy, the competitive drive of established organizations. Together with the experimentation of entrepreneurs, it creates a lot of turbulence in the economy, masking much of what is going on.

CHAPTER FOUR

THE TURBULENT ECONOMY

Capitalism is by nature a form of economic change and not only never is, but never can be stationary

Joseph Schumpeter

F ew of the 2,000 participants at the White House Conference on Small Business held in January 1980 realized that a major economic discovery had just been made public when a speaker quoted the results of a recent study by a Massachusetts Institute of Technology (M.I.T.) professor, on job creation in the U.S. economy in the seventies. What caught their attention was the statement that most new jobs in the economy were being created by small business, an idea that seemed far-fetched at the time, but which greatly pleased the participants.

David L. Birch, the M.I.T. professor, had finalized his study a few weeks before and had not even bothered to show up at the Conference. His most important finding, the astonishing turbulence of the U.S. economy, was barely noticed, overshadowed by its conclusion on the role of small business in job creation. Yet his path-breaking research provided an important missing link in understanding economic growth. The competitive drive of established businesses and the innovative drive of entrepreneurs are continually changing the production side of the economy. Understanding the resulting turbulence allow us to find out more about what makes the economy grow.

At the time, David Birch was director of M.I.T.'s Laboratory on Neighbourhood Changes. To learn more about neighbourhood businesses, his research had led him to analyze Dun & Bradstreet's credit files. Over a period of a few years, he built a huge file of all U.S. businesses recorded by Dun & Bradstreet and followed them for a period of eight years. Analyzing the evolution of the business population and their employment over a period of several years led him to analyze a reality never observed before by economists: the inner workings of the production side of the economy, the five million plus businesses that constitute the private sector of the economy.[1]

What Birch found was not merely that small businesses were creating a disproportionate amount of the new jobs in the economy, but more importantly, that the economy was characterized by a high level of job churning and business churning.[2]

Much scepticism greeted these results, especially those about small business. Birch's methodology came under severe attack. Dun & Bradstreet's credit rating files were not a conventional source of data for most economists. Furthermore, Birch's conclusions on the role of small businesses, and their aggressive promotion by small business advocacy groups, raised suspicions at a time when small businesses were considered of little relevance in a modern economy.[3]

The controversy attracted other researchers, sometimes called job-counters. Using sophisticated methodology and better databases, the job-counters confirmed David Birch's basic findings on the turbulence of the economy and on the proficiency of small businesses at creating jobs.[4] In the process, they explored a new avenue of research that allows us to understand better the workings of the economy, why its production side is so turbulent, and why small business plays such a key role. The growth process, widely distributed in the economy, just as it is in our mythical garden, occurs in a context of continual change.

THE TURBULENT ECONOMY

Within the next five years, more than half of the jobs that exist today in North America will have disappeared, having been made economically obsolete. They will be replaced by different jobs, which will be better adapted to the needs of the economy. Whether there will be more or fewer jobs depends on the dynamics of the economy, which vary greatly between regions.

Thus, the half-life of a job in an advanced economy is less than five years, and during that period, the job can have several occupants. Jobs come and go. For every net increase of one job in the economy, five new jobs are created and four old jobs disappear. Just to keep job levels constant, a region must replace approximately half of its job base every five years.

New businesses are fundamental to this rejuvenation process, creating a large proportion of the new jobs. The other prime sources of new jobs in the economy are rapidly-growing small businesses.[5] They compensate for the other sectors of the economy, where there is a constant erosion of jobs.

The two tables on the following pages present a picture of the U.S. economy during the mid-eighties, its last expansionary phase, as seen by the job counters. Talbe 4.1 refers to the jobs created between 1984 and 1988, as a percentage of all jobs in the private sector. Table 4.2 refers to what happens to individual business establishments during these four years. Job-counters typically distinguish to between large and small businesses and between what happened to them during that period: births, closures, expansions, and contractions.

As table 4.1 indicates, private employment in all firms increased by 13% that period. The importance of new establishments in creating jobs

FIGURE 4.1
JOB CREATION OVER FOUR YEARS OF EXPANSION
(1984-1988)

	Firms by size (# of employees)					
	1-19	**20-99**	**100-499**	**>500**	**All Firms**	**Total growth**
Jobs created						
Births of firms	36%	26%	29%	36%	33%	257%
Expansions	20%	16%	13%	10%	13%	102%
Sub-total	36%	42%	42%	46%	47%	359%
Jobs eliminated						
Contractions	6%	9%	9%	8%	8%	61%
Closures	31%	24%	25%	24%	26%	198%
Sub-total	37%	33%	34%	32%	34%	259%
Net contribution	19%	9%	8%	14%	13%	100%
% of total jobs, 1988	20%	17%	14%	49%		
% of new jobs, 84-88	28%	12%	9%	52%		

is evident. After the four years, they generated a third of all jobs. Existing establishments that were expanded create less than half as may jobs, 13 per cent.

34% of the jobs were eliminated (an annual rate of 9 per cent!). Thus the net gain for these four years of expansion were only 13 per cent. Closures were more than twice as important a job-killer as contractions. (In a recession, the reverse holds.)

Major differences are also noticeable by firm size. In this period of expansion, very small establishments and large establishments lead the way in job creation. During a recession, small firms hold their own while large firms retreat. But the most surprising factor is the overall turbulence. Even in a period of expansion, it took 359 jobs to be created for every net gain of 100 jobs.

FIGURE 4.2
**WHAT HAPPENS TO BUSINESSES OVER FOUR YEARS OF
EXPANSION**
(1984-1988)

Firms by size (# of employees)

	0-20	20-99	100-499	500 +	All Firms
Births	38%	33%	41%	48%	39%
Expanded	19%	23%	19%	15%	19%
Did not change	31%	27%	27%	26%	30%
Contracted	11%	17%	13%	11%	12%
Closures	35%	28%	28%	21%	30%
Total	100%	100%	100%	100%	100%

Source: Small Business Administration, Office of Advocacy

Table 4.2 looks at what happened to businesses during these four "good" years, whether they expanded, contracted, closed or were born. More than one-third of the firms were created uring the period. On the other hand, nearly as many disappeared. Only 31 per cent of the businesses did not have a significant change in employment. What is also surprising is that there were not much difference between firm sizes. The turbulence is well distributed in the economy.

Some of the other findings of the job-counters who have tramped in Birch's pioneering footprints since 1980 are worthy of mention.
* Smaller firms create more jobs than large firms, particularly in fast growing regions. On second thought, this makes sense. Our garden analogy leads us to expect that the small but growing firms will do more than their share, as they are slowly replacing the large firms.[6]
* Most jobs are created by a small percentage of businesses, less than 15 per cent of the total. These "fast-track" businesses grow in a bumpy fashion, with a lot of stops and starts, mostly under the helm

of an entrepreneur. Along with new firms, they are mainly what makes the economy grow.[7]

- Job disappearances and firm disappearances are more or less constant not only over the years, but across regions. Only the rate of formation of new firms affects them. Furthermore, the higher it is, the more closures there are. New firms are fragile and represent a large share of the closures.

- Few businesses escape this turbulent life. The typical pattern is characterized by consecutive periods of expansion and contraction of varying severity. Over a period of several years, the overall change can be highly significant. Whether a firm is large or small, multi-unit or single-unit, does not really matter. The turbulence is shared by all.[8]

This turbulence is masked by the placid appearance of the overall level of the economy. The demand side of the economy, which is measured reasonably well by national income statistics, is fairly stable, fluctuating along with the business cycle. Spending patterns are much more constant than production at the level of the firms. Fluctuations on the production side are absorbed by buffers, namely change in personal income buffeted by saving and unemployment insurance. Changes in production are buffeted by inventories. Thus, the stability of aggregate demand does not betray the intense wavering at the level of the firm, from where the income of households is derived. Below the surface of aggregate supply, a world of agitation similar to the Brownian motion of particles suspended in water can be observed. This has led one observer to talk about the working of the "invisible foot", which, analogous to Adam Smith's famous invisible hand, kicks workers and firms around, generating a continuous churning in the jobs market.[9]

The forces that create such turbulence and which trip up some businesses and propel others are the entrepreneurial drive of new businesses and the competitive drive of established businesses, responding to market pressures and to their own expansion needs. Competition and innovation are the forces of change. Innovation is generated by the myriad of entrepreneurs attempting to break the status quo by entering into markets with something new and unsuspected, and expanding in new markets on the strengths of earlier innovations. Competition is brought about by the moves and tactics of established businesses that defend their turf and expand it with better product offering. That can mean lower prices, better distribution, improved products, etc. In a sense, competition forces established corporations to innovate, although, unlike entrepreneurs, innovation is not their raison d'être.

Competition and innovation maintain a continuous redefinition of economic activities, hence the turbulence. But the changes that result are improvements over the present situation, and it is this continual improvement of what is produced that brings about economic growth. The turbulence does not hide a mere churning of jobs: it leads to economic growth. The sapling in the forest that is buffeted by the wind and other elements throughout its life adapts to the stresses and grows large and strong. Innovation and competition provide stresses which force businesses to change and adapt, resulting in an enlargement of the circular flow.

THE TWO REALMS OF THE ECONOMY

The conditions that prevail in the environment of the entrepreneur are very different from those faced by the corporation already established in the marketplace. The realm of the entrepreneur is fraught with uncertainty. Their organizations are young and fragile; their resources are strained. It is do or die. But it is also a realm of great triumph. It is a realm where one finds hustling, knocking on doors, initial public offerings, moving to new premises, the Jaguar, triple digit profit gains, the Chamber-of-Commerce award, and at the outer limit, the corporate plane and Boards of Directors. The challenge is to break even and then to grow sufficiently strong. The reward system in the entrepreneurial realm addresses successful start-ups, innovative new products, breakthroughs. Creative leadership is more critical than managerial skills. Although it represents only a small proportion of the total jobs in the economy, the entrepreneurial realm creates the majority of the new jobs.

The realm of production is the existing, the established — a world of slower change where one encounters both the big and the small. It is managerial America, managerial Europe, big business, Business Leaders Council, trade unions, GATT negotiations, meetings with the President or the Prime Minister, commercial paper, the Dow Jones index and the products advertised on television. But it is also much of Main Street, the small town law partnership, the insurance agencies transmitted from father to son, the family farm, the laundromat, and all the small business world, the established businesses that have found their niche and are coasting along. Their challenge is to be competitive, through innovations that yield better products and service and lower costs. The reward system in the production realm is aimed at efficiency, reducing costs, improving products and service, making better use of capital and labour, expanding market share, etc. The production realm controls more than 90 per cent of private sector production. It creates a high proportion of jobs, but it also loses them at nearly the same rate.

The two realms overlap, as Figure 4.1 illustrates, making it hard to distinguish where one realm stops and the other starts. The entrepreneurial realm spawns the organizations that populate the realm of production. But there are no steadfast rules to clock them as they cross over into the production realm, especially the smallest ones. Moreover, entrepreneurs sometimes are encountered in the production realm. They are mostly entrepreneurs who remain as innovative as they were in their early days, despite the growing inertia of the large organizations that they have built. Nevertheless, the fit between an entrepreneur and a large organization is seldom good. Edwin Lamb, the entrepreneur who built Polaroid, was never too comfortable with his huge organization, and he let others manage while he worked in his laboratory. Henry Ford moved into the production realm on the strength of his Model T, but he was no match in this arena for Alfred Sloan, the quintessential manager who ran General Motors. Many chief executive officers try to run their company as an entrepreneur would. But they are not doing the job of an entrepreneur. A CEO runs an organization. This is not what an entrepreneur does in the entrepreneurial realm.

Nevertheless, most successful entrepreneurs have some managerial talent. As an organization grows, their entrepreneur role gradually recedes and their managerial role expands. Planning and coordinating the activities of others become more important than innovating. The passage from the entrepreneurial realm into the production realm typically occurs a few years after the corporation has taken off, when the activity and creativity of the entrepreneur become relatively constrained by the "production" needs of the organization. At that point, the entrepreneur sometimes leaves the corporation and a professional manager, often with the same drive, takes over and pursues "the dream" with efficiency and competence.

FIGURE 4.1
THE TWO REALMS OF THE ECONOMY

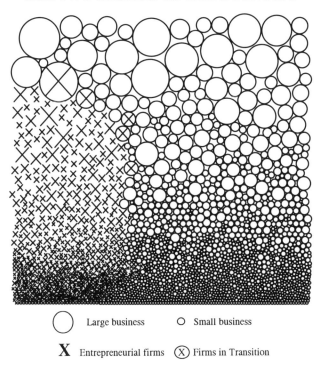

◯ Large business   ○ Small business

X Entrepreneurial firms   ⊗ Firms in Transition

THE REALM OF PRODUCTION

The realm of production accounts for most of the production side of the economy. In terms of output, it is also dominated by a limited number of large firms. These firms are run by managers according to bureaucratic rules. But their large size, their diversity and the overall stability of their balance sheet often masks a turbulent domain. Competition forces them to pursue ruthlessly a constant battle to reduce costs, increase productivity, improve their products and service. Senior management continually tinkers with their portfolio of activities, shrinking some operations, expanding others.

Most of the small businesses that also populate the production realm are to be found in a more placid domain, characterized by well-defined niches sustained by local demand. Their employment is relatively more stable, except for predictable, seasonal variations. But nevertheless, their environment changes, forcing placid small business to evolve. The changes are slow. But take a walk through your neighbourhood shopping centre and notice how much it has changed over a 10-year period. Some stores have closed, new ones have opened, some have expanded, changed owners, or acquired new equipment. Beyond these self-evident changes, one could also discover job redefinitions, new technology, the switch to part-timers, new opening hours, etc. Cumulative changes are significant in the placid world of the small local business: continuity, more than stability, characterizes it.

The production realm is driven by the rule of competition. Sustained improvements in the product offering are demanded by the marketplace. The technical qualities of the product (how well it does its job), its attractiveness and its relative price must be improved or the competition will better it.[10] Failure on any count will allow competitors to drive even the best managed organization out of business.

Competition varies over the life cycle of a product. Technical improvement is particularly critical in the early years of a product's life, as the product typically passes through a phase of significant technological improvement. Thus, competition on product performance dominates the early phase of its life cycle, and this tends to favour younger and more flexible organizations. This is when the production realm is most prone to incursion by entrepreneurial firms. This is why Apple was able to become a big player in the computer industry, piggybacking on the personal computer.

As the products mature, fundamental technical improvements become more marginal. The product explodes into differentiated versions, as the market gets segmented. Prices become more critical and lower costs take over as the dominant concern of established firms. Reducing costs is done in various ways. Economies of scale are achieved by expanding the markets where the product is sold. Economies of scope are obtained by enlarging the product line and combining the production and the distribution of products having commonalities. Higher productivity is achieved through capital investments in machinery and equipment, better technology that improves production methods and processes, better design, etc. An important contributor is better management, allowing, for instance, a low level of defective output, or operating equipment at the optimal level. As we will see later, Japan's main advantage in the mature car-making industry has been better management, leading to superior production techniques.

Competition requires continuous change within an organization. Continuous is the key word. Innovation has to be relentless. Competition demands an unending upgrading of products and compression in unit costs, leading to better prices and better products. That applies to both General Motors and to the neighbourhood convenience store. Their priority is to maintain their competitiveness. Forgetting this simple rule can lead quickly to the demise of an organization. How different is the realm of entrepreneurs.

THE REALM OF ENTREPRENEURS

Successful entrepreneurs arrive with a better mousetrap at the right place and at the right time. By developing a superior substitute, they are able to root new activities in the economy. The uncertainty associated with this rooting process creates much turbulence. Until they have proven their worth in the marketplace, new businesses are very fragile. Indeed, about half of them disappear within five years. Most of those that make it pass quickly to the realm of production, as small businesses.

But some of the new businesses remain entrepreneurial for a longer period, and turn into fast-growing companies, the success stories of the advanced economies. Their growth stems from a combination of good ideas, good leadership and good management. They have a vehicle to grow, a will to grow and an ability to grow. Their ride is not necessarily smooth, with periods of contraction often following phases of expansion. But eventually, organizational concerns become dominant and the firm slips into the production realm, and competitiveness replaces innovation as the most visible force that shapes it.

The rules that prevail in the realm of entrepreneurship are quite different from those in the realm of production, where competition relies on such factors as teamwork, additional resources and improvement in the margin. Entrepreneurship commands other rules. Innovation is often a solitary experience. The entrepreneur tinkers in his basement and comes up with the ultimate mousetrap... or develops the ultimate chocolate chip cookie. He must then parlay that idea into a business. Resources are limited. He is not a proven manager. His product is not established and he has no reputation as a reputable supplier.

But if he succeeds in rooting its activity, the rewards are often generous. Money starts to flow into the organization. Social recognition follows. Then the challenge becomes building up the business, expanding, recruiting, developing systems where none existed, etc. The entrepreneurial task is not over until the organization is large enough to translate these tasks into managerial activities.

THE ENGINES OF GROWTH

What makes the entrepreneur begin this process and what makes him succeed? What makes an organization compete, defend its turf, expand its business, enter new markets. The opportunities, brought about by technological advances? The availability of capital? The availability of labour? Or is it mainly the rules of the game? The social conditions that drive the entrepreneur to tinker, to experiment, to invest all that he has, to keep on striving to grow even after the first success? The organizational pressures and the financial pressures that drive senior management of large organizations to be more demanding, to push for higher profits and for expansion? What are the engines of growth? What makes the entrepreneur run? What makes large organizations run?

For entrepreneurs, it is the pursuit of success, with its redeeming benefits. They respond to their social environment. "This is the way to make it". For established corporations, survival gets translated into a growth imperative. The competitive tactics that drive them to improve their product offering are essential to their survival. Modern economics is ill at ease with such explanations, for they are beyond the reach of economic analysis. Social conditions and organizational behaviour belong to sociology, not to economics. Economists tend to take them for granted, with the blanket assumption that entrepreneurs and established businesses are maximizing profits.

Economists also focus on other factors to explain growth. Factors of production, namely labour and capital, are stressed. Technology is also deemed a major element, as it determines the level of production that can be obtained from a particular combination of labour and capital. So far, our analysis of growth has not dwelled on these elements, as we emphasized entrepreneurs who innovate and existing businesses that compete. To innovate and to compete, they rely on labour, capital and technology, which can be thought of as the raw materials needed to sustain economic activities. But that does not necessarily mean that these factors are critical in the growth process. Do they matter?

DOES CAPITAL MATTER?

The answer is "Yes, but...". Capital is essential, but it is there, widely available. In a modern advanced economy, it is not a critical factor. There is a lot of capital. Furthermore, to entrepreneurs and small business, its price is relatively immaterial . As we will see later, their complaints have to do with access to capital, less on its costs. Investors do not trust them sufficiently, preferring safer investments. Among large corporations, the cost of capital is rarely a competitive factor that makes a difference. (Japanese corporations, which have access to much lower priced capital, owe most of their success to other factors.)

The truth of the matter is that capital plays less an active role than commonly assumed in the growth process in an advanced economy. Capital is not a catalyst for growth. It is only a raw material behind economic production. Not only is it widely available, but its cost is sufficiently low to be a secondary factor in the growth equation. Facilities offer a good analogy. Adequate facilities are essential to the good operation of a company. But facilities problems can be resolved and seldom do they hamper the long term growth of a company.

The passive role of capital explains the relatively weak correlation between investments and interest rates which puzzles economists.[11] Investments are correlated with output measures, such as GNP, suggesting demand as an important determinant.[12] Interest rates matter much less, and only indirectly, through their influence on the demand for certain goods. (When interest rates increase, the demand for housing and for consumer durable goods falls. Consumer credit is also adversely affected. Thus, interest rates have a bearing on capital goods purchased by households. Moreover, high interest rates can lead to an increase in the exchange rate, and to a drop in the demand for domestically made goods. These demand-side effects are the major consequences of high interest rates. Although they have an impact on corporations and on entrepreneurs, it is not related to the higher cost of their funds.)

The cost of capital is not a critical variable in most entrepreneurial decisions to start a business. Capital is only one of the factors of production that has to be assembled by an entrepreneur. Key employees and first clients are much more important. The relative scarcity reflected in the higher cost of capital has little bearing on the financing of a new venture. Most entrepreneurs rely on their own funds and that of friends and relatives for the equity component of their capital needs. For the rest of their needs, they are somewhat flexible and can do with leaner buffers. Only through their effect on the demand side of the economy do high interest rates affect significantly the rate of business formation.

Most established businesses are also not overly affected by the cost of capital for their operations. Nobody likes high interest rates and business complains loudly when they occur. But the cost of capital is not a large expenditure for most corporations. For non-financial corporations, interest expenditures represented between 3 per cent and 4 per cent of total costs in the 1982-1983 period, a period of fairly expensive money.[13] A small increase in such expenditures seldom endangers most corporations. If the stakes are significant, it will not hesitate to raise capital despite its higher costs.

Moreover, the major cost that a corporation considers when making an investment is not the cost of capital, but rather the risk of losing the capital, that is, the business risk. This calls for an explanation. The cost of capital to corporations is reflected in the bank lending rates and in the interest on corporate bonds. For the past 15 years, this cost has been in the area of 7 per cent to 14 per cent, depending on market conditions. After inflation, that cost is of the order of 3 per cent to 6 per cent. But the internal return that corporations routinely demand for their investments is hovering between 20 per cent to 30 per cent.

The difference between what capital costs and the return which is demanded is to allow for the cost of the business risk or the risk premium. If the investment turns sour, the corporation is stuck with unproductive assets and with debt. The risk premium is generally correlated with expected future business conditions, and not significantly with the cost of capital. Moreover, the risk premium is a much more significant cost than the basic cost of "leasing" the capital. This explains why a change in real interest rates has little impact on corporate investments.[14]

Corporations worry about high interest rates. Indeed, the wailing of business leaders dominates the business press in periods of high interest rates. But beyond the natural needs for a whipping boy — and central banks make nice targets — business people worry mostly about the demand side of their business. Recessions are dreaded because demand can fall precipitously. Tight money can choke the economy through its effects on the demand side. Falling demand, rather than interest rates, mostly affects business decisions.

Indeed, capital can best be seen as a passive resource harvested by the production realm according to its needs. Its costs fluctuate, but with limited direct impact on corporate decisions. Furthermore, capital now flows fairly well between the capital markets of the industrialized economies, adding stability. The Euromarket, a large pool of international capital unregulated by any specific country, links national markets together through short-term capital flows. In practical terms, the industrialized countries now share the same pool of capital, over which no single country has a large influence. Central banks can influence capital flows. However, they are constrained by the impact of their policies on the value of the exchange rates, which effectively limits their autonomy.

Structural policies can create permanent differences between the real level of interest rates for domestic borrowers among countries. But, except in the case of Japan, the differences are minor. Japanese corporations have access to very low cost capital. But their total cost of doing business is affected by numerous other factors which, in the final analysis, turn out to be more significant.[15] Furthermore, because of the connections between the markets, the costs of capital in various countries moves more or less in harmony. For all practical purposes, the capital markets of the advanced economies are integrated.[16] At equivalent levels of risk, capital is cheap and abundant. It is no longer a critical element of the growth process in industrialized countries.

All of the above requires a major caveat for the entrepreneurial firms. The availability of equity capital for small private firms is somewhat deficient, the result of the inefficiencies of the venture capital markets. For small investments in equity, uncertainty is much too high to allow for a proper evaluation of the risk involved. Local conditions become highly significant and can result in very different supply conditions existing between regions and countries. These variations can have an important impact on the productivity of the entrepreneurial realm. We will get back to this issue

DOES TECHNOLOGY MATTER?

The same general conclusion applies to technology. Technology, or more specifically R&D budgets, have become sacred cows among advocates of economic growth. But is R&D in such a short supply? Although it is a very important element underlying economic growth, one that provides opportunities, technology is abundant and readily available when needed. We generally have the R&D budgets that are warranted. The bottlenecks to growth are not to be found in a lack of technology, just as capital was not guilty of holding back the economy. Let me present the argument.

Consider first, product improvements and the introduction of superior substitutes. Enterprises and entrepreneurs attempt to differentiate their products from the competition in a positive way, generating a relentless drive which entails a continuous scanning of potentially accessible opportunities. Some of these opportunities are offered by technology, but others are not related at all to technology, such as fashion and design. Entrepreneurs and enterprises are condemned to tinker with what is available, and some of the tinkering will involve technology. The search for a superior product is brought about by the growth process and not by the availability of technology.

The most famous example to that effect is the modest horseshoe, a seemingly simple product. When there was a significant market for horseshoes, from the middle of the 19th century to around 1920, tinkerers improved horseshoes and there was a continuous flow of patents filed to protect their rights on their innovation. When automobiles and tractors replaced horses in the 1920s, filing stopped abruptly. There was no further need for inventiveness, and therefore, inventiveness fell. When there is a need, technology responds.[17]

Productivity is also driven by demand, and not by the availability of technology. The need to lower costs and improve productivity and the quality of the products is ever-present in the managerial mind and has nothing to do with technology. In fact, technology is one of the tools to achieve these goals, along with capital investment, training, improved management techniques, etc. Depending on the relative payoffs, corporations will invest in any of these tools.

Technology is market-driven, and not vice versa. Corporations and entrepreneurs invest in technology when they need to and when there is a commercial payoff. R&D does not create opportunities. But it can provide solutions, both in terms of better consumer goods and better capital goods.[18] This conclusion has major policy impacts, to which I will return in subsequent chapters.

Naturally, entrepreneurs and managers profit from an enlarged pool of technologies to explore. For instance, the development of computers and integrated circuits has opened new fields of exploration to find ways to improve products and processes. Did it accelerate economic growth? The answer is yes. Without the technological advances of the past 200 years, we would not have achieved our present standard of living. The proper question to ask is what brought about these technological developments. The ongoing search of entrepreneurs and enterprises for better mousetraps was a key factor. In this chicken and egg situation, technology is the egg.

Breakthroughs in basic research enlarge the pool of potential technological solutions. There is a theory on the fringe of economic science, known as the Kondratieff cycle, which postulates that long-range technological waves, spurred by fundamental discoveries such as the internal combustion engine and the semiconductor, regulate economic growth. The theory has many fatal flaws, such as its rigidity concerning the duration of the cycles and the difficulty of integrating some basic discoveries which most unfortunately do not fit the pattern. But its basic proposition, that fundamental discoveries provide a strong long-lasting spur of economic growth, has validity.

However, most of these fundamental discoveries can be attributed to the growth process and to entrepreneurs and enterprises looking for a better mousetrap. Some of these discoveries belong to "scientific entrepreneurs" who pursue research, for fame and to satisfy their compulsive need to understand, but with little thought of deriving commercial products. But these are exceptions. The major discoveries, such as the internal combustion engine and the aeroplane, were developed by entrepreneurs searching for better mousetraps, and they revolutionized the twentieth century. The initial research on semiconductors was conducted at Bell Lab, a fundamental research laboratory. But it was only when an entrepreneur, William Shockley, transformed the basic idea into a commercial venture that the semiconductor industry took off.

The problem with basic research is that it yields "knowledge" and there are insufficient market incentives to sustain a sufficient level of development of knowledge by the market economy. Knowledge is a public good, whose commercial applications are available to all. Why would an entrepreneur or a profit-minded corporation pay for a public good? Furthermore, basic research that has an impact on fundamental knowledge rarely has immediate applications in products or production methods. Who should have paid for Einstein's research on relativity? There is little financial incentive for any individual corporation to conduct basic research, since the results will most likely be available to all and there will not be any commercial payoff.

Basic research is a fountainhead that rejuvenates the pool of technologies harvested by entrepreneurs and by enterprises. But it does not bear directly on the economic growth of a region or a country. However, by supplying new knowledge to the world, it sustains the global economic growth. What is not evident is that fundamental knowledge is on the critical path. I will argue that there are sufficient inventories of knowledge banked in the laboratories of this world to feed entrepreneurial appetites for many years to come.

INNOVATION, COMPETITION AND ECONOMIC GROWTH

The enlargement of the economic output of a region or a country is the result of a process widely disseminated in the economy, a process that takes two basic forms. First, new activities are imbedded in the economic fabric, generally by entrepreneurs, and then expanded. Second, ongoing activities are improved by their producers, resulting in a superior product offering. In both versions, the effect is the same. The income of the suppliers of the "factors" used (labour and capital) is increased, and as a consequence, aggregate demand is also increased. Throughout the economy, producers respond to this additional demand with an enlarged production.

Rooting a new activity can be difficult. First, it has to provide a product considered superior by a sufficient number of customers. Second, the entrepreneur must have enough reserves (buffers) to make it through the unprofitable start-up period. Thirdly, he has to be at least a half-decent manager.

The task may seem difficult, but our modern advanced economies are swarming with would-be entrepreneurs. Every year in North America, close to one per cent of adults undertake an entrepreneurial venture. This is roughly fifteen million Thildas per year hanging out their shingle in Canada and in the United States.

Not all these activities have the same potential. Import-substitutes offer the greatest potential for growth. First, these products are tradeable and thus tend to have large potential markets on which a large export-oriented corporation can be built. Second, the new products tend to be innovative, as they must be differentiated from the well-established imported competitors. This enhances their potential. Thirdly, they give rise to the multiplier effect, providing an additional kick to the local economy. And finally, and most importantly, they rejuvenate the import basket of the region, in a little understood positive sum game whereby the total level of imports of the region remains constant, although the importation of the competing products falls.

Established businesses contribute to growth mostly by improving their product offering in their ongoing attempt to stay competitive and to ensure their survival and their development. Faced with competition, they are on the lookout for opportunities to improve their situation. They must adapt to survive.

All this creates turbulence on the supply side of the economy. Jobs are created and jobs are eliminated as producers and entrepreneurs tinker with the economy. But the process yields growth. If our goal is to learn to manage growth, to better distribute it, to accelerate it in backward areas and to calm down the anxieties of our time, we must learn how this process can be influenced. We have to find out how entrepreneurs are inspired to start their businesses. We have to find out the ideal conditions that will allow an entrepreneur on the fast-track to expand his business more rapidly. If capital matters little in the final analysis, and if new technologies are brought about by growth- seekers and not vice versa, we have to find other levers that will allow us to master the process.

CHAPTER FIVE

THE REALM OF THE ENTREPRENEURS

"He has to slough off yesterday and to render obsolete what already exists and is already known. He has to create tomorrow."

Peter Drucker

T ed Turner, Steve Jobs and Thilda Thabet have much in common. They all decided one day to take the plunge and start a new business. They felt strongly that there was a need in the marketplace for a new product which they set out to offer. They met scepticism, but it left them undeterred. Costs were higher than expected, it took more time than planned and the initial business was slower than expected. But they kept going. Ted Turner and Steve Jobs made it into the big league and are now both famous, although Jobs was more or less thrown out of the firm which he founded. Thilda also left her business to go back to her husband's food service business and it is one of her sons who is now carrying the family entrepreneurial banner. They all have memories of the beginning, and especially of their first sale. And they all say that they would do it again.

We should know a lot about entrepreneurs, who they are, what makes them run, how they can best be supported. Unfortunately, the entrepreneur remains a mysterious species. Pete Kilby, a specialist in economic development, has compared the entrepreneur to the Heffalump, the strange animal encountered in Winnie-the-Pooh stories. Many say that they have seen the Heffalump, but nobody seems to agree on his looks. People have been trying to trap one for ages, but without success. Similarly, our search for the entrepreneur is long and arduous. The interest in this elusive species is sufficient to generate several books a year. But it seems that we are still far from the lair of the entrepreneur.

THE ENTREPRENEURIAL TASK: CHANGING THE STATUS QUO

The word entrepreneur was introduced by a Scottish economist, Richard Catillon, in 1725.[1] Etymologically, an entrepreneur is someone who undertakes something. One hundred years later, Jean-Baptiste Say defined the term more rigorously as "the agent who unites all means of production". The entrepreneur promotes a concept and coordinates the necessary resources: labour, capital and technology.

Early in this century, Austrian-born Joseph Schumpeter further clarified the concept, defining an entrepreneur as a person who breaks the existing flow of production by introducing a new productive activity.[2] He made a clear distinction between this role and the role of the capitalist, who only provides a particular factor of production, namely capital. The entrepreneur's role is much broader.

Schumpeter saw the contribution of the entrepreneur as central in the process of economic growth. The entrepreneur is at the core of a "creative destruction" mechanism which ensures the rejuvenation of the economy by replacing old activities with new ones.[3] For Schumpeter, even the business cycle could be traced to the entrepreneur. The cycle starts with an innovation that allows an entrepreneur to enter the market. His success draws imitators who expand the market. Investments increase, stimulating the economy. Then competition sets in, putting pressures on prices and profits drop. Investments fall, depressing the economy. But as the product matures, another entrepreneur comes to the market with a superior product and starts the cycle again.

The motives driving Schumpeter's entrepreneur are quite complex. In many ways, the entrepreneur is a social deviant; he is ambitious; he is self-confident.

> "First of all, there is the dream and the will to found a private kingdom, (...) a dynasty. (...). Its fascination is especially strong for people who have no other chance to achieve social distinction. The sensation of power and independence loses nothing by the fact that both are largely illusion.
>
> Then there is the will to conquer: the impulse to fight, to prove oneself superior to others,... The financial result is a secondary consideration, or, at all events, mainly valued as an index of success and as a symptom of victory...
>
> Finally, there is the joy of creating, of getting things done, or simply of exercising one's energy and ingenuity."[4]

Few people have managed to write it better since 1911.

WHO IS THE ENTREPRENEUR?

Was Thilda, our failed restaurateur, an entrepreneur? I believe so. She plunged into a risky proposition to set up a new activity in her community. Schumpeter, however, would disagree because Thilda did not innovate significantly. She merely borrowed a concept and dressed it in local costume. Peter Drucker, another Austrian- born investigator of the entrepreneurial spirit and one of the most astute observers of the modern capitalistic organizations, would also disagree. He believes that one can be an entrepreneur only by breaking with the past. Thilda did not break with the past. On the contrary, she just brought a tried-and-true restaurant formula to St-Georges.

Against these Austrian purists stand the populist values of North America, which bestow the title of entrepreneur to all who start a business and often to those who develop a significant new activity within an organization.[5] For many, an entrepreneur does not even have to be an innovator. Implanting an activity is what counts. The individual who starts a business faces the unknown, whether he is proposing a new type of computer or merely bringing a new restaurant formula to the neighbourhood. Or proposing a new type of television programming on a local TV station, the base for Ted Turner's media empire. No matter how revolutionary his venture, the entrepreneur is confident that the market will accept it. He faces some uncertainties, about the how, the how much and the when. But uncertainties exist in all ventures, and the entrepreneur, whether the name is Steve Jobs, Ted Turner or Thilda Thabet, is confident he can handle uncertainties.

I take the broad view of the entrepreneur in this book. An entrepreneur detects an opportunity in the marketplace and assembles the necessary resources to implant an activity that offers a response to the perceived need. Whether the resulting product is an original design is secondary. What is unique is the response to a market opportunity with a new activity, and not whether the specific product is original.[6]

Nevertheless, one can still distinguish between the nobles and the commoners. Steve Jobs and Thilda Thabet share similar experiences. Yet, Steve Jobs ushered the personal computer into contemporary society. Undoubtedly, he will pass into history as a great entrepreneur and deserves credit as such. That somebody else would have brought personal computers into our lives if Steve Jobs hadn't is immaterial. Whoever does it is the grand winner. History is vain, and it glorifies those who usher in progress, and forgets the commoners like Thilda.

But not all great business celebrities are entrepreneurs. Unfortunately, being a great entrepreneur sounds somewhat more prestigious than being a great manager. A line has to be drawn somewhere. Was Alfred Sloan, who built General Motors, an entrepreneur, or one of the greatest managers of this century? How about Thomas Watson Jr., to whom we owe IBM? And what was John D. Rockerfeller, who created Standard Oil, from which came companies such as Exxon, Sohio, Mobil and Socal?

John Rockefeller was an accountant who discovered the potential of oil and set up a company to tap this potential. But his skill as a financier, which overshadowed his entrepreneurial talent, led him to build Standard Oil. Alfred Sloan was definitely a great manager, not an entrepreneur. He was selected as the first president of the newly-formed General Motors in 1919 because he was one of the best managers of the period. He proved it subsequently, fashioning an efficient organization and a winning product strategy. There are some entrepreneurial features in such tasks, but calling Sloan an entrepreneur is stretching the concept, especially in comparison with Henry Ford. Ford, despite being a poor manager, was the quintessential entrepreneur. But when Sloan and Ford competed as the heads of two large organizations, Sloan was the decisive winner.

Thomas Watson Jr. was an entrepreneur who turned out to be a very good manager. In 1918, when he was in his early thirties, Watson took over the Computing-Tabulating-Recording Corporation and reoriented it as the International Business Machine Corporation. And for the next 30 years, he applied his talents as a superb manager, to build one of the best marketing organizations in the world. His entrepreneurial talents surfaced again in the forties, when IBM was known as an office product company selling mechanical tabulation machines. Although he did not have too much faith in these new machines called computers, he made sure that IBM was involved in these electronic machines being pushed by mathematicians in Philadelphia and Boston. Thus IBM was in the front row of the emerging computer industry, while General Electric, RCA and the other large electronics companies all missed the boat.[7] (It is the same trick that Steve Jobs, with much smaller resources, pulled on IBM some 40 years later.)

Some managers can be good entrepreneurs. But if they are only entrepreneurs, they do not stand much of a chance succeeding as business leaders, for entrepreneurs do not manage organizations and, indeed, are often bored by such responsibilities. It is within the domain of the manager to lead an organization, develop its product base and channel its resources into promising fields.

THE ENTREPRENEURIAL TASK: SUBSTITUTION

Entrepreneurs are on the prowl, dreaming, scheming, and then bringing their projects to life. There are always entrepreneurs scanning the marketplace for opportunities to tap, to offer substitutes superior to what is already available. The entrepreneur identifies an opportunity, designs a project, assembles the necessary resources, and starts a new venture. Many other actors come onto the stage, but in less central roles: clients, employees, suppliers of capital, technology, etc. But it is the entrepreneur who detects the opportunities by scanning the marketplace and who decides to do something about it. Whether he succeeds in building an organization out of his venture depends on several factors, such as his ability as an entrepreneur and also as a manager, for very rapidly, a budding organization demands managerial skills at the top.

But the key factor is the potential of the product. There is always room for improvement of an existing product. An entrepreneur finds it easy to break away from tradition and offer a substitute which is significantly different from what is available. The attributes that make the difference are not necessarily technical. It can be a lower price or superior service or, in the case of a local service, a better location.

For tradeable goods, being a local producer often makes the difference. Starting a business to compete directly with established producers is risky, but routinely done. Most product managers in large corporations can name small competitors that have recently entered some of their markets. Moreover, initially, entrepreneurs who start small are often not detected, allowing them to get a good foothold before their larger, established competitors take them seriously. IBM did not start to work on its personal computer until 1980, four years after the Woz started tinkering.

Technology is often the spring-board used by an entrepreneur to offer a superior substitute. Technological advances continually redefine products and methods of production, but often established businesses are committed to older technology and are technological laggards. The story of Apple is a case in point.

It is not that established organizations are blind to the new technology. In fact, they often discover the new technology at the same time as the entrepreneurs but remain prisoners of older technologies into which they have invested so much. Thus, they watch helplessly as their product position is slowly eroded away by a superior product developed by an entrepreneur tapping a new technology.

TV news provides an example of such a duel which is being won by the entrepreneurs. Satellite communication technology harnessed by local TV stations is slowly engineering the demise of network television news in North America. Remote mobile facilities also allow local stations to reach the scene of an event more rapidly and with more cameras, but at much lower costs than the networks will ever be able to manage. Then, they sell by satellite their "news" to other local stations. Because each station is able to tailor the editing of news to its local audience, they can produce news programs that handily compete with network news. Although lacking the savvy of the network news, they are not only more popular, but also cheaper than network news.

The symptoms are clearly those of substitution: lower "small-town" salaries, more flexibility, proximity to customers, and better deals to advertisers. The demise of network news will not happen overnight. But technology offers entrepreneurs an opportunity to offer a better substitute, and they are drying up the advertising markets of the network news. Meanwhile, the networks are paralysed with their "old" technology, watching the parade passing by. It is only a matter of time before the "network television news" as we know it today joins LIFE, movie house Weekly Newsreels and the New York Herald Tribune in the Hall of Fame of past glories.

INNOVATORS AND COPYCATS

The challenges of entrepreneurs are not all the same. There are many more entrepreneurial successes in the restaurant business than in the computer business. Indeed, one can say that there is a shortage of entrepreneurs in many sectors while there is a surplus in others. Who needs another restaurant, or another television station?

Such concerns call for a way to distinguish between the aristocrats and the commoners. Two fundamental distinctions can be made: whether the substitute is innovative or merely a me-too product, and whether it is a tradeable good or a local good.[8] Applying these distinctions gives rise to four types of entrepreneurs.

- **Innovative basic entrepreneurs**: High product risk, much uncertainty about the demand, difficult starting conditions: very few entrepreneurs. (Jobs and Wozniack)
- **Innovative local entrepreneurs**: High product risk, some uncertainty about the demand, good starting conditions: the level of entrepreneurship depends on the local market's openness to experimentation. (The McDonald Brothers)

- **Copycat basic entrepreneurs**: Low product risk, some uncertainty about the demand, difficult starting conditions, must catch up with the leader: a good entry mode for low-cost producers. (Compact Computers)
- **Copycat local entrepreneurs**: Low product risk, low demand uncertainty, but a tight market, good starting conditions: abundant entrepreneurship (Thilda)

What makes some types more abundant than others has much to do with the uncertainty of their ventures, the most uncertain being less frequent. The uncertainty depends on the product risk (will it perform?), the specific demand (is there a market?), and the starting conditions (how easy is it to monitor product performance and the marketplace?).

Innovative entrepreneurs make technological leaps, offering something new, while copycats apply known ideas in a new terrain. Innovative entrepreneurs are not necessarily high-tech. Products at the technological frontier make up a small proportion of total demand, at most 10 per cent.[9] Indeed, most innovations are not high-tech. They often consist of new ways of doing things. The McDonald's story is a typical case of innovative entrepreneurship with little technological content.

What Ray Kroc did was develop a well-managed franchise system which gave birth to the McDonald's chain of restaurants, a significant entrepreneurial achievement for a 43-year-old ice cream equipment salesman. No fancy technology was used, nor did Kroc's contribution depend on a product idea, for the original McDonald brothers were already flipping burgers. After he took over their business, he added a well-thought-out franchise system, efficient cooking methods, a coherent product line, and the cleanliness and fast service which is a hallmark of the McDonald's marketing strategy. Kroc's successful formula gave McDonald's years of lead time over imitators.

The copycat entrepreneur faces an easier task. The existence of a market has already been demonstrated, and the product has been defined. The copycat either follows in the wake of an innovator or applies a proven formula to a new location. Little innovation is involved, although risks still abound. Thilda merely applied a tried- and-true formula to a new environment. But new markets often demand a tailored formula, which does not always work, as Thilda discovered.

As a general rule, it is easier to succeed as a copycat entrepreneur than as an innovator. The lawyer's offices, hairdressers' salons, specialty shops, fashion boutiques, service stations and McDonald's franchises are relatively easy ventures, accessible to common folks. The major uncertainties in these ventures have to do with local market conditions and with the management ability of the entrepreneur. This is why franchisers such as McDonald's always do a thorough market study before selling a franchise, and offer management support services. The reduced level of uncertainty explains why copycat entrepreneurship thrives in the local sector, a market easy to understand and to study.

Basic entrepreneurs face distant markets and far-away competitors and confront a tougher challenge than local entrepreneurs. This applied in particular to basic copycat entrepreneurs who have to differentiate their products, as they cannot rely on location to survive. Their challenge is still significant. Hundreds of basic copycat entrepreneurs started personal computer companies in the late 1970s, after Apple showed the way. Only a few of them survived, and in particular Compaq, one of the greatest copycat success stories ever.

The "local" entrepreneur has it a bit easier, and that's why there are many of them around. Thilda knew the local market conditions for restaurant services, something easy to assess by casual observation. She knew the competition and knew that no other restaurants were being planned in town. Her bank manager shared that information and felt fairly comfortable with the venture since he did not expect any major surprise from the marketplace. A hands-on entrepreneur, in the restaurant all the time, she could get the feel of her clientele and see how her staff was doing. She had instant feedback. Her bank manager was in the same situation. Indeed, he knew enough about the restaurant business to monitor how well his loan was doing just by dropping in once in a while.

The basic entrepreneur faces a different environment. It's harder to assess distant markets, and feedback is not instant. The challenge is even greater if he is an innovative entrepreneur — a Steve Jobs — providing a new product. Innovation and distant markets add much complexity to his task.

First, he gambles that his product will better meet the needs of the marketplace than competitive products. That is high risk. Numerous concepts were proposed when the personal computer came of age, from build-it-yourself kits to the now-standard IBM PCs. The market tested them and only two basic designs survived, those of Apple and of IBM.

Second, the entrepreneur also bets that there is sufficient demand for the new product. Apple, Atari, Altair and Osborne were among the ventures that tested the size of the market for personal computers. Only when signals from the marketplace indicated that something big was brewing, did IBM, the epitome of good management, decide to design a personal computer.

Third, an innovative entrepreneur tries his hand at producing something new, that neither he nor anyone else has ever done before. He has to establish and meet performance standards in terms of quality and reliability. He cannot inspect a competitive product to determine how it is built, because his is the only one. Obviously, a lawyer opening an office faces much less uncertainty about how to go about his business.

The innovative basic entrepreneur finds himself alone, surrounded by uncertainty. As a result, trial-and-error reign in the trenches where he challenges the established order. Because of that heroic challenge, we can consider them justifiably the noblest of all entrepreneurs. Indeed they are the only ones that meet the expectations of those aristocratic Austrians, Joseph Schumpeter and Peter Drucker.

THE CHARACTER OF THE ENTREPRENEUR

The cottage industry of entrepreneurship studies that developed in the quest for Winnie-the-Pooh's Heffalump has accumulated a considerable inventory of entrepreneurial portraits.[10] But a walk through the gallery does not help our search much. Howard H. Stevenson is the Director of Harvard University's Centre for Entrepreneurial Studies. In 1983, he summed up the results of his search for the Heffalump at a conference on entrepreneurship.

> ... the search for a single psychological profile of the entrepreneur... is bound to fail. For each of the traditional definitions of the entrepreneurial type, there are numerous counter examples that disprove the theory. We are not simply dealing with one kind of individual or behaviour pattern, as even a cursory review of well-known entrepreneurs will demonstrate. Nor has the search for a psychological model proven useful in teaching or encouraging entrepreneurship. Whatever the psychological roots of the entrepreneurial spirit may be, it is my belief that it is primarily a situational phenomenon.[11]

Thus, the emergence of entrepreneurs depends more on the soil and the climatic conditions than on the seeds.[12] The entrepreneur arises as a result of a particular situation. His environment leads him into an entrepreneurial behaviour. This does not imply that any wimp can be an entrepreneur. Indeed, we know that entrepreneurs are typically inner-directed people, wanting to be their own boss and not needing anybody else to drive them. They rely on themselves to achieve their goals. Surprisingly, entrepreneurs are not, as a group, high-risk takers. Rather they are good calculators and careful risk-takers. Indeed, many of the preparations leading to their venture are undertaken to reduce risks.[13]

HOW ENTREPRENEURSHIP ARISES

What makes an individual break with his or her present situation, and invest a significant amount of time, money, credibility and honour in a venture? If we know what draws someone and how we can make the environment hospitable to feeble new ventures, we can "grow" entrepreneurs.

The entrepreneurial motivation is widely spread. Indeed, most of you reading this book have at some time in your life thought about going out on your own, about starting a business. Most of you have brushed the idea away. But some of you have not shelved the dream, but will think about it all your life, never daring to break with the comfort of the present. Only a few of you will plunge, as Thilda and Steve Jobs did.

The motivations drawing one to be an entrepreneur are numerous and varied. The potential reward of success is an important element.[14] In any community, the entrepreneurial route stands as one avenue to success. Would-be entrepreneurs notice that business owners are respected in their community. Somebody who "makes it" is definitely not a loser. Success-ful entrepreneurs demonstrate that they are achievers, that they can do it. This is particularly evident today with women entrepreneurs. They are making a big statement, to husbands and companions, to classmates, to former colleagues and to former bosses who did not promote them. The entrepreneur does not say it publicly; the entrepreneur just demonstrates it, powerfully.

There are other motivations. Successful entrepreneurs are their own bosses, a powerful magnet when one desires to assert oneself. Being the boss is also not a bad job. Bosses usually make good money, own nice cars and have bigger houses. More importantly, they work in their field of interest, doing what they want to do.

An opportunity meeting a deep-seated motivation usually provides the trigger for the entrepreneurial decision. The decision "to come out of the closet" tends to result from a combination of circumstances and opportunities.[15] The entrepreneur is at the right place at the right time, a favourable situation which is seldom solely a matter of luck. He has usually thought about it, and he has moved on favourable ground, to be at the right place, just in case. Then typically, an event occurs that triggers the decision. The triggering event is not always pleasant. A person may get fired, face few job opportunities, and so decide to create a job for himself. Not surprisingly, there is a correlation between the rate of creation of new firms and bad economic times. Other common situations are the opportunity of a leave of absence, the sudden availability of financing, a first contract or the attainment of a technological breakthrough. Finally, many entrepreneurs just push themselves into a decision by gradually increasing the work load demanded by their tinkering "in the garage" until they realize that they must work full time at it.

These triggering events do not fit neatly into a theory. But careful observations of entrepreneurial ventures can suggest fertile conditions.[16] Favourable soil and weather conditions help a seedling grow into a strong tree. Similarly, favourable entrepreneurial conditions make it easier for an event to trigger a decision which will become a successful venture. Chapter Six looks at these conditions.

CHAPTER SIX

GROWING ENTREPRENEURS

If there hadn't been an Apple I, there would not have been an Apple II

Steve Jobs

S t-Georges de Beauce, a town with 25,000 inhabitants, is located 70 miles south of Quebec City, the last town on the road to the U.S. Thirty miles south is the Maine border, where one encounters mostly lakes and forests. Nobody can quarrel with the affirmation that St-Georges is close if not squarely in the middle of the boondocks.

But St-Georges is also one of the fastest growing areas in Canada. Oil hasn't been found and neither the Japanese nor Walt Disney have set up a local operation. There is no booming metropolitan area nearby to fuel its growth. It does not have the cultural mix that breeds new ideas, nor does it attract immigrants with entrepreneurial drive. What St-Georges has done, in this remote corner of north eastern America, is to breed entrepreneurs who have developed its economic base and fuelled a spectacular growth of its local economy.

Meet the 1990 local fast-track companies of St-Georges: Canam Steel, the second largest North American manufacturer of steel joists; Manac Inc., the second largest Canadian manufacturer of trailer vans; Procycle Inc., the largest Canadian manufacturer of bicycles; R.G.R. Inc., the largest Canadian manufacturer of denim cloth; and Groupe Hervé Pomerleau, one of the five largest construction companies in Canada. All these companies were born in the late sixties or in the early seventies by local entrepreneurs. And just behind them is another crop of younger firms, with a younger set of entrepreneurs at their helm. Thilda's son, 30 year old Pierre, runs a company of 55 employees, making wooden flooring, a typical entrepreneur of the second generation. Not bad for a town of 25,000 "at the end of the road", 30 miles from one of the most depressed areas in the United States.

St-Georges is a fertile ground for entrepreneurs. Fifty miles from there, in towns which are as big or bigger, and which are better located and closer to turnpikes (St- Georges is served by a curvy two-lane highway), one looks in vain for entrepreneurial effervescence. What happened in St-Georges is a local phenomenon. It demonstrates that when establishing their firms and targeting them for grander horizons, entrepreneurs respond very much to local conditions. This is indeed what creates the wide discrepancies between cities, why Seattle is bigger than Portland, why San Francisco was overtaken by Los Angeles, why Toronto is doing better than Montreal, and why St-Georges is growing so amazingly fast. It was not branch plants, nor better infrastructure, or climate, nor the special character of those born in St-Georges. What made St-Georges such a fertile ground for entrepreneurs?

FERTILE SOIL FOR ENTREPRENEURS

Fertile soil for growing entrepreneurs is characterized by three critical elements: incubators, models and sponsors. The **incubator**, usually the entrepreneur's former employer, is where he learns his trade. This is where his concept for the venture takes form, where he starts collecting information and putting down matters. Some organizations make good incubators, and some make very poor ones. Learning to differentiate between them is important.

Models, the second element of fertile entrepreneurial soil, show the way to the entrepreneur and to those who deal with him. "Others have made it, people not much better than me," thinks the entrepreneur. Powerful models get potential entrepreneurs out of their closets. Most of us dream at one time in our life of starting a business. If we had lived in St-Georges, the odds would have been higher that one morning, we would have said: "let's go".

Sponsors consist of the first clients who believe in the entrepreneur. They vindicate his vision on the eyes of doubters, as well as help him finalize his product and get clients. They also provide cash.

FIGURE 6.1
FERTILIZING THE SOIL

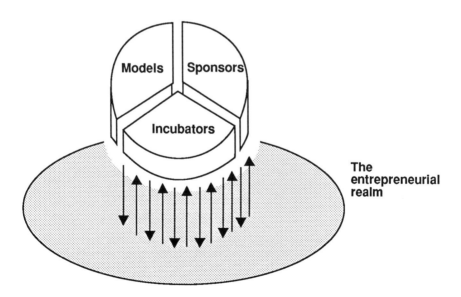

85

These three elements, (in our gardening analogy, the soil conditions) interact to facilitate entrepreneurial success, and this success breeds a new round of incubators, models and sponsors. This self-generating mechanism is at the root of the entrepreneurial effervescence that built Silicon Valley and Route 128. But more than fertile soil is needed. Climatic conditions also aid healthy growth. A good gardener checks for a constant input of technology, a constant input of business nutrients and good social support. We will come back later to the climate.

INCUBATORS

The term "incubator" is often used to describe specialized small business industrial malls, where a new business shares space with other start-ups and benefits from numerous support services, such as low-cost secretarial services, marketing assistance and the preparation of business plans. Many of these "incubators" are subsidized, allowing tenants to benefit from lower rent. These are artificial incubators, as artificial as the mechanical incubators one finds in hospitals.

Mothers are nature's incubators, and they usually deliver normal healthy babies. The same applies to the realm of entrepreneurs where new businesses usually emerge from a natural incubator as normal healthy start-ups.[1] Artificial incubators are as useful for entrepreneurs as artificial incubators are for babies, very important for premature, fragile beginnings, but unnecessary for healthy start-ups. In the following pages, we will concentrate on the natural incubators of new business.

Entrepreneurs learn their trade on the job, or more specifically, on their previous job. Walk down Main Street and check where the owners of the shops and stores were working before becoming an owner. Most likely in a similar business, as an employee. The world teems with local copycat entrepreneurs like Thilda and we do not have to worry about their reproduction.

We are more concerned with innovative entrepreneurs and with basic entrepreneurs, which are harder to breed and whose contribution to economic growth is more important. These entrepreneurs venture into activities which do not depend on local demand. But they still had to learn their trade and develop their ideas while holding a job in an incubator.

The incubator provides the entrepreneur with many of the building blocks needed for his ventures. While employed, he acquires knowledge and credibility in a particular line of business. He learns about the marketplace, the products that sell, marketing practices and techniques, and upcoming developments. He becomes knowledgeable about the technology of the products, not only their features, but also their production methods, their strengths and their weaknesses. Finally, the entrepreneur gets to know who matters in the industry, the important clients, the key distributors, the potential mentors. He builds his credibility with these people through a network of contacts and references. In the first phase of his venture, many key people who side with him will be acquaintances from the days in his incubator.

It is during this incubating stage that the entrepreneur develops the concept for his venture. He doesn't generally plan to replicate what his present employer does, as it is typically beyond his means and capabilities. (However, in fast-emerging industries like the personal computer in the 1977-1979 period, that could happen.) As a practical person, curious and alert, he sees opportunities in the marketplace. Once in a while, he detects one that makes sense for him. It could be a product or service idea or more generally an area of opportunity. The idea floats around while he collects information, makes inquiries and tries to make more occupational contact with the area of opportunity. A would-be entrepreneur manages his luck by trying to be the right person at the right place at the right time.

The drop-out rate is very high at this stage. Many potential entrepreneurs just keep on dreaming. Others call the whole thing off: family responsibilities, exciting work, a promotion and the fear of going ahead are only some of the numerous motives for abandoning the dream. This explains why few entrepreneurs get into business after they reach their 40s.[2] Those who have not succumbed to the temptation by then are most likely dreamers who will just keep rerunning their fantasy. Most entrepreneurs go into business in their 30s. Few start at a younger age because of a lack of experience, personal resources, business contacts and credibility. (This is why I am not too keen on programs that assist the young unemployed to start their own businesses. They should get a job in a good incubator. Time will do the rest.)

An event on the job often triggers the entrepreneur's decision to leave the incubator and start his business. Getting fired or being asked to move to the Kalamazoo branch are good reasons. Quarrels or bitter disagreements on decisions taken by the company also add to the straws straining the camel's back. Eventually, the proverbial final straw causes them to leave.

A fertile ground for entrepreneurs will have good incubators, which spew forth a large number of basic and innovative entrepreneurs. What makes a good incubator?

Rapidly growing high-technology firms head the list of top incubators on many counts. First, they are in growing industries where opportunities continually mushroom. Their small size and loose organization give a would-be entrepreneur exposure both to the market and the technology. A potential entrepreneur will manage to be where it matters in the organization to confront the numerous strategic choices in product design, marketing and technology. The flux, pains and difficult decisions of rapid growth not only provide frustration but also help build the entrepreneurial character.

However, high-tech is not a must. Practically any fast-growing organization fits the bill as a good incubator. What matters is exposure to high opportunity commercial areas. When the fast-food industry exploded in the early seventies, pioneering organizations such as Kentucky Fried Chicken and McDonald's served as incubators, not only nationally, but also to franchisees at the local level.

Mature firms undergoing changes can offer good incubation opportunities. Would-be entrepreneurs can get exposed to technologies or to markets (less often to both, as the organizations are too large.) Restructuring in large companies increases their potential as incubators. In the process, they are giving their managers opportunities, providing a potential entrepreneur with open windows on the challenges and turmoil of their industry.

Head and divisional offices are also good incubators. Headquarters are more attuned to changes in the marketplace than are other types of establishments. They house all the critical functions needed to design a good response to an opportunity. Product and sales management jobs provide ideal perches from which to watch and learn about the marketplace. Although sales offices and branches lack exposure to all managerial functions, particularly the design and production functions, contacts with clients and market problems make up for it.

Conversely, establishments cut off from the marketplace, such as branch plants, do not offer good incubation. Moreover, managers in branch plants are usually not too interested in the marketplace. Entrepreneurial aspirations dry up very fast in such an environment.

Colleges and universities are usually entrepreneurial deserts, despite the pretentions of their presidents. Professors and researchers suffer from a lack of exposure to the marketplace. Their research projects, although incorporating state-of- the-art technology, typically miss market needs by miles. They are much better at advising, and usually do well as consultants.

This does not mean a university cannot instil entrepreneurial values in its students. Stanford's School of Engineering was the most important element behind the rise of Silicon Valley in the 1950s and 60s because of the entrepreneurial spirit it transmitted to its students. Many graduated with the firm intention of starting their own business, and with the conviction that they could succeed because other alumni had. After a stint in an incubator to get the necessary market exposure, experience, credibility, etc., many went into business for themselves.

Research organizations, laboratories, research institutes, and the like, are also low on the list of good incubators because of their distance from the market. This has nothing to do with the researchers themselves, among whom many potential entrepreneurs can be found. Instead, it's because they get exposed to so few realistic opportunities. Their research orientation does not put them in contact with the marketplace. Oxford and Cambridge in England offer a relevant demonstration. The British government has sponsored several laboratories near Oxford, bringing more than 20,000 PhDs to the area. Yet there has been little entrepreneurial effervescence near Oxford. On the other hand, the presence of a few good incubator corporations near Cambridge has given birth to over 100 high-technology companies.[3] Although research labs have limited incubating talents, applied laboratories, where actual products are designed, are very good incubators.

One way to analyze the effects of incubators is to trace the genealogical links between organizations. The genealogy of Shockley Laboratories is well-known. William Shockley led the team that invented the transistor at Bell Laboratories, near Princeton, N.J. In 1956, he returned to Palo Alto, his hometown, to establish his own company. One year later, most of his key employees left to found Fairchild Industries, which rapidly became the leader in semiconductor technology, and produced the first integrated circuits. The growing pains of that organization must have been something, for in 1966, Fairchild nearly blew up. Three major spin-offs emerged, National Semiconductors, Intel and Advanced Micro Devices, which in turn, spawned some 20 more high-tech companies in the area.

MODELS

"If that jerk can start a business, anyone can". The name of the jerk is lost in the penumbra of one of my visits to St-Georges. This is unfortunate, because he must have been quite a good model for at least one entrepreneur. A model shows the way, indicates that it can be done and, by his own experience, demonstrates how. The closer an entrepreneur is to the model, the more effective the model is.

Somebody once asked me why I write about the Thildas and not more about famous entrepreneurial heroes such as Steve Jobs and Ray Kroc. The answer is simple: understanding the Thildas is more important, for their experience is much closer to what most would-be entrepreneurs will go through than those of the big successes. Moreover, the Thildas are more effective models than the Steve Jobs, to which few would-be entrepreneurs relate during their incubation stage.

In fact, when the great entrepreneurial heroes started, they most likely identified more with the Thildas of this world than with the entrepreneurship Hall-of-Famers. An effective model is not necessarily one's hero, just somebody that shows the way.

The model is above all a living demonstration that the potential entrepreneur's own goal is realistically attainable. Models help trigger entrepreneurial decisions by lowering the uncertainty and self-doubts about success. They comfort entrepreneurs in the inevitable difficult periods during the start-up phase. Some say that the entrepreneurial experience is 90 per cent stamina and perseverance in the face of adversity, and 10 per cent everything else. Models keep the entrepreneur hanging in there during the tough periods.

Models also influence all those who have a financial or emotional stake in a venture, who also look to reassure themselves and to diminish the uncertainty. The "jerk" was also a good model for those who dealt with the St-Georges entrepreneur. Lenders tolerate a higher level of uncertainty because they have seen it before. Suppliers have actual case histories on which to base their credit conditions. Clients do not hesitate to be pioneers because they have seen similar ventures succeed.

Models also provide support to the friends and family of the entrepreneur. A typical entrepreneur generally worries quite a lot about the reactions of the people close to him, in the initial stage of his business. He worries about their reactions, and about his risk of failing them. Models answer many of his hesitations and his apprehensions that he is risking too much and is sacrificing the interests of his spouse and children. Moreover, when the going gets tough, models become the light at the end of the tunnel for the entrepreneur's entourage.

Finally, models are important for the informal investors who are behind the majority of new ventures. Forget for the time being about venture capitalists. At least 300,000 businesses get started every year in United States and Canada. Venture capitalists invest in fewer than 1,000 of them. Most of the money for new ventures comes from the entrepreneur's own resources and from the pockets of amateur investors, parents, in-laws, friends, mentors and acquaintances who have some loose change and faith in the entrepreneur. Success stories provided by the models loosen up this "loose change".[4]

These investments are sometimes called "love money". That is a misnomer. Altruism may motivate some of these investors. But good old "greed" is a more important motivator. Sharing the dream of the entrepreneurs is common. Furthermore, these investments provide tax-free interest payments, a sort of tax-shelter for parents and in-laws. Over half of the business start-ups involve some kind of friendly loans, on which the interest is not declared for tax purposes.

SPONSORS

We all have seen that dollar framed on the wall behind the cash register. The first sale. Entrepreneurs forget many things about the period when they started their businesses, but seldom do they forget who was their first client.

First clients provide an important psychological boost to an entrepreneur, as a testimonial to his foresight. The cash that they bring is also important, as few businesses start with bundles of capital. Starting the flow of sales revenue is critical to cash-tight ventures.

For a basic firm that sells tradeable products, the first clients are critical for they bring a lot to the fledging organization. Sponsors often help define and finalize the entrepreneur's product, especially a high-tech one. They test prototypes and help the entrepreneur correct defects. A kind of partnership often develops, the equivalent of a mentor relationship, the sponsor providing financing, technical assistance and credibility.

A sponsor also helps to market the product. He plays an important role in establishing the reputation of the new venture by word-of-mouth.

Moreover, he provides crucial references, especially when reliability and performance are important.

In high-technology ventures, sponsors (or beta-sites, in the jargon of venture capitalists) are all but essential.[5] Most venture capitalists will not commit funds to a high-tech venture unless a beta-site has been found. Indeed, many ventures start with a beta-site, the first contract being the trigger. The would-be entrepreneur sticks to his incubator job while developing the product and talking with potential clients. When a client gets serious and starts talking of a development contract, all the pieces rapidly come together: the beta-site is committed. The entrepreneur quits his job. Venture capital comes on line. Key employees make their move. The Rubicon is crossed.

Sponsors gain through such arrangements. It allows them to tap the creativity and accumulated knowledge of technological resources at relatively low costs. They also avoid committing internal resources to technological fields that are not part of their core areas. When he teams up with a new venture, a sponsor decides to rely on untested outside resources, a decision that requires a high degree of confidence. The corporate culture must condone the implicit risk of dealing with an untested venture. Not all large organizations allow such decisions. But as the industrial arrangements in manufacturing move towards more flexible patterns along Japanese lines, major manufacturing corporations will concentrate on their core technologies and build networks of sub-contractors and suppliers for peripheral technologies. This tendency bodes well for start-ups as it institutionalizes sponsorship in the management creed.[6]

A study of more than 100 high-technology start-ups by my colleague Roger Miller indicates that sponsors come from all sectors of activity, from banks and government agencies to old-line industrial organizations and high-technology companies. Large corporations can be spawned from such sponsorship arrangements. Hydro-Québec, one of the largest utilities in North America, has traditionally relied on private engineering firms for the constructing of its hydro-electric facilities. As a result, Montreal is home to two of the world's largest engineering firms. In relying on local firms to design and manage the construction of its huge hydro-electric system, Hydro-Québec built up their capacity and expertise, which they then went on to sell throughout the world. Ontario Hydro, a utility similar in size and whose development paralleled that of Hydro-Québec, opted for a different strategy, relying on internal staff for its major engineering tasks. Today, not only has engineering employment at Ontario Hydro peaked, but it has generated few spin-offs and no major engineering firms can trace their development to critical Ontario Hydro contracts.

THE CLIMATE FOR NEW VENTURES

Incubators, models and sponsors sustain a self-generating process. New firms tends to be good models, better incubators and more willing sponsors than established firms. But this self-generating process can be influenced by climatic conditions which enrich the entrepreneurial environment. These conditions relate to technological inputs, business inputs and social support, as shown in Figure 6.2.

Technological inputs relate to the types of technologies available locally. New ventures always rely on particular technologies, which they absorb during their incubating period and right after being founded. Steve Jobs did not know much about microprocessor technology when he founded Apple. But he teamed up with Stephen Wozniak, who was working at Hewlett-Packard. They attended the monthly meetings of the Homebrew Computer Club, where hobbyists exchanged ideas. A lot of work on semiconductors and advanced microprocessors was going on in Silicon Valley in 1976 and 1977. Curious tinkerers such as Steve Wozniak had good access to the technology.

Business input was provided when Jacob backed his nephew Albert, when a few venture capitalists got behind Steve Jobs, when Thilda's husband helped her, when bank managers coached new businessmen, when brokerage firms underwrote initial public offerings, when lawyers handled business start-ups, etc. Business input is smart money, and much more.

FIGURE 6.2
THE ENTREPRENEURIAL PROCESS

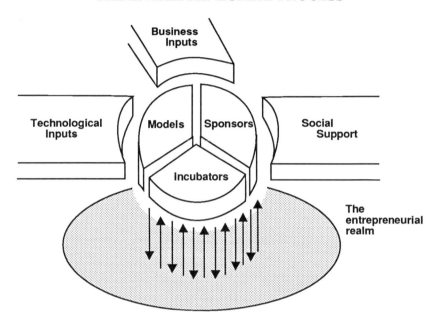

Social support is society's recognition that entrepreneurs matter. This recognition is reflected in numerous ways; in laws, in political attitudes, in the values transmitted at universities, in the standing of business as a career, etc. Some communities, and indeed some countries at different periods, are more supportive of Horatio Alger stories than are others.

TECHNOLOGICAL INPUTS

Most technological inputs in a region come from its industrial base. Organizations continually absorb new technologies. They also diffuse their technologies, in numerous ways: employees changing jobs, client-supplier relations, sponsor relations, incubation of entrepreneurs, etc. This is why some cities and areas are more able to fertilize the entrepreneurial mindset. The more of a crossroads a city is, the more technological flux one can expect. Cities where cultures meet, such as Miami, Los

Angeles, Montreal, London, Toronto and San Francisco, enjoy this technological current. New York is highly favoured by its traditional role as the Gateway to America.[7]

Technology is any applied knowledge, from how to structure a musical comedy or how to run a large hotel to the design of a test instrument to measure sound distortion. It includes applications derived from the latest scientific discoveries, such as microprocessors, gene-splicing and the like. New technologies, whether high-technology or low, often have the potential to generate whole new industries, whereas old technologies, (e.g. musicals, hotels, cars, plastics, etc.) have already yielded most of their important commercial applications.

Technologies play a fundamental role in the growth process. In the production realm, technology keeps large organizations competitive. In emerging industries, it plays a big role in sorting out the dominant players, although it is not essential for winning. IBM became the leader in computers without ever having been the technological leader, mainly on its strength in marketing.

Entrepreneurs generally follow either one of two generic strategies to break into a market: lower price entry (e.g., Compaq Computer in its early days) or superior product (e.g., Lotus). Low technology products usually adopt a lower price strategy. When technology rather than price is the determining factor, the "better mousetrap" route is the only way to go. Technological leadership, which can be provided only if an organization is closely tied with advanced applied research, is important mainly in emerging technological fields. In other fields, parity is enough. Organizations remain competitive by matching the technological prowess of competitors.

Thus applied research conducted in local firms greatly enriches the climate for entrepreneurial activities in the same sectors, through incubation, sponsorship and models. Basic research is a different story. Being far from the marketplace, it is not a good incubator, neither a good source of sponsors nor models. Although basic research is important to applied research, the links between the two are usually not intense. Japan excels in applied research, but is much less of a powerhouse in basic research. Moreover, the results of basic research are shared among scientists of all countries. The sudden discoveries in superconductivity in a great number of universities around the world in 1987 exemplify this phenomenon.

Therefore, we should be sceptical when confronted with the claims that research institutes are significant catalysts for local economic growth.

Some applied research institutes that work at the frontier of development, can play a critical role in the emergence of new industries. A case in point is Lincoln Laboratory, a contract research laboratory affiliated with the Massachusetts Institute of Technology, where the first experimental mini-computers were developed for the U.S. Department of Defence. It was from Lincoln Laboratories that a group of engineers spun off to adapt their technology for commercial uses. These engineers established the Digital Equipment Corporation, now the second largest computer company in the world.

But most research institutes are neither the paragon of excellence that they claim to be, nor are they active in emerging fields that have direct contact with the marketplace. Nothing can replace the intimate knowledge of the marketplace achieved through the actual development of products in a highly competitive timeframe. And in emerging fields, research institutes that are not among the world leaders cannot be good sources of competitive advantage to local entrepreneurs. Runners-up are losers in high-technology.

Four broad propositions can be made concerning the role and importance of technological inputs. First, they are important mostly in areas of technological effervescence, the high-technology areas of today. Second, technological leadership comes from applied research, not basic research. Third, people matter very much, especially young engineers and scientists. The foremost contribution of universities relates to their educational mission, not their research activities. Finally, research organizations contribute to local economic growth only to the extent that they are well-immersed in the marketplace. Very few research institutes qualify.

BUSINESS INPUTS

Venture capital is a highly-touted way of providing start-up money to entrepreneurs. The venture capital industry as we know it today started in Boston in 1946, when a professor at the Harvard Business School, General George Doriot, established the American Research Development Corp. (ARD) in cooperation with some of Boston's major financial institutions. ARD invested in several local high- technology ventures. Its big breakthrough came rather inauspiciously in 1958 when a medium-size investment of $72,000 for 65 per cent of the equity helped start Digital Equipment. Today, this investment would be worth $5 billion, making it by far the best ever made by a venture capitalist.[8] But the major role of

ARD was as an incubator of young venture capitalists who went on to establish their own firms in the 1960s, giving rise to the U.S. venture capital industry.

The foremost contribution of a venture capitalist to a new business is not financial. The money always helps, but an entrepreneur usually can get money elsewhere. What he needs most at the outset is smart money, the presence of the investor as a wise associate, who can advise, guide, provide contacts, and vouch for the venture's credibility. One of the most important contribution of a venture capitalist is also to expose the entrepreneur to rich financial development networks during the start-up phase. Thus, when additional equity financing is needed, the presence of a business mentor, doubling as an early shareholder, greatly eases the search for the second round of financing.

Another major contribution of the venture capitalist occurs later in the corporation's life. This is when detached observers have to prevail on the entrepreneur to make organizational changes, as the venture evolves into a growing organization. This operation can be delicate. It deeply touches the entrepreneur who must realize that his company, his baby, has a life of its own. I once saw one of the toughest entrepreneurs I ever met start to cry in front of his peers, when confronted with the inevitability of major changes in the way he ran his own company, of which he was still the majority shareholder. Not all entrepreneurs can accept this change. The slow ouster of Steve Jobs from "his baby" has been well documented. His partners from the early days, the venture capitalists, had to make this painful decision. The business press regularly announces the departure of CEOs from the companies they founded. Behind such departures can be found the tough business acumen of venture capitalists who put the interests of the organization ahead of those of the founder.

First-round venture capitalists are thus a most precious breed for stimulating the entrepreneurial realm. Not only are they rare, but it is very difficult to replace them by ersatz investors, such as government-supported venture capital funds. The key contribution of the venture capital institution is the experienced businessperson, with a good nose and plenty of contacts, and not the money. Most government-supported venture capital funds have the money, but not the talents. Good first-round venture capitalists command compensation packages which are astronomical by everyday standards. These individuals are not interested in working for government agencies and prefer to stay in the private sector where they do not have any trouble raising private capital. They also keep an important share of the profits, typically 20 per cent, and thus do not need government support. Conversely, if they were that good, the managers recruited by government-supported funds would be able to raise their own money from non-government sources.

Despite all the attention it attracts, venture capitalism is a marginal way of supplying smart money to new ventures. Most of the large new venture capital funds that have mushroomed in the 80s specialize in financing ownership transfer, particularly through leveraged buy-outs and acquisitions. This is very different from the pioneering investments of ARD, which specialized in financing start-ups. Such investments are relatively small, typically only a few hundred thousand dollars, and often less, well below the threshold that now interests most venture capitalists. Most of the recently- created venture capital funds come in at later financing rounds, where the "smart" input is less critical.

Venture capital professionals are expensive, and so is their methodological approach to investments. As a consequence, they demand high returns, and only a limited number of sectors qualify on that basis. The return potential must be high and the size of the investments, significant. On these counts, high-technology and leveraged buy-outs are appealing. And it is also the reason most ventures do without the venture capital industry.[9]

Thus entrepreneurs tend to rely on "informal smart money" from the local business community and acquaintances. Indeed, the smart entrepreneur will seek out a "smart" partner as a minority shareholder. The local business community, lawyers, accountants, etc., can play a big role in creating a good climate.

Governments also get into the game, with various programs that attempt to fill the managerial and financial gaps of start-ups. Indeed, in North America, the new or expanding small manufacturing firms that do not benefit, sometimes substantially from these programs, are rare. But my experience with these grant programs is that they are relatively inefficient, of value mostly in last-resort situations when the entrepreneurs have nowhere else to turn and nothing to lose. These programs have serious drawbacks.

First, grants tend to consolidate the entrepreneur's sole ownership of his venture, since he does not have the same need to take financial partners. This is bad. Second, these programs choke the informal smart money investment, or at least, price it out of the manufacturing sector. Third, they tend to lead to bad decisions, as the entrepreneur and the government agent who runs the program, form an awkward team at the helm of a new venture.

Indeed, there is a fundamental conflict between the entrepreneur and the bureaucrat. The cultural gap between the two is usually wide. Differences in age, education, values, and work methods are usually significant. The entrepreneur is usually older, less educated, less "polished", more practical and short-term oriented. In addition, he is a workaholic who identifies solely with his company. He is intuitive and puts a high value on his experience and his hands-on knowledge of the marketplace. The bureaucrat is more systematic, more analytical, more objective, and relies on written documentation.

Their respective roles and the relations that bind them also conflict. The entrepreneur's fundamental function is to take calculated risks; he weighs the pros and cons of every move. The analyst's function is to ensure that the funds for which he is responsible are spent wisely and according to the "rules". Thus he evaluates the entrepreneur's project carefully, with explicit objective rules. From the entrepreneur's perspective, it's not just another project, but the financial and emotional investment of his lifetime, his "baby". On the defensive, the entrepreneur normally takes a negative attitude toward the bureaucrat and criticizes the program as bureaucratic, slow, complex, and having "too much paperwork".

But the entrepreneur wants the money and will go through all the required motions to get it. Thus, entrepreneurs flock to these programs, despite their shortcomings. Nevertheless, one of the first things an entrepreneur does when his firm grows is to delegate the responsibility of dealing with government officials to a junior employee.

SOCIAL SUPPORT

Have you ever noticed that towns which have an episcopal seat or a Superior Court courthouse tend to do less well, in terms of economic development, than towns of similar size lacking these institutions? Administrative towns dominated by a professional elite discourage entrepreneurship. Towns run by their commercial elite encourage it. Administrative towns are often cleaner, better looking and on the surface, wealthier. Commercial towns are crasser, brassier, less orderly. But they are also more dynamic. As expected, entrepreneurial effervescence thrives in greedier, more vulgar and less structured environments such as

Jacobsville, as opposed to the more staid administrative centres and company towns, where the proper order of things is not defined by the pocketbook.

This is not new. In the eighteenth century, the old administrative centres of Great Britain (such as Nottingham and York) were all passed over by a group of more dynamic commercial towns (Manchester, Leeds, etc.). Jane Jacobs in The Economy of Cities tells us about two pairs of cities with comparable endowments, but highly different potential, Manchester and Birmingham in 19th century England, (Manchester being by that time institutionalized), and Atlanta and Birmingham in the U.S. in the early 1950s. Despite many advantages, both Manchester, England, and Birmingham, Alabama, were surpassed by their more dynamic rivals.

Social support covers a wide range of institutional characteristics. But it ultimately boils down to the openness of social institutions to change in the economic order. Since any change can affect the distribution of power within the society, it tends to be resisted by the establishment. A community has to accommodate the rise of new organizations, and accept the decline of others. Are there barriers to hinder the former and props to shore up the latter? Does the community, and its business elite, let the sun shine where it may?

Widespread belief among the political elite in economic progress as a way to improve the welfare of society translates into positive social support for economic growth. This shows up as openmindedness toward new technologies, financial support for education, investing in basic research, using long-term planning horizons, and so on. Lower personal taxes and fewer regulations also improve the entrepreneurial environment. Lower income tax, and in particular lower marginal rates, lead to more savings and to more investment in high risk ventures. Less regulation lowers the barriers to entry to new firms. Governments in a society where the entrepreneur is held in high esteem will be more prone to introduce such policies. When historians talk of the climacteric conditions that explain the relative decline of Great Britain as an economic powerhouse, they refer in part to a lack of this kind of support for progress.

Boston and Palo Alto illustrate what a commitment to progress can achieve in the long run. Boston has more colleges and universities par capita than any other city in North America. At the end of the nineteenth century, its banking and industrial communities joined to establish the Massachusetts Institute of Technology, whose purpose was to provide technical personnel to local industries. Even today, high- technology business leaders communicate to the area's universities their anticipated needs for scientific manpower. The financial community of Boston is likewise involved. The Bank of Boston has always assumed a leadership role in promoting the region's economy. After the Second World War, the financial community was instrumental in setting up ARD, which gave birth to the local venture capital industry.

Leadership can come from outside the business community. In Palo Alto, where Stanford University is established, Frederick Terman, an engineering professor who went on to be President of the university from 1952 to 1964, provided the leadership, and more than anybody else, was responsible for the blossoming of Silicon Valley. When he was the dean of the engineering school, he convinced Stanford to turn over 1,200 acres of land into the Palo Alto Industrial Park. His students became the early Silicon Valley entrepreneurs. David Packard and William Hewlett established one of the first plants in the park. So did the Varian brothers, whose company developed the kryston, the predecessor to the transistor and which now employs 4,500 people in Silicon Valley. It was also natural for William Shockley to locate his new company in the Palo Alto Industrial Park when he came back to California in 1956.

A healthy social support system also holds entrepreneurs in high esteem. This is not an endorsement of big business, but rather of progressive firms, firms that grow and innovate. The CEOs of such progressive businesses become local folk heroes. People listen to them and respect them. They set an example for ambitious young people. In such a supportive context, being an entrepreneur is a highly rewarded function in society.[10] This is not naive Horatio Alger stuff. On the contrary, regions that share such attitudes are bound to generate more entrepreneurs and thus, grow faster.

Finally, healthy social support is reflected as a flexible legal framework for innovative and smaller firms. Nothing illustrates this better than Italy. For decades, Italy was considered the problem child of Western Europe. Its political system, and the governments it produced, were unstable, ineffective, disorganized, and had little control of the economy. Moreover, its social framework gave much power to unions and emphasized such things as job security at the expense of inefficiency.

But in parallel, Italy strongly encouraged its small business sector, through numerous initiatives and involuntarily, through a leaky tax collection system. Firms with fewer than 15 employees were exempt from many laws and regulations. As a consequence, small businesses boomed in Italy, over the years weaving a dynamic fabric of firms of all sizes. The impact on the economy is there to see. In the late eighties, the Italian GNP reached the level of that of Great Britain.[11]

Developing values that yield a social commitment to growth and progress takes time. Their emergence needs strong and persistent commitment by the social elite, educators, writers and commentators, the political class and leaders in business and in labour unions. The commitment should be reflected in all facets of the social framework, from the quality of primary and secondary education, to maintaining a just balance between the power of organized labour and the needs of industrial adaptation and competitiveness. Commitment implies fundamental choices, which are not always easy.

GROWING ENTREPRENEURS

Entrepreneurs thrive in a soil where incubators, models and sponsors abound. Fortunately, these three elements are replenished by the growth of new firms. Climatic conditions, namely technological inputs, business inputs and social support, maintain the effervescence. Conversely, choking any one of these sources can have a chilling effect on growth.

Jane Jacobs recalls the gradual drying-up of entrepreneurial dynamism in Rochester in the 1920s and 30s. Eastman Kodak had emerged from the entrepreneurial ferment of the turn of the century, when the chemical industry was very much high- tech. But Eastman Kodak strongly discouraged spin-offs, suing former employees who tried to go into a business even remotely related to photographic film. In doing so, it sent a powerful message to the community. A benevolent employer and a corporate citizen with a social conscience, Eastman Kodak did not foster values conducive to change and to entrepreneurial opportunities. Rochester had everything necessary to become a dynamic city, except the social support for the entrepreneur. When Robert Wilson invented holography in Rochester, he did not find any local backers and had to team up with the Batelle Institute from Columbus, Ohio, to form Xerox. Ironically, a few years later, Kodak went into the copier business, as a late-comer.

The entrepreneurial realm has to be alive and well to maintain the health of an economy. Its role is to replenish the economic fabric and to increase the number of activities which structure the production realm. By supplying a continuous stream of new activities, the entrepreneurial realm produces a very rich economic fabric with growth potential widely distributed in organizations of all ages. In such a fertile soil, the economy becomes a very diversified garden, containing trees of all ages.

The attention that we have paid so far to the entrepreneurs, does not belittle the economic importance of the established corporations spawned by an earlier generation of entrepreneurs. Indeed, most of the economic production is generated by established firms, and so is a significant share of economic growth.

Let us digress for a few chapters to review the role of established corporations in the economy. It will help us to better understand their limits, especially those of the large corporations, and put in a better perspective the critical importance of the rejuvenating entrepreneurs.

THE LIMITS OF
LARGE CORPORATIONS

CHAPTER SEVEN

THE ECONOMIC MACHINE

"Change is relentless. The basic motivations of management, however, tend to remain intact. Throughout the history of big business, managers have aimed for growth and control of markets. These pressures on management have been part of every major move forward, from small to large business, from large to related and from related to unrelated.

Milton Leontiades

Welcome into the large corner office, on the top floor. There is a desk at the far end and a small conference table near the entrance. To the right, a "living-room" area with couch and coffee table has been arranged. Several paintings hang on the wood-panelled walls. There is a computer terminal on a side table, next to the desk, tuned to a stock market channel. On the desk, the most important tool of the CEO, the telephone.

Welcome to the production realm, with a view from the command post. This is the office of Tom Roberts, Chairman and Chief Executive Officer (CEO) of the fictional ProXi Corporation. ProXi is a diversified industrial company, active in opticals, office furniture, and control systems, with sales approaching $1.2 billion a year.

Tom Roberts is in town today. He has been working in his office since eight o'clock, sorting through his mail, scribbling comments in the margin, and dividing it into three neat little piles. At 9:30, he discusses the follow-up actions with his executive assistant and takes a phone call from Frankfurt.

Tom then walks in on an ongoing budget committee meeting, chaired by the chief operating officer (COO), the number two man at ProXi. The senior corporate officers are going through the preliminary capital budget for next year.

Over lunch, Tom meets with the president of the Office Furniture Group and the outside counsel to discuss the antitrust implications of a proposed acquisition. At two o'clock, he is back at the office, to make a few telephone calls.

At 2:30, the COO and an assistant walk in to review various operations. At 3, they move to the conference room, where the president of the Control System Group presents an action plan to turn around the performance of his group. Acceptance of his budget had been delayed pending this meeting. Questions are asked by the senior officers from head office, while Tom sits silent. The meeting ends at 4:15, with conditional approval of the plan. The Group people leave the meeting smiling.

More telephone calls. Short meetings with the corporate counsel to go over the material for next week's Board Meeting, and with the Public Affairs V.P. to discuss the corporate position on a pending bill in the legislature. At six o'clock the CEO leaves, with a bulging case of papers, but he knows that tonight he has only to review the speech that he will give tomorrow afternoon at a local community college. Tom reads the speech on the way home, in the back of his limousine.

This is how generals spend their days in the corporate game. Talking on the phone, reading memos, attending highly-staged meetings where the underlings do most of the talking, thinking about the Board meeting, participating in community affairs, controlling what the corporation says, comforting the movers and shakers.[1]

Their years are built around the budget cycle, the main planning tool of a corporation, which generates a flurry of meetings every autumn. Despite many attempts to make it more sophisticated, the budget is still the tool around which every manager commits himself and which is used to monitor performance on a continuous basis.

Tom Roberts' year is also paced by the quarterly results and by formal meetings. Nine Board meetings; the annual meeting of shareholders; an April meeting with financial analysts in New York, just before the annual tour of the operations of the company, a late spring ritual. In between Tom Roberts squeezes four weeks of vacation, which are almost a cliche: two weeks for skiing in Europe in March, two weeks with the kids in the summer.

Meanwhile, the corporation hums along. Seven thousand five hundred and twenty-two employees, according to the annual report, walk in every morning and know exactly what to do. The three groups, coordinating 23 (soon-to-be 24) profit centres, operate in North America, Europe and Singapore. ProXi's capital budget is $117 million this year, profits up by 17 per cent, to $85 million, a good year. The stock is high, one of the best price-earning ratios in the industry. No crisis looms, except that the President of the Control System Group will have to be replaced. Tom Roberts hates pushing old friends aside.

THE PRODUCTION REALM

This chapter is about the production realm, the large corporations that dominate it and their contribution to economic growth. The production realm is the machine that generates most of what is being produced by an advanced economy. It builds the cars, operates the banks, bakes the bread, flies the planes, fills the stores and publishes the books. Indeed, if it were not for the entrepreneurs, the production realm would be the whole economy. Millions of firms populate the production realm, each with its technology, its products, and its market. In North America, the number of firms in the production realm is somewhere between 5 million and 6 million.[2]

The production realm is dominated by a limited number of large corporations, each with at least several thousand employees. Using as minimum size, sales of $200 million per year, (with two exceptions; financial institutions, $1 billion in assets, and retailing and wholesaling, $1 billion in sales), the production realm of the advanced economies of Western Europe, North America and the Pacific Rim is dominated by less than 10,000 large corporations, of which ProXi is a valid representation. The largest corporations have several hundred thousand employees. Most of these 10,000 corporations are multinationals, operating in several countries. Altogether, they account for over half of the production of the non-communist world, and for over 90 per cent of its international trade. About 40 per cent of them are based in the United States.

The presence of these large private organizations is a fundamental characteristic of the advanced economies. Never in history have there been so many large organizations spanning countries and continents and adapting not only to different environments, but to fairly tumultuous changes in these environments. ProXi Corp. is fairly typical. The company is publicly owned, with a controlling interest resting in friendly hands. It is diversified in several fields, and has several groups, divisions and subsidiaries.

If there are problems in the production realm, they are associated with such corporations, the way they are structured, the way they are run and mostly their ability to adapt. Fortunately, they are intensively scrutinized by some of the best intellects in the world.[3] We know much about what is good and what is wrong with them. The challenge is to make them perform better.

OPERATING IN A TURBULENT ENVIRONMENT

Never in modern peace time have such worldwide perturbations shaken the economic environment as the shocks sustained by the advanced economies since 1970. Double digit inflation, which sent all kinds of incorrect signals to management and workers and created the false illusion of prosperity; interest rates that climbed above 20 per cent; two dramatic increases in energy prices, in 1973 and in 1979, multiplied energy prices by ten; consumers' reactions to these higher prices, which changed consumption patterns which had been stable for decades; then, oil prices dropped by half in 1985-1986, creating another set of winners and losers.

Exchange rates fluctuating over 50 per cent in a few years were also big shocks to multinational corporations which derive half of their earnings from abroad. Exporters suddenly became uncompetitive and had to rapidly reshuffle their production plans. The debt crisis also loomed over the international economy. Several hundred billion dollars of debt from countries such as Argentina, Brazil, Poland and Mexico threatening to default, rocked the international banking system like never before. Then, suddenly, the Communist world crumbles in a matter of months.

Finally, the old North American and European industrial structures were shaken by the profound inroads in their traditional markets by Japanese and other Asiatic manufacturers. Whole industries were stunned: automobiles, consumer electronic appliances, steel, semiconductors, etc. The spectre of international trade wars looms high, the same type of trade war that precipitated the Great Depression in the 1930s.

What is interesting is that most large corporations have adapted rather smoothly to these shocks, whose impact cannot be discounted. Whenever there is a sharp discontinuity in the environment, opportunities arise. Aggressive competitors try to capitalize on these opportunities to fundamentally alter the competitive structure. Laggard corporations not reacting rapidly enough become highly vulnerable. This is the new environment of the production realm that has emerged.

Can the production realm thrive in such an environment? Has industrial America taken the climacteric mood that led the British economy to stagnation in the early part of this century? Or is it passing through a period of great turbulence from which the production realms will emerge shaken down, leaner, more flexible and more or less intact?

THE COMPETITIVE GAME

To understand the production realm, its competitive drive and its contribution to growth, one has to understand the management process of large organizations. A productive organization owns assets, masters technologies and is generally deployed in several markets. Three major constituencies make demands on it. Clients demand good products at competitive prices. Suppliers of capital and in particular, shareholders, demand financial returns. Employees demand good compensation and challenging careers. CEOs and senior management do the arbitrage between these competing constituencies. They command the deployment of the assets of their organizations to generate the surpluses which will be distributed among the constituencies. Maintaining the productivity of the asset base is the challenge of CEOs.[4]

Strategy has been a commonly used term in management only since the late seventies.[5] Yet, corporate management is very much a matter of strategy as the frontier of management technology has moved to the challenge of being adaptive and creative in the competitive game. To obtain sustainable competitive advantages, corporations give great importance to how they are structured and how their production and marketing resources are deployed. Since large corporations routinely operate in more than one field of activity, strategy is also concerned with moving resources internally from one industry to another, from one competitive theatre of operations to another one. The strategy of an organization determines which businesses it should be in, and within each business, how best to ensure and enhance both short- and long-term profitability. Competitive strengths and weaknesses have to be carefully assessed. Available resources have to be identified and properly managed. Ensuring and enhancing profitability is a complex exercise.

Corporate strategies are typically set every five to ten years, and reviewed formally during annual strategic planning exercises, where priorities and objectives are defined and structures are reviewed. The objectives at that level are broad, bearing on markets and market segments, products and production level. The annual budget is then prepared, to deploy corporate resources within the guidelines of the strategic plan.

The outcome of this process fixes the markets and the products of the corporation and its sales and profit objectives at the operating level. These objectives drive the organization throughout the year. The plan and the budgets are prepared neither from the top down nor the bottom up, but interactively. The role of senior management is to obtain ambitious objectives and extract strong commitments to achieve them. Typically, the process involves the management of the organization for several months every year. The planning cycle usually drives the expansion into new markets and new products, magical routes to increased sales and profits. The operating budget serves as a monitoring instrument throughout the year. Regular reports filter to the top, comparing actual performance to budgets throughout the organization.

The budgetary exercise also involves R&D and capital expenditures. The R&D budget is generally institutionalized and determined mostly by rules, such as a percentage of sales, or so much above last year. Within this budgetary envelope, allocations are made to specific projects, taking into account the demands of the organization. Most of the R&D budget is allocated to projects that have strong sponsors within the organization.

This is a critical bias of large organizations that causes R&D activities to be oriented mostly toward cost reduction projects and toward product improvements. Conversely, it is more difficult to finance projects that stray too far from present activities, as they do not find strong sponsors. There are exceptions to this. Organizations whose centre of gravity is the mastering of a specific technology are more adventuresome within the range of possibilities of that technology.

Nevertheless, one should not be fooled by the potential impact of corporate R&D expenditures. Most R&D expenditures are spent in enhancing productivity and making marginal improvements to existing products. Only a small proportion goes to new product development or basic research. For several decades, General Motors has consistently been the leading R&D organization in the United States, on the basis of its budget. For the past 30 years, General Motors has spent (and still spends) as much on R&D as the whole American drug industry. That does not make it a path-breaker. GM research is targeted mainly at improving productivity and existing products, the name of the game in the production realm.[6] The results are for everybody to judge.

Capital expenditures budgets have a greater strategic importance than R&D budgets, for they are used to control the expansion of the corporation into new activities. Thus these budgets are tightly controlled by headquarters. Indeed, heads of divisions and subsidiaries who sometimes control operating budgets of several hundred million dollars, typically have to go to their bosses for capital items of a few hundred thousand dollars. This ensures that decisions to enter new fields of activity are made at the top.

Management is a lot more than the planning and budgetary exercise. Implementation and control are critical. In times of crisis, contingency systems take over, and many rules stemming from the budgetary and planning exercises are superseded. Symbolic management also plays an important role. Signals sent downward by the leaders of the organization have a profound impact on the way the organization performs. Corporate culture is also given much attention, as the values that characterize an organization are as important as leadership in determining the organization's ability to change and be flexible.[7]

The strengths and weaknesses of this modern system of management are well known. The strengths should not be underestimated. They allow the efficient management of very large organizations active in several countries and in a wide variety of products. We sometimes forget the size of some of these organizations, which comprise several hundred thousand people, speaking different languages, active in a wide variety of business fields. These sizable organizations are also fairly democratic, much more so than the large government bureaucracies. Most managers participate in determining their annual objectives, which become their corporate commitment. Performance is measured and rewarded. Naturally, not all organizations are well managed. But the method is the same.[8]

ADAPTING TO MANAGE DIVERSITY

The greatest strength of the system may very well be its capacity to adapt and evolve. Management practices and structures are continually being improved upon. Management studies are now one of the most important fields of social research. The competitive drive also forces corporations to experiment with new approaches. As modern economies become more complex and corporations span an increasing number of different markets, modern management has to tackle the challenge of managing diversity.

To do so, organizations have evolved from the traditional Army-type hierarchical structure, to much more complex models. Divisions have appeared, to handle families of products. In the largest organizations, divisions are regrouped in largely autonomous groups. This allows senior management to decentralize decision making, allowing efficient operations in highly different environments.

Flexibility is also obtained through decentralization, specialization and subcontracting. Service contracts for standard activities as diverse as maintenance of equipment and buildings, data processing, cafeteria operations and building security have become the norm in large organizations. Specialized manufacturing is being subcontracted. Large corporations are relying on "body shops" to provide them with technical personnel, for activities where the demand fluctuates. This trend has spread to numerous sectors, from computer programmers to nurses for the winter months in southern resort areas.

More and more professional activities in large organizations are farmed out to professionals, working either in small "boutiques" or from their homes.[9] From the perspective of a large corporation, paying only for the services needed and having the freedom to chose the person it wants for a specific job, is a vastly superior alternative to having full-time professionals on the payroll. The transaction costs, finding and hiring the persons, are less than the benefits of the added flexibility.[10]

114

Other structural trends are appearing. Cross-ownerships and industrial alliances which have been extensively developed in Japan, are on the rise in Europe and appearing in North America. Whether they will spread is still uncertain. But this continual search for the perfect organizational structure underlines the fact that the production realm is well aware of its shortcomings as it faces a rapidly changing environment.

Competition is the driving force behind the evolution of the production realm. A continuous stream of new entrants, leaner and more creative, rejuvenate it. The relative positions of players are always shifting. Lamentations over the difficulties of the dinosaurs, the U.S. Steels, Krupps, and Renaults of this world, will not change the ineluctable march of the forces of change. Indeed, Noburo Makino, a Japanese business author, has calculated that the average life "at the top" for a large Japanese corporation is something like 25 years. It is tough to stay large, independent and healthy for many generations. Indeed, the majority of the large corporations are taken over or fade away within 50 years.[11] For instance, of the 500 large industrial firms listed by Fortune magazine in 1954, less than 250 remained on the list as independent firms in 1990, 36 years later!

CORPORATE CONTRIBUTION TO GROWTH

Large corporations not only represent a large part of world-wide production, but they are also significant contributors to economic growth. Indeed, they account for most of the economic growth contributed by the production realm. But their contribution is achieved mainly through the expansion of their own activities, as opposed to the implant of new activities which characterize the entrepreneurial contribution. Understanding this distinction is most useful in establishing the relative role of corporations and entrepreneurs in the economy.

Consider a decision of our fictional firm, ProXi, to double its share of the U.S. sunglasses market, and its concurrent decision to expand production capacity in the United States. Does this expansion contribute to economic growth, or isn't ProXi just taking away sales from other domestic producers, transferring the jobs from one community to another? This is an important question.

ProXi's optical group is a dominant player in the sunglasses business, competing in particular with Bausch & Lomb's RayBan. To achieve its strategic objective, ProXi introduces a new line of glasses and invests in an aggressive marketing campaign.

Gradually, it takes market share away from Bausch & Lomb's RayBan. To meet the demand, ProXi adds a second shift at its Tallahassee plant. But on the other hand, it forces cuts in production at the RayBan plant in Rochester, N.Y. At that point, the net effect on the U.S. economy can be seen as nil, the gains in Florida being cancelled by the losses in upstate New York.

But ProXi's new models are superior sunglasses. Indeed, this is the reason for their success. This superiority results in an expansion of the market, more people buying sunglasses than before. In other words, ProXi's gains are larger than RayBan's losses, causing the increase in Tallahassee to be somewhat larger than the reduction in Rochester. This net gain generates its multiplier effect, which increases total consumption in Florida, and, as the ripple spreads, elsewhere in the U.S. Ultimately, it generates enough demand to re-equilibrate all markets. For instance, Rochester feels it through a small surge in the sales of Kodak films. This takes away some of the slack created by the contraction at RayBan.

What ProXi has just done is add another thin layer of activity in the production realm. As one can expect, RayBan will react to ProXi's invasion of its turf. It will fight back with a new colour of lenses or increased productivity, lower costs, or lower prices. In reacting, RayBan attacks ProXi's and other companies' turf. In doing so, it also adds another thin layer of economic activities. Multiply this by the number of divisions and independent corporations in North America and you have an idea of the contribution to growth continually added in thin layers by competition in the production realm.

David Birch's analysis of job creation suggests that at least two-thirds of the net annual new jobs in the economy are added by the production realm, through expansion of activities. Thus, this thin but continuous layering of additional products and services, fuelled by increases in productivity and product quality, is a major contributor to economic growth. It also replaces the jobs lost in the production realm through normal erosion of the competitiveness of some activities.

Competition brings forth a relentless pressure to reduce costs and to be more efficient. Moreover, in highly competitive markets where prices of all competitors are related, the competitive drive urges organizations to differentiate and improve their products. So every year, the ProXi sunglasses become a little bit better, more attuned to current fashion, more scratch resistant, etc.

THE LIMITS OF THE PRODUCTION REALM

But ProXi will have difficulty learning to do something other than what it does presently. To be innovative in any significant way is one of the major problems of organizations, and it is doubtful whether all the improvements to management will ever change this. ProXi can learn to be more competitive, but it has problems with path- breaking innovations. It will learn to make cream-coloured, four-phase, ultra-violet cured, scratch-free, aviator sunglasses. And maybe ProXi will license its brand name to a jean designer, who will tap some of the ProXi goodwill with another brand of jeans, ProXi jeans. But it will be difficult for ProXi to go beyond this, as it has major problems with path-breaking innovations.

Deep inside ProXi, there are many curious, practical people who regularly spot opportunities for new products, some of which could turn out to be path-breaking innovations. In its various R&D departments, ProXi has 65 professionals and technicians. But most of their work is concentrated on improving products and production methods, such as designing aviator glasses for Japanese noses, adding a fifth phase to the cream-coloured sunglasses and reducing breakage. Their jobs are not to fiddle with new concept ideas; their jobs are to keep ProXi humming along profitably by doing what is being asked and by meeting their budget objectives. Moreover, there are departments in each Group looking for new products for ProXi. Thus, in practical terms, there are many less opportunity scanners at ProXi than meet the eye. Up there in the corner office on the top floor, Tom Roberts might think that innovation is under control within ProXi, but deep in the bowels of the organization, people know what the real priorities are.

The consultants at Arthur D. Little wrote a fascinating book, *Breakthroughs*[12], about the difficulties of translating innovations into products in the corporate world. They examined 12 of the most significant commercial breakthroughs of the past 20 years in America, Japan and Europe. Astonishingly, the authors confess that they could not find a single company that succeeded in developing an "environment for creativity" (their expression). One company, the 3M Corp. (formerly Minnesota Mining & Manufacturing Corp.) was the object of particular attention because it is recognized as the world leader in management techniques and structures to foster innovation. But 3M nearly failed in the case of their most famous innovations of the past 20 years.

"In the company most often praised for an environment supportive of "innovation", 3M Corporation, we saw in action a corporate culture that, over a period of five years, appeared at times to discourage and stifle the Post-It Note Pads, the most pervasive office product breakthrough since Scotch Tape."

The Post-It Note Pads are the little yellow sticky note pads now common in offices. The long genesis of this product tells a lot about the difficulties large organizations have, even those with the best of intentions, in making room for entrepreneurship. It is a story worth being told.

3M's fundamental strength is the mastering of technologies of coating and binding materials. No other organization in the world masters these technologies as 3M does. 3M coats glue on Scotch tape and ferric oxide on magnetic tapes for computers. The 3M R&D labs are staffed with scientists who spend their lifetime fiddling with coating materials.

To ensure creativity and foster the development of new products, 3M allows its scientists 15 per cent of their time to conduct projects of their choice. They are able to scan the world for opportunities. So, in 1964 (remember that date), Spence Silver, a scientist at 3M, found, in his free time, the glue which is the basic feature of the Post-It Note Pads, a glue that does not stick too well and which stays on one surface when the material is peeled. The glue can be characterized as a non-aggressive adhesive, a poor glue indeed. Where can such a glue go in an organization looking for the perfect glue?

Spence Silver made a fool of himself for several years, fighting to get 3M to develop products with his glue. (Luckily for 3M, good corporate man Silver convinced them to spend $10,000 for a patent.) One product proposed by Spence Silver, a sticky bulletin board, was finally tested. It bombed.

In 1973, nine years after its discovery, the glue was picked up by a "new venture team", one of those special groups set up within 3M to discover new products. A year later, the specific idea of the Note Pads came to Arthur Fry, a member of the group. While singing in the choir at church, he thought how useful it would be to have a sticker to keep the bookmarks in place in his hymnal. Arthur Fry had the key idea of putting the glue on the paper instead of the bulletin board. Great expensive high-technology thinking. Within months, the technical problems were solved and the first prototypes of the stickers were all over the laboratory offices.

But getting from there to the market was another ordeal of several years. In late 1978, marketing told the venture team that the Note Pads had flunked their market tests. "Bananas", said the venture team, which then redid the market tests. The product was finally launched in 1979 and was an "instant" success. It had taken 15 years.

The incredible thing about this story is that 3M is structured from top to bottom to be innovative, with 15 per cent roaming allocations, new venture teams, new programs for innovation, honours for innovators, and a strong corporate belief that a quarter of their sales in five years will come from products not yet invented. Moreover, glue is their thing; they are always looking for new glue products. It took 15 years for this great glue to be put to use. A simple idea, replacing the impractical pin with glue to stick paper onto something.

If Spence Silver had been a frustrated would-be entrepreneur, he would have slammed the door and left 3M carrying his gluish ideas along with him. The non- aggressive glue would have fallen into the public domain. Spence Silver would have knocked on doors with his sticky bulletin boards. Some of the Thildas of this world would have tinkered with the sticky bulletin boards, and either in their basement or at church, would have thought about the great glue switch, from the board to the paper. The pads would have appeared in Kalamazoo or St-Georges instead of St.Paul. The first sales would have been considered a positive market test, and a new business would have been on its way. Whether the offices of America would have had the opportunity to enjoy the sticky little yellow pads before 1979, nobody knows for sure, but it is highly probable. Furthermore, nobody can deny that the route for incubating a new innovative product is still arduous even in the most creative large corporation. What about the others?

THE IMPORTANCE OF NEW PRODUCTS

The hubris of large corporations demands sustained growth. Increasing profits command a higher value for the stock of a corporation. A high stock price not only ensures fatter bonuses for senior executives, but also guarantees the independence of the corporation as it puts its price out of the reach of would-be bidders. To sustain growth, large corporations seek first and foremost activities with above-average growth potential.

New products offer such potential. The high-growth phase of new products is typically short, 5-to-15 years. But this is the period when a large corporation does what it can do best: expand production and develop distribution channels to reach potential customers. Growth rates over 100 per cent a year in the early growth phase of products are common. As the market saturates, the growth in demand slowly tapers off to gradually track the normal rate of expansion of the economy. There is a need for only so many television sets in a market.

At that stage, competition becomes tougher and maintaining market shares is based on improving the product appeal by adding bells and whistles. Using lower cost labour, either younger workers or workers from abroad or from rural areas, the copycats start nibbling at the low-end segment of the mass market, with cheaper alternatives. They spoil the market. The fun is gone. The CEOs attention gets attracted by the hopes of newer products with more zest in their future.

Most corporations wish for a continuous stream of new products developed internally, which the company can then take into their growth phase. But that does not happen. Innovations are constrained by the interests of the organization. Invent a better mousetrap and try to sell that to your boss at 3M: no way, mousetraps are not their business. Steve Wozniak tried to sell the Apple I board to his boss at Hewlett- Packard: "no way, HP is in the instrumentation business." So the Woz slammed the door and his young friend Steve Jobs, who fortunately did not have any business at the time, took the time to harvest the technology that gave us the personal computer.

Large corporations are usually good at innovating only within their centre of gravity. The centre of gravity of an organization is defined by the strategic functions which generate the fundamental competitive advantages of an organization. Thus IBM will be innovative in the marketing and applications that have fuelled its growth since the early fifties. Proctor & Gamble innovations will tap its mastery of the channels of distribution for packaged goods with new products to move down these channels.

Corporations whose centre of gravity is defined by a technology should be the most innovative, as they can focus on finding new applications for their technologies. Yet, as the case of the Post-It Note Pads indicated, it is difficult for any organization to break away from its corporate focus. Thus, IBM can make stupendous technical advances in developing the next generation of computers. But it took outsiders, Jobs and Wozniak, to break away from existing commercial grooves and conceive the personal computer. It is not that IBM could not have done it. Indeed, it had the technology, the researchers and the funds to do it. But those who had power within IBM had corporate blinkers which kept them focused on the next generation of computers, and unfortunately, in their vision, that generation was just an enhancement of the existing computers of the period. Personal computers had to be ushered in by two kids.

Thus, although large organizations argue that they are innovative and generate new products, they will tend to stay in their grooves. This greatly limits the number of innovations and breakthroughs that come out of the production realm. New activities will be generated, but mainly within the narrow confines of their centre of gravity.

Large organizations have difficulties in adding new work beyond derivatives of their present product line. There are not that many managers who will buck the system, to push new ideas that do not fit into the "efficient management" plans for this year. In the 4,000 or so large corporations of North America, there might be some 40,000 points of innovation, that is "entrepreneurial" senior managers who are on the lookout for opportunities and are political enough to pull off a new venture. (This is a very generous estimate.) That does not compare with the entrepreneurial realm. There are 250,000 entrepreneurs starting businesses every year. Although there are many copycat entrepreneurs among them, there are enough who are innovative, who get great ideas while singing at church, and who will encounter less resistance than they would in large organizations.

Thus, on the basis of the numbers alone, small businesses and new businesses win easily at the innovation game. But they also win by default. Large corporations that have problems with innovation have a way out: they can acquire firms that have innovated. It is much easier for large corporations to write a cheque for an acquisition than to listen to the Spence Silvers and Steve Wozniaks of this world.

BUYING GROWTH AS A CORPORATE STRATEGY

Mergers and acquisitions valued at more than $1 million occur at the rate of 3,000 a year in United States and Canada, nearly as many mergers and acquisitions as there are large corporations with sales of over $200 million.[13] In half of the situations, the buyers are growth-minded large corporations; the sellers are controlling shareholders of smaller corporations with underdeveloped products.

For a large corporation, growth by acquisition is much easier and much more rapid than internal growth. Furthermore, it is a process controlled by senior management and thus much more manageable than internal growth. An acquisition is a handy lever to pull in order to meet ambitious growth objectives. Whether the acquisition route is an efficient way to grow is debatable. Cursory analyses of the financial performance of acquisitions often report dismal results.[14] However, if the efforts at internal growth were analyzed using the same criteria, similar dismal results would most likely be obtained.

One has to look at the global performance of corporations to assess whether the acquisition route to growth is efficient. There is some evidence that acquisition-active corporations do better than passive ones.[15] But this is a chicken-and-egg story. The active corporations may make acquisitions because they are better managed, which gives them better access to financial resources. Or conversely, the acquisitions may allow them to post superior performances.[16]

Thus, for the economy as a whole, the impact of acquisitions is mixed. Acquisitions in unrelated fields have led to diversified corporations. Econometric analyses indicate that diversified corporations are less profitable than less diversified corporations and that corporate productivity falls with diversification. The trend toward diversification has reversed in the seventies. Indeed, there is evidence that some of the gains in manufacturing productivities achieved in the 1980s in North America have been caused by the "de-diversification" trend in larger corporations.[17] This means that acquisitions can be good for the economy, when they invoke "de-diversification". Buyers can be more efficient in developing the full potential of the acquired product line, a net contribution to the growth of the economy. This effect seems to dominate in most of the smaller acquisitions. The classic acquisition was McDonald's, a restaurant operation with a good concept, but operated much below its potential. It was purchased by Ray Kroc, who expanded the concept and greatly enriched it.

But the empirical evidence indicates that many acquired operations fare poorly under new ownership. Buyers often cannot properly manage the acquired operations. Business magazines such as Fortune, Business Week, and Forbes delight in following these corporate disasters, particularly among the largest corporations. EXXON lost several hundred million dollars in the 1978 acquisition of Reliance Electric, an electric motor company which it sold at a loss in 1986. Sohio dissipated over a billion dollars on the purchase of Kennecott in 1980, a company which a few years ago, had greatly overpaid to acquire Carborundum, a large old-line abrasive manufacturer. Most of the Kennecott and Carborundum operations have now been closed or sold by Sohio at a loss.

However, buyers seldom lose everything. Acquired operations continue, although often at a reduced level. Buyers realize the economies of scale and of scope in combining certain activities with their own. What saves many deals are the jewels that buyers often pluck from acquired operations, a trade mark, a management team, some hidden assets, etc. This can make a transaction financially and organizationally rewarding without making a contribution to economic growth. By analogy, if I were to buy out a competitor and close him down, just to access his technology, I could make a profit, although the economy as a whole might lose.

Robert Reich, a Harvard professor, has argued that many buyers engage in "paper entrepreneurialism", restructuring the liabilities side of the balance sheet, changing the capital structure, then reselling the assets, with good timing in relation to the mood of the stock market.[18] What a corporation does in the real world does not really matter to a paper entrepreneur. The corporation is merely a vehicle. The deal is strictly financial. But at every transaction, the paper entrepreneur takes a profit for himself, milking the assets or the buyers who are usually the unsuspecting investing public. Because paper entrepreneurialism weakens the financial structure of the production realm, it has a negative impact on growth, although it enriches some shrewd "entrepreneurs".

Acquisitions are also financed by depriving other stakeholders of some of their patrimony in the acquired company. In a study of well publicized acquisitions, a Harvard economist, Lawrence Summers has concluded that most of the premium that the shareholders of the acquired companies received is later paid by employees, clients, tax payers, borrowers and communities.[19] The acquirers renegotiate the contracts or understandings that these stakeholders have, in order to cut cost and finance the acquisitions. Salaries are cut, senior management is pruned, sales contracts are renegotiated, suppliers are pressured to cut prices, plants are closed unless the community comes up with a good deal, borrowers see the value of their collateral diminished, as debt is accumulated, pension funds are stripped of their surplus, etc. Higher interest expenditures lower the tax burden. Finally, employees realize that they are now working for a company in a much weaker financial situation, which constrains their future demands. All these new arrangements do not create wealth: they are merely transfers from one group of stakeholders to another. To the extent that the transfers weaken the company, they have a negative contribution to the economy. But they can also strengthen the company by pruning in competent management and inneficient operations. Thus, such exercises, however traumatic, can be beneficial to the economy.[20]

Acquisitions are a legitimate avenue of growth for corporations. Faced with internal growth and acquisitions, most CEOs argue that they pursue both, although acquisitions will usually contribute more to new sales. Moreover, the internal growth to which they refer is mostly a result of getting the juice left in existing product lines and activities. Internally, generating new activities to sustain the growth of the corporation for the next 10 to 20 years is a minor strategic avenue in most corporations, despite all pretensions to the contrary.

An exception can be made for corporations whose centres of gravity are the mastering of technologies. They might rely more on internally-generated new products. But the saga of the sticky yellow note pads within 3M indicates how difficult that route is in the large organizations that dominate the production realm. With millions of entrepreneurs creating new activities in smaller businesses and in the entrepreneurial realm, acquiring the successful ones in their early stages of growth is a much more efficient strategy for a large corporation. Implicitly, such a strategy recognizes that a large organization is not the best environment to generate a new activity. The realm of the entrepreneur is much better suited to this.

PORTFOLIO MANAGEMENT

Strategic management in large corporations can be thought of as incorporating two fundamental functions: driving the organization in such a way that all its units meet superior performance targets, and managing a portfolio of activities to sustain the organization. Managing the portfolio implies selecting its composition through acquisitions and divestitures, and channelling development capital to the units with higher potential. It also demands restructuring some activities to increase their potential.

Divestitures, the counterpart of acquisitions, are becoming trendy. The recent aggressiveness of corporate raiders on the stock market contributed to this growing trend. Most of the recent large divestitures were brought about by financial restructuring of corporations, either to protect corporations against raiders, or to finance the successful acquisition of a corporation by a raider. Many acquisitions are financed in part by the sale of some of the assets of the acquired companies. In particular, leveraged buy-outs, where a management group buys a subsidiary, a division, or sometimes the whole company, as in the case of Macy's and Beatrice Goods, rely mostly on the divestiture of selected units for basic financing.

Strategic divestitures, for purposes other than raising money, are frequent.[21] CEOs realize that some activities would fare better if they were independent. Some corporations also decide to channel their investment budgets into a limited number of activities, making some of their present activities redundant, often those with lower growth potential. The stock market generally approves these strategic divestitures.

Acquisitions and divestitures are also at the core of some radical corporate transformation strategies. None has been more spectacular than the five-year transformation of the American Can Corporation in the mid-eighties. This corporation with sales of more than three billion dollars in 1982, went from being a large manufacturer of packaging products such as cardboard boxes and steel cans to being a financial conglomerate named Primerica. From 1982 to 1986, it sold practically all of its old operations, while a whole array of activities in the financial services sector were acquired. The stock market liked it; its stock price went from $12 to more than $50 a share. By reshuffling its portfolio of activities, the value of the corporation went from $900 million to $4 billion. Then, in a fitting ending, it sold itself to a large consumer finance company, which renamed itself Primerica.

The economy gained from this transformation; the activities under-lying both the old American Can and the new Primerica are better managed under their new ownership. Indeed, careful pruning of ineffi-cient activities from large corporations has become an important phenom-enon in the production realm, with a significant positive impact on the economy. As the emphasis moves toward service and flexibility, smaller organizations are often more effective. Large corporations sell back to local managers their smaller non-critical establishments. The trend is evident in food retailing. Many large food retailers are franchising individual stores to their managers, while they concentrate on what they do best, wholesale distribution and brand management. Individual store owners, managing 20 to 30 employees, and giving their clients the attention they demand, are much more efficient than salaried managers operating under the constraints of a large corporation.

Selling corporate stores to independent operators shows how large corporations adapt to the competitive pressures by altering their structures and their modes of operation. Indeed, the production realm adapts to the changing economic environment, sustaining a fundamental trend toward decentralization away from the large organization model. Smaller organizations are more efficient at tackling production functions previously done by large organizations. Pressed by competitive pressure, the production realm is making room for these more efficient, smaller organizations.

Many commentators have concluded that the corporation is becoming more entrepreneurial because it is becoming more adaptive. But entrepreneurs are good at weaving new activities into the economic fabric, something that large organizations are not as good at. A performance-oriented, large-scale organization is a tough place to grow a new activity that starts small, defiant, and fragile.

The major challenge of the corporation is different: to continually improve its competitiveness. It does this by improving its products and reducing its costs as well as by optimizing its structure — the portfolio of activities that it manages and the way it organizes itself to manage them. But many commentators question the motive of senior management, whether they are really pursuing better competitiveness. The focus on short-term performance is the object of severe criticism. Can the large corporations maintain their competitiveness if their major concerns are dominated by the next quarter financial results? This is the governance issue, the question of what goals are pursued by senior management, who sets these goals, who monitors their achievement, and who demands corrective action when needed. If the North American production realm is losing in the inevitable competition with the Japanese and European production realm, it is because of fundamental flaws in the governance of its large corporations.

CHAPTER EIGHT

TROUBLES IN THE PRODUCTION REALM

"The bourgeoisie, during its rule of scarcely one hundred years, has created more massive and more colossal productive forces than all proceeding generations together."

Karl Marx and Frederic Engels, 1848

I n 1984, a joint venture of General Motors and Toyota, the New Motor Corp., otherwise known as NUMMI, started operations in an old General Motors plant in Fremont, California. The plant, which had been shut down for several years, divided its production between GM's Nova and Toyota's Corolla. This fairly unique venture was seen as an opportunity for General Motors to learn about Japanese production methods and practices. Toyota managed the plant, which used conventional technology. Its employees were all former employees of the General Motors plant and bona-fide members of the United Automobile Workers union.[1]

Surprisingly, productivity turned out to be 50 per cent higher at NUMMI than at other General Motors plants. A 50 per cent difference is impressive. But the surprise was not that the Japanese obtain higher productivity in their plant. Indeed, GM knew that the Japanese were getting higher productivity in Japan, and it set up NUMMI to learn more about it. The astounding thing was that GM was surprised that the Japanese could do it in America. GM not only had totally underestimated their Japanese competitors, but it had not realized that the Japanese had developed over the years a much superior production process.

General Motors was the biggest car company in the world. Senior management knew that it was facing a strong competitive challenge from Japanese car manufacturers. But the Japanese successes in the automobile industry were attributed to factors specific to the Japanese: Japanese work ethics, lower capital costs, Japanese subcontractors, just-in-time inventory, robots, docile unions, lower labour costs, etc. The playing field was not level: indeed the Japanese were cheating.

NUMMI debunked this rationalization. Taking over a problem factory, the Japanese showed the world how they were doing it, on GM's own terrain. Nobody at GM dared to think that their success was due simply to better manufacturing management. Until NUMMI, GM, the largest U.S. corporation, did now know that one of its prime competitors could get 50 per cent more output per worker using GM's own facilities, tools and workers. They did it by training the workers, by arranging them in small teams and giving them responsibility, by inserting team leaders between foremen and workers, by insisting on zero-defect quality, and stopping the whole production line if a defect was not corrected, etc.

The NUMMI joint venture will not last for ever. Half a plant is not optimal either for Toyota or for General Motors. General Motors has learned all that it had to learn. Thousands of managers and union leaders from all over the GM operations have visited the NUMMI plant, to find out how Japanese manage a factory, how they train and motivate workers, how they structure the rules of operations, etc.

Why did it take a $300 hundred million plant to discover that the Japanese had a much superior manufacturing approach? Why did General Motors have to go through this humiliating venture to be shown how to build cars? How come nobody in senior management knew that the Japanese had developed way back in the 1950's, a superior production method and had been using it for more than 25 years, beating the hell out of their American competitors in any market where they were facing each other directly? Will the U.S. have to invite the Japanese to build semiconductor plants, VCR plants, machine tool plants, just to show American management how to do it?

THE GOVERNANCE ISSUE

What kind of questions were asked when General Motors' Board of Directors met?[2] For the governance of corporations lies ultimately with the directors. Senior management respond to them. They select the principal officers. They decided on their annual pay and on their bonuses. They are responsible to the shareholders, ensuring that the corporation is well managed. What did they do when they learned the truth: the Japanese way of building automobiles, and nothing else, was mostly responsible for the higher productivity and the superior quality obtained by Japanese manufacturers.[3]

There is a deep malaise within the North American production realm, and it has to do with the governance issue. Are the large North American corporations properly governed? Are they pursuing the proper objectives? Are they really striving to improve their competitiveness? Are they run by the best people? Are the directors able to make tough decisions? Are they sufficiently independent from management? Do they know enough to call the shot? Are they responsible, or merely cruising along, collecting fat director fees in the process?

Several criticisms are directed at large North American corporations: a focus on the short-term, complacency in the Boardroom, empire-building and paper entrepreneurship and finally, lack of respect for manufacturing. These criticisms are not to be dismissed lightly. There is more than a grain of truth in each of them.

The planning system of the large corporations, to which we alluded in the previous chapter, encourages a short-term focus. As a consequence, large organizations have difficulty institutionalizing a decentralized initiative-taking spirit that stimulates the organization to explore new avenues and new activities. Such free-wheeling management would conflict with the demands of a management system focused on keeping the organization competitive on a day-to-day basis.

This conflict is basic. The performance of a manager is assessed first and above all on his ability to meet his budgetary targets, very much a short-term outlook. The rewards for undertaking a long-term project are ill-defined and often illusory. Not only are the risks of failure higher, but by the time a long-term project blossoms, the manager who initiated it has often been promoted to another job. Furthermore, the uncertainty and the complexity of projects with long incubation periods demand that they be well understood by senior management, to obtain a long-term commitment. But senior management, which manages the reward system, cannot be expert in all fields. The uncertainty stemming from their lack of familiarity is compensated for by more prudent assessment. The safe way to perform in a large organization is to stick to measurable short-term achievements. Nobody will punish you if you pay only lip service to long-term development. An ambitious manager will have been promoted by the time the chickens come home to roost.

Public companies must also be concerned with quarterly results, another constraint which biases the organization toward the short-term. The principle is the same. Senior management is monitored chiefly by financial analysts, who base their assessment mostly on the quarterly profit performance. The fear of an undervalued stock price, which makes the organization vulnerable to take-over, increases the influence of the stock market over senior management's outlook. Thus, not only the management systems, but also the motivations at the top are biased toward a short-term focus.

The consequences are fundamental. Long-term risk is avoided. Corporations will prefer to buy an existing operation, rather than building one from scratch. In times of budgetary constraints, expenditures directed at the long-term development of the corporation, such as training and R&D, will be cut, as the system will barely notice it. The financial side of the organization, the bean counters who control the numbers, become very influential in the organization, taking over from operating managers.

But can these short-term biases be avoided? Can they be compensated for by corrective moves. The answer is yes, and indeed, much is already done to achieve this. But before going to that, let us hear about the other criticisms.

Are directors really overseeing senior management? This is a valid interrogation. Not that many insiders sit on the Board, benefiting from much superior information. In fact, insiders are slowly losing their importance on Boards to outside directors. But are these outside directors really independent? There is nothing to gain from being tough on a Board, except being ostracized by fellow directors. Indeed, the money is not there: it is at most a part-time job, a day or two a month. Furthermore, management controls the nominating process. As a consequence, very seldom will mavericks be found on Boards. Indeed, CEOs would be foolish to appoint troublemakers to their Board. (They have enough problems with ex-CEOs and their friends who sit as directors.) Very few large corporations have external directors with a large financial stake in the long-term future of the corporation, because such stockholders are rare.

Management control of the Board is not bad per se. In Japan, management controls the Boards of Directors, more than in the United States. But when this control is combined with the short-term focus of the organization, problems can arise.

The tough decisions, replacing an inefficient CEO, turning down a merger offer, setting the basic strategy of the organization, are Board decisions. But directors seldom have the legitimacy to stand up to senior management. Who are they to say no to them? The Japanese have a solution. So do the Europeans. The large financial institutions that have a big stake in a corporation, either as lenders or as stockholders, are influential on Boards. There is a check-and-balance mechanism.

Robert Reich, the Harvard professor, coined the term paper entrepreneurship to describe the unproductive empire-building of CEOs who build inefficient organizations merely because bigger is better. There is no indication in the literature on management and economics that "bigger is better", that large firms are more profitable than small firms. But to grow is the only way to go. There are all kinds of pressures in an organization which demands growth. And nowhere are these pressures felt more than at the top. So CEOs are looking for growth. And nothing beats acquisitions for fast growth. Acquisitions do not create wealth, or add any activities in the circular flow. Acquisitions merely rearrange ownership. But then, the acquirers have to pay for the acquisitions, and that demands actions.

The acquirers can improve the management of the acquired firm, and generate more profits and wealth from the new operations. Thus the acquisitions can be financed mostly from improved profits. But the empirical evidence arrives at a different conclusion: acquiring firms are usually not as good as the former management in running the operations. Instead of riding the road to more efficiency and to something "better", acquisitions lead the other way. The acquiring corporations buy growth, but at a price. So over time, it has to rearrange its balance sheet to pay for it: sell some units, borrow short term, borrow long term, issue stock, etc. Conditions in the financial markets will dictate the proper moves. Paper cntrepreneurship: when the stock market is up, move fast; when the market goes down, move fast; when long- term interest rates fall, move fast.

Large empires with feet of clay were built by empire builders who were good at paper entrepreneurship. When rough times came, the empires cracked and stumbled. IT&T, Gulf & Western, Litton, corporate names that were once famous and powerful. US Steel, renamed USX, derives three-quarters of its revenues from oil, the results of acquisitions made when the price of oil was much higher than today. General Motors has spent billions to buy its way into aerospace and data processing, and in the process, has lowered its earnings.

What is wrong with empire-building is the loss of focus. The direct costs are not that big. Sometimes, there are gains. But there are significant opportunity costs. While American CEOs huddle with their lawyers and investment bankers to plot the next offensive, Japanese managers hone their management practices.

Thus it is not surprising to find that the art of manufacturing things is loosing its popularity in corporate America. The Berkeley Roundtable, a loose association of California economists, has been arguing that the main weakness of the American economy lies with the decline of manufacturing.[4] The NUMMI surprise occurred because people in the Boardroom did not really care about the factory floor. The fast track to the top in large corporations does not pass through the factory. Legal works, planning, marketing, finance, yes; but seldom managing people to get them to manufacture things more efficiently.

The production of goods is very important to all advanced economies. Trade between countries still involves mainly manufactured goods. The relative efficiency of the manufacturing sector is the main determinant of the terms of trade and of the relative wealth of most advanced economies. According to the Berkeley Roundtable, America, no more the premier manufacturer of the world, is losing ground.[5] CEOs have more pressing concerns.

EXIT OR VOICE

What can be done to correct these flaws? One has to look at the governance of corporate America, and in particular the few thousand publicly-owned corporations that dominate the production realm. Institutions, pension funds and mutual funds own about half of the stock of shares of these firms. Since most of them do not have a controlling shareholder, in theory, these institutional shareholders have the dominant voice in the governance of these corporations. The fact that these institutions are large, sophisticated, professional investors make them suitable for such a role.

Unfortunately, in practice, institutional investors play a limited role in the governance of the corporations that they control. Surprisingly, this situation is of their own volition. They do not play a role because they do not want to play a role. The governance of corporate America is not in the hands of its principal shareholders — it is left to management, by default.

One of the sharpest minds in America, Professor Albert O. Hirshman, of the Institute of Advanced Studies at Princeton University, offers some insight on this curious behaviour. Faced with a situation that they do not like, persons or institutions can react in two ways: Voice or Exit.[6] The Voice behaviour reacts by attempting to change the situation and eliminating the cause of the displeasure. The Exit behaviour is that of those who quit, sell out, move away, turn the page, etc. Voice is fighting, exit is fleeing. In a "voice" posture, a person is loyal: when he is unhappy, he voices his opinion and demands change. In an "exit" posture, a person must keep his options open: he can leave if he is unhappy.

The whole philosophy of North American institutional investment demands that institutions be in an exit posture. An institutional investor has only one loyalty, a fiduciary loyalty toward those who supply the funds that it manages. What an institutional investor values are the exit conditions, the actual value of its stockholding in a corporation and its liquidity. It does not have any loyalty to the corporation in which it invests. Indeed, it prizes itself on being independent, so that personal relationships will not cloud its judgment. To stay at arm's length from the corporations into which it invests, not only will it keep its stockholding small so it remains liquid, but it will also voice no opinion on management. If unhappy, it sells. The exit posture is very much the American way, "Take it or leave it". Thus, institutions care little about the corporations behind the stocks that they own. What concerns them is the market and how well relative to the market a stock should do.

A voice posture is different. The investor is loyal to the organization. Thus, he can have a larger stake, as liquidity is less of a concern. He also ensures he will be heard when he is unhappy. He is concerned about the Board: a voice shareholder ensures that management does not control the nominating process. Furthermore, he ensures that directors' main loyalty be to the shareholders and not to senior management.

Voice investors do not necessarily sacrifice any financial reward because of the lower liquidity of their investment. Indeed, there is evidence that a voice approach ensures higher return than an exit approach. This is not surprising. Most of the great investors are voice investors: Warren Buffet, the Tisch brothers, the Pritzker family, Roy Disrey, etc. Individuals who have great wealth seldom let the market handle it: they stick their noses in their investments.

This is also the way that the governance of large corporations is structured in Japan and in Continental Europe. The financial institutions that have a stake in a corporation, either as lenders or as stockholders, participate in all the major decisions, from the choice of the CEO to large investments, corporate mission, financial goals, etc. The governance of the corporation is not in the hands of senior management.

For instance, in Germany, the three largest banks vote 70 per cent of the shares of the largest 425 firms and have representatives on the Supervisory Boards of most of them. They are locked into a long-term relationship. The stock market has little influence on the management of the companies.[7] A similar situation prevails in Japan. Stocks traded on the exchanges represent a relatively small amount of the total capital base of large corporations. Real governance power lies with the financial institutions that are allied with any corporation.

There are benefits to having voice investors. The focus is no longer on the short-term, as the alliances are stable over time. The absence of liquidity makes it impossible for voice investors to withdraw quickly. There are far fewer concerns about raiders, for the voice investors usually control the company. Finally, the directors' main loyalty is toward the shareholders, which allows them more independence from senior management.

There are also problems associated with generalized voice investment. Voice investors assume real power. What a rise of voice behaviour among institutions implies is a transfer of power, from the senior management oligarchy to Wall Street, financiers, banks, insurance companies and other financial institutions. The bias toward the short-term might be de-emphasized, the Boardrooms of America could become less cosy, CEOs could dream less of big acquisitions and more of improving productivity on the factory floor. But other warts will appear.

There is no perfect system. Most European countries have voice investors controlling their largest corporations. Looking back at the past 20 years, it is hard to tell whether the overall performance of their production realm has been superior to that of North America. There are some merits in having management running scared, in always watching one's back. Moreover, cosy "long-term" relationships can develop between voice investors and senior management. In many instances, the typical exit North American investors, with their short-term outlook and their total lack of loyalty, would offer better governance just by keeping senior management off-balance about what they would do next.

Much has been written recently on corporate raiders. The rash of mergers, acquisitions, and corporate restructuring has generated its own apologetic literature. According to one side, corporate sharks are disembowelling good but dull companies, to make quick profits. According to the other side, investors are making the rationalizations and corrections that complacent or incompetent management did not do. Both situations are effectively encountered, but there is still no consensus on the overall effect. Nevertheless, something good can be said about such a dog-eat-dog system. No public corporation can be complacent and the CEO's attention has to be even more focused on maintaining good results to ensure the autonomy of his corporation.

THE YELLOW PERIL

Japanese CEOs do not have such a worry. Their governance is dominated by voice investors, making hostile take-overs a rarity in Japan. The performance of the past 20 years also suggests that they have something going for them. But is it the governance of their large corporations, or something else, that enabled them to develop the superior management system that so startled General Motors officials at NUMMI?

In fact, it is a combination of circumstances. Japanese culture encouraged certain techniques, such as workers' motivation, team work, flexibility, attention to quality, etc. In the fifties, Toyota pioneered several innovative manufacturing techniques which spread to the rest of the automobile industries and to other industries.[8] They also borrowed heavily from abroad. An American, William E. Deming, is famous in Japan as the father of statistical techniques designed to ensure a high level of quality control. The Deming Award, a kind of Oscar for manufacturers, is highly prized in Japan.

Competition also helps. Domestic competition in Japan's economic base is fierce. There are several competitors in most Japanese export industries. Moreover, government encouraged this competition.[9] Differentiating products and reducing costs through innovation were the driving forces of competition. Out of this emerged not only highly-prized exportable products, but also a highly-efficient production system. Hong Kong, Korea, Singapore and Taiwan followed a similar route.

But the Asiatic invasion of European and North American markets should be put in perspective. For instance, Japanese exports to the U.S. represent less than 2 per cent of total U.S. GNP. It appears bigger because Japanese manufacturers have made inroads in highly specific markets, and their U.S. competitors howl loudly.

But is the competition unfair? Over the years, the Japanese have used a combination of various factors as competitive advantages: lower labour costs, better quality production, better designed products, better management, and a toughness that surprised many corporations. Many Japanese exporters also benefited from a protected home market to hone their skills and reach a size sufficient to compete internationally. Strategically, this was an important advantage, and Korea and Taiwan in particular imitated it. U.S. manufacturers were not damaged significantly by not being able to enter Japanese markets.[10] Indeed, many did not even try. They were hurt however, by having to face stronger Japanese competitors.

Thus, a protected home market was strategically useful. But other factors, and not unfair ones, were much more important to the success of the Japanese in the U.S. Highly satisfied customers can testify to the quality of the Japanese cars, to the cleverness of the Japanese cameras, to the design and quality of Japanese sound systems, office copiers, machine tools, heavy equipment, etc.

A favourable exchange rate also had a significant impact. It is tough to beat a structural price advantage. Japan, and the other Asiatic "Dragons", have pursued a typical export-led development strategy which counts on a favourable exchange rate which encourages exports and discourages imports. But such a strategy can last only a certain time, until the exchange rate becomes impossible to maintain at an artificially low rate.

Japan has traditionally run small, but chronic, surpluses in its trade with the United States. But from 1983 to 1987, the surplus ballooned to unprecedented heights, due to a surge in the value of the dollar brought about by high interest rates in the U.S. The yen started to fall relative to the dollar and finally the Japanese discovered the potency of exchange rates. Labour costs in North America are now lower than in Japan for manufacturing operations.[11] The exchange rate has finally got the best of Japanese cost advantages. The balance of trade between Japan and the U.S. is slowly turning around.

Export-led development strategies count on a favourable exchange rate to stimulate demand for local production. A surplus in the balance of trade usually results. But trade surpluses do not last, no matter how competitive and productive a country pretends to be. The exchange rates will ultimately adjust to wipe them out. When Japan runs a chronic surplus in its balance of trade, foreign money piles up at the central bank. These funds are depleted only by exporting capital. But there is a limit to a country's acceptance of a chronic outflow of investment capital, or other countries' acceptance of a high level of indebtedness toward the Japanese. Increasing pressures on the exchange rate generate a correction.

The market adjustments are not instantaneous, and most governments try their best to foil them or delay them. The time of reckoning came for Japan around 1984 when the Japanese government "decided" to let the value of the yen rise. In less than four years, the yen more than doubled in value relative to the U.S. dollar, a stiffer trade medicine than any tariff. Japanese Toyotas suddenly became more expensive in America, and American computers, a little cheaper in Japan, etc. It takes several years for all the price effects to be felt. The Japanese corporations moved fast. Starting in the early eighties, they sought to protect their market shares by establishing manufacturing plants in the United States. This was the only way to protect their North American market share as their production cost advantages in Japan were gradually offset by a rising yen.

No large country can maintain a substantial, chronic disequilibrium in its balance of trade (or more precisely in its current account balance).[12] High-growth developing countries such as Korea and Taiwan can postpone the day of reckoning by posting substantial growth performance, repaying foreign debts and building up reserves. Exchange controls can also help the central bank to keep a lid on the growing pressures. But that cannot last forever. The exchange rate will eventually rise and offset some of the cost advantages that allowed a country to export much more than it imported.[13] Export-led strategies eventually peter out. Japan is weaning itself out of such strategy, relying increasingly on domestic demand to fuel its growth. It was about time. Until the 1980s, Japan's GNP growth rate was systematically more than double that of the United States and Canada's GNP. Japan has now joined the major leagues. Its GNP is now growing at the same rate as that of Canada and the United States.

Temporary disequilibria are inevitable. The world economies are full of buffers which defer adjustments. Before they can take place, some corporations benefit from their cost advantages and manage to establish beachheads in new markets. But these situations are fairly limited. Indeed, most U.S. manufacturers do not have any significant Japanese competition. But that does not mean that the competitive environment cannot suddenly change.

THE CHALLENGE OF FLEXIBILITY

Large corporations that span several countries and several industries have learned to immunize themselves from sudden competitive changes. But large fluctuations in the exchange rates are a different story. From 1980 to 1985, the U.S. dollar gained 50 per cent against the major currencies, only to lose it in the next three years. Technological development can also set an industry in turmoil. For instance, computerization of controls are now rapidly transforming entire industries. Flexibility is the new password. Corporations ensure that their operations can be rapidly adapted for sudden change in their environment.

The changing practices of the American automobile industry illustrate this pursuit of flexibility. For a few years in the seventies, the "world car" came to symbolize the dominant strategic concept for U.S. car manufacturers. To benefit from economies of scale, basic international models were to be introduced, with minor cosmetic adaptations for each national market. They were to use many standardized parts and components and to rely on integrated plants spread around the world, and in particular, in low-wage developing countries.

The "world-car" strategy failed. It was a logistic and managerial failure. Quality went down. International procurement did not work. Plants in low-wage countries did not materialize. Furthermore, the standardized models were not well accepted in most countries, despite the cosmetics. The "world-car" concept was replaced by the Japanese model, a flexible one.

In the 1960s, the Japanese stumbled on the production techniques developed at Toyota, which were based on great attention to quality, low inventories, worker participation in floor decisions and close relationships with fairly autonomous suppliers.[14] Innovations and product improvements by suppliers were rewarded. Smaller runs traded off some economies of scale to a better fit to market needs. This model yielded flexibility and attention to quality, two factors which came to be highly prized as the automobile markets fragmented in the late 1970s and the early 1980s. As the American manufacturers scrambled to compete with the Japanese and the Europeans in the early 1980s, when the dollar surged in value, they had to do away with the traditional mass-production techniques and borrow the Japanese model of production. This model is emerging throughout North America, in most industries that manufacture mass production goods.[15] That it took more than 25 years to discover the superiority of this system and adopt it can be interpreted as the greatest failure of the U.S. manufacturing industry.

Competitiveness in the production realm now demands flexibility, which allows producers to adapt to fast changing situations. Competition is rapidly teaching the virtues of flexibility. The debate on the productivity of the North American production realm, a major public concern in the mid-1980s, is now slowly fading. North American corporations are learning to be more flexible. They now respect the managerial skills of the Japanese. The rise in value of the yen has also alleviated the pressures on costs. There are still some problems. The governance issue is far from being resolved. Just by comparing cars made by the big 3 North American manufacturers with those made in Japan, we can visualize the difficulties of North American firms to master the leading edge in design and in quality control. But progress is being made. Things are moving in the right direction.

TIRED ECONOMIES

The production realm is the economy that we all see, the economic machine that delivers the bread, cleans the shirts, and builds the schools. It is the economy that exports and imports. It has important sectors dominated by large firms, which benefit from economies of scale. Competition in the production realm gets firms to improve their products and increase their productivity. New machinery, technological development, training of workers, and simply learning more about manufacturing and delivering a product improve the product offering.

The production realm is composed of organizations of all sizes. Smaller organizations are more flexible, but they age less well than large organizations where the "people flow" is more regular. An aging small organization loses flexibility. But in their search for bigger economies of scale and optimal efficiency, large organizations also get locked in particular processes and patterns and lose flexibility.

The loss of flexibility is the major problem of the production realm. No organization is perfectly flexible. Any organization, large or small, is vulnerable to a drift toward being a high-cost producer with standardized products, thus becoming vulnerable to competition from lower-cost, innovative competitors. Organizations without the flexibility to counter-act these competitive threats lose market share to new competitors. Moreover, old organizations often cannot generate enough new activities on their own to replace those that disappear. Thus, the production realm, and in particular the large organizations within the production realm, depends on a steady diet of new activities through acquisitions.

However, very seldom can a large organization fully replace the key activities that made it a large corporation. Long range foresight is needed to ensure its constant rejuvenation. The hurdles are numerous, and indeed even the most enlightened organization cannot avoid aging. Performance falls as an organization comes to rely on increasingly mature and soon declining activities. Old trees die. Fortunately, corporations, and in particular the larger ones, are usually spared this ignominy. They get merged into or are acquired by younger, healthier organizations.

Without a continuous influx of new blood, the production realm tires rapidly. Old trees are not replaced. Younger aggressive organizations do not keep the pressure on the more mature ones. Such tired blood explains the decline of industrial nations. Could it be that Great Britain, in the middle of the nineteenth century, started to suffer from entrepreneurial anaemia, a sickness that accelerated after the Second World War when the country slipped at a more rapid rate? An anti-business culture, high taxation rates on entrepreneurial income and on "loose change", an overvalued currency, unfavourable labour codes, high regulatory barriers, widespread monopoly shielded from competition and the lack of social support for entrepreneurs, slowly choked the rejuvenative forces of the

British economy, while the government was pouring hundreds of millions of pounds into a tired production realm suffering from a severe case of anaemia.

REGIONS AND
COUNTRIES

CHAPTER NINE

NATURAL GROWTH

"A rising tide floats all ships"

Anonymous

To grow is natural for a modern economy, as long as entrepreneurship is unshackled and competition is allowed in the production realm. New activities will be imbedded in the economy, production will be expanded, costs will be driven down, products will be improved. However, growth rates can vary widely, depending on the local conditions, that is, on the state of the garden.

Furthermore, most attempts by governments to accelerate economic growth are of dubious effectiveness. The Japanese have witnessed the average annual growth rate of their economy decrease by half within less than 10 years, without really knowing why: had they lost the magic recipe, or had their citizens been spoiled by their past achievements? Most likely, no. What happened was a change in the material conditions that fed the growth process, a change brought by growth itself. The fact of the matter is that so little of practical use is known about the economic growth of advanced economies that most government efforts are ineffectual — rain dances. Nevertheless, some countries and some regions are doing much better than others. We look in this chapter at how the turbulence generated by entrepreneurs and by businesses influences growth conditions.

First, let's limit the scope of our inquiry at the regional level, such as New England, Southern California, Quebec, Scotland, etc. Regions are traditionally defined by political, administrative or historical reasons. In economic terms, the criterion to define a region is the level of intra-regional trade. Geographers established the limits of a region where trade with the region is nearly equal to their trade with the neighbouring regions. Inside the boundary, internal trade is higher. Outside, trade with other regions is higher.

Economic regions are generally characterized by a central city, Boston, in New England, Montreal in Quebec, etc. Beyond the suburbs of the central city, a ring of secondary cities and smaller towns and villages complete it. Central cities play a major role in economic development.

IT STARTS MOSTLY IN CITIES

Jane Jacobs, one of the most astute observers of economic growth, is known for her provocative ideas about development. One of her most controversial propositions is that urbanization preceded agriculture in the development of civilization. Orthodoxy among development specialists and experts on prehistoric time postulates that agriculture was needed to generate the food surplus essential to feed urban dwellers and thus had to precede the first permanent settlements.

But this proposition is not based on more empirical facts than is Jane Jacobs' counterview. Jane Jacobs argues strongly that only urban settlements could have provided the conditions leading to the discovery of agriculture. She argues that the first settlements were small trading posts, run by tribes or bands adept at maintaining good relations with the nomadic tribes of hunters which were the dominant form of social organization in early history. The trading bands obtained their food from their own hunting and harvesting in the wild around their post, and from purchases from nomadic tribes with whom they traded. Wild grain was such a traded commodity. It is highly conceivable that seeds fell on the ground around the trading post and grain started to grow. Some people noticed and started to experiment. Over time, clearings, then fields around the trading post were seeded by entrepreneurial traders.

Jane Jacobs maintains that agriculture could not have been developed without a permanent settlement, which offered suitable conditions for this act of entrepreneurship. The conditions were present: a demand for a more reliable substitute for wild grain, tinkering entrepreneurs and a permanent trading post where observers stayed around for the growing season. The technology was then passed to nomadic tribes who brought it to rural areas, where there was less of a need to cultivate grain.

Jane Jacobs buttresses her argument by noting that the major agricultural advances in the Middle Age originated around the major cities and then spread to the countryside. Innovation and cities are intimately tied to the entrepreneurial process, and explain why most economic growth passes through cities and that there are "good" cities and "bad" cities. Understanding what is at work is essential to good management of economic growth.

CITIES AT WORK

Cities have exploded in size in the past 200 years. It is not a coincidence that sustained economic growth started at the same time as large cities started to develop. Cities offer three important advantages for entrepreneurship. First, a city offers a local market of sufficient size, presenting good opportunities for local production. Second, it provides "socially deviant" entrepreneurs with better social conditions to start businesses, raise funds, convince clients, and if they fail, to withdraw in the anonymity of the city. Third, a city is a cross-road where creative people meet and exchange ideas. It is this last function that more than anything else, makes cities good seed-beds for developing new activities.

Cities are places where "networks" converge. Essentially, a network is an established pattern of communications or exchanges between individuals. The pattern ensures higher efficiency.[1] Businesses and entrepreneurs make use of networks to carry out their activities. Some of the networks are physical, such as the flow of goods in and out of factories to warehouses and stores. Others deal with information. Managerial networks serve to control activities. These formal patterns of communication encompass such functions as the administrative and financial systems of businesses, the communication industry and the legal and judicial process. These networks allow a city to work.

From our perspective, that of growth, another category is more important — the development networks. Based on personal contacts, development networks handle complex and unstructured information. When a person refers to my "network", he refers to a development network. They are effective at dealing with the new and with changes. They handle uncertainty, whether it is about concepts, about products or about people. Social interactions, such as face-to-face meetings, play a big role in the operation of development networks. They are important channels for learning, whether it is about a new idea, about what works and what does not, about people, about a new play in a downtown theatre or about an entrepreneur selling a new concept to investors. Learning is necessary to reduce the uncertainty and evaluate. Development networks handle these interactions and the social learning underlying them.

Managerial networks are quite different. They handle standardized information and the patterns are routine. They are less and less dependent on the social interactions of a city. Modern communications and improved transportation systems have greatly expanded the scope of managerial networks, allowing the geographical spread of managerial activities. An executive in New York can now monitor a plant in Phoenix, using information transmitted between computers. More and more professionals work from home, communicating via their computers and telephones. In the past 30 years, the efficiency of managerial networks has increased by leaps and bounds, allowing a major reorganization of activities — from downtown to suburb, from large cities to small cities, from metropolitan areas to rural areas.

Such deconcentration cannot be done as easily for activities that rely on development networks. Frequent face-to-face interactions are too important and cannot be decentralized. Unstructured and often unplanned meetings are great learning places and cannot be conducted over the telephone. Thus, vibrant cities, which have dense development networks, will continue to be the most productive wellsprings of entrepreneurial activities.[2]

Nevertheless, improvements in communication technology will greatly affect the role and relative importance of cities in the future, as lower-order activities that rely mostly on managerial networks become more footloose. Cheaper air travel, more efficient telecommunications and computers favour decentralization of the production and distribution activities controlled through managerial networks. This trend favours smaller cities, low-cost cities and regions with an attractive climate. But large cities will continue to matter, for creativity, for uncertainty, and for change. Providing rich development networks is one of their important functions.

Because they are large and consequently more impersonal, cities are also better adapted to dealing with the new and the unexpected, providing entrepreneurs with a good terrain for experimenting. Their citizens are used to dealing with strangers. Furthermore, the entrepreneurial drive is supported by social conditions. Entrepreneurial success is a good social ladder. Finally, the entrepreneurial task of assembling the human and financial resources needed for a venture is easier done in such an environment. Indeed, the more a city has experienced growth in the recent past, the more it is used to change and the better is the environment for the entrepreneur.

Indeed, the only thing working against cities is their higher cost structure. Everything is more expensive in cities, including workers, rent, services, taxes, etc. Indeed, this is the reason why most cities spawn, beyond their suburbs, a belt of smaller towns and villages where cost-sensitive activities are located. This high cost structure is affecting especially older line basic producers. So they tend to relocate their labour intensive manufacturing and back-office operations in smaller towns, away from the cities. But decision-making and creative functions and the white- collar and professional employment that support them stay in the city. Without the city at its core, the belt would wither away. This is why economic development starts with cities.

This is not to say that a small town such as St-Georges cannot be a hot bed of entrepreneurship. Indeed, soil conditions - models, sponsors and incubators - are as effective in small towns as in large cities. But much better climactic conditions - the technological environment, the business input and the social support - can be achieved and sustained in large cities. (And conversely, they can also be absent).

NATURAL GROWTH, FROM A REGIONAL PERSPECTIVE

A regional economy can be seen as a complex system of exchanges, a self-sustaining circular flow. Local production typically provides between one-half and two-thirds of the economic goods demanded in the region, the rest being imported from other regions and from other countries.

The regional economy sustains a flow of exports in basic activities, where it has efficient producers that can sustain competition coming from other regions. Most of these producers can be traced back to local entrepreneurs who in the past have solidly rooted basic establishments in the economic fabric, although the ownership of some of them may have passed to outsiders,namely to large corporation "buying growth". Other basic establishments were implanted locally as branch plants by outsiders, providing the region with a mix of well-implanted competitive establishments, along with struggling younger establishments in the process of becoming rooted in the economic base.

The growth process is generally imbedded in the economic structure. Entrepreneurs succeed in implanting new activities; managers in the production realm succeed in improving their product offering. Whenever such development occurs in the economic base, the regional demand expands. The combination of these two elements is generally sufficient to compensate for the natural erosion of "old" activities. The rate of growth will depend on local conditions and on the structure of the economy of the region.

Growth rates are never measured in large numbers in advanced economies. Dynamic regions, such as California, can sustain real average growth rates of more than 5 pere cent for several years. At the national level, where the growth rate is an aggregate of that of the regions, the economy expands between 2 per cent to 4 per cent a year on the average. Such rates might appear small, but are sufficient to double real income within one generation. The "catching-up" economies in developing countries benefit from the advanced economies' markets, product ideas and technologies. They can grow by 10 per cent and more, allowing them to double their income every five to ten years. Indeed, this is what has happened in China in the 1980s, with some of its regions doing even much better.

FEEDING THE GROWTH PROCESS

The growth process in a region feeds on three major elements: technological progress, the accumulation of capital, and expanding external markets. Technological progress, broadly defined, encompasses any advances in the ways products perform and in the ways they are made, and is much more than high-technology. It is the "better idea": it includes a better designed chair as well as an advanced portable computer and an improved automatic landing system for airports. Technological progress continually offers new possibilities which are harvested by entrepreneurs and by managers. It results in additional production in the region and to the extent that some of that production is basic, in additional exports.

A better machine can be a substitute for a better idea. Capital investments can lower costs, allow for lower prices, and sustain an expansion of the exports of a region. It is an important competitive approach in the production realm and for fast-track entrepreneurial firms. Like technological progress, growing on capital investments is a push approach, in the sense that it results from conscious decisions of local businesses.

The third source, expanding external markets, is different, as local businesses are often passive actors. The Miami cut flower industry benefits from the boom in New England without having anything to do with that boom except helping people to celebrate it. External markets can expand for various reasons: economic growth, currency appreciation, changes in tastes, etc. Most of them are exogenous, making expansion of export markets a "pull" contribution, although the decision to enter a market that later expands can be an important and conscious strategic decision.

Other factors can sustain the growth process. Labour is one. For instance, legal and illegal immigration provides low wage labour in a region allowing entrepreneurs and established producers to capitalize on low price competitive strategies. Some of the dynamism of Southern California can be traced to the availability of "chicanos" labour from Mexico. The climate is also an attractive asset for some regions, drawing retirees and tourists, as Florida clearly demonstrates. About 100 years ago, the availability of fertile land was very important and it fed the growth of many cities and in the Mid-West. Nevertheless, technological progress, capital investments and expanding markets are by far what feed the growth process in most advanced economies.

From a long-term perspective, import-substitution is the major route of expansion for the economic base, for it not only provides a stream of activities with high potential for eventual exports, but it also replenishes the import basket of a region and thus its reserve of entrepreneurial opportunities. Import-substitution is often hard to detect and to observe, for it can span several years. By the time a firm starts to export, few people remember that such expansion was written on the wall several years before when the firm introduced a local substitute to an imported good. Who remembers that before building its media empire, Ted Turner operated a second-tier television station which competed with the networks by televising the Atlanta Braves games? Or that before the Apple II, there was the Apple I, a product targeted to San Francisco computer hobbyists as a substitute to the Altair board, imported from Albuquerque. Import-substitution makes its mark slowly, over a long period of time, as it presides over the rooting of a new activity with export potential in the local economic fabric.

Import substitution as a critical mechanism is also often marked by the response of the local economy to growth in the economic base. Growth starts humbly, by import substitution, followed eventually by exports. But, then the multiplier kicks in, as local demand expands and the local economy responds. All this is accomplished with much turbulence and is difficult to follow, except over long periods, when the increase in output and in employment becomes evident.

OFFSETTING THE LOSSES

The turbulence also masks the continuous downsizing and the disappearance of activities, offsetting some of the gain from growth. Whether the economic base of a particular region is a winner or loser depends on several factors. The mix of activities in its economic base is the most important one. Competition is much more intense in older basic industries, where costs and prices come to play paramount roles in the competitive game. Old industries tend to be high wage industries with a technological base which evolves only slowly. They constitute ideal targets for low cost regions and for low cost entrepreneurs that rely on "radical" technologies. In the mid-seventies, regions which depended on steel production were crippled as demand stagnated and low cost producers from developing countries and new entrants relying on electric furnaces made severe inroads into their markets. There was not much the old line establishments of Pittsburgh could do except retrench, invest massively and upgrade their technology. Employment in the industry shrank by half in eight years, although total volume shipped barely moved. This is the type of restructuring faced by old basic industries.

Other factors affect the dynamism of the economic base. A region where the economic base is dominated by branch plants is less dynamic than if it were dominated by firms with local head offices. The vitality of the entrepreneurial realm, which depends on this complex combination of role models, sponsors, incubators, good business and social supports and the availability of technology, is also paramount in the long term.

In a healthy region, new industries and expanding younger industries compensate for the job losses in the mature industries. The important characteristic to watch is the regional portfolio of industries.[3] In a well-balanced regional economy, sunset industries are offset by sunrise industries. To achieve this balance, a region must count on a vigorous entrepreneurial realm to spawn the sunrise industries.[4]

Moreover, as an industry matures, there is a tendency for productivity - output per employee - to increase, leading often to a dramatic reduction in employment. Two-to-one reduction is not uncommon in mature basic industries. Higher productivity is the best way to stay competitive in mature industries. Indeed, the phenomenon is generalized and it is slowly leading to the demise of the blue-collar workers in advanced economies.[5] Blue-collar workers in manufacturing, which constitute the mythical bedrock of the industrial revolution, now represent less than 9 per cent of the labour force, two-fifths of what it once was. Their high cost brought about their demise.[6] The use of more machinery, the rise of the specialized craftshop and the decentralization of manufacturing to lower-cost countries should shrink the blue-collar work force in manufacturing to something like 5 per cent of the labour force. The North American economy is well beyond the halfway point in this transition. There were once fifteen million blue-collar workers in North America. Early in the next century, their number will sink below 5 million.

The parallel with farming in the first half of the century is striking. About 100 years ago, farmers represented 40 per cent of the labour force in the U.S. as it did in most other industrial countries. Their numbers have shrunk dramatically, to below 4 per cent, although farm output stands at a record level.

Traditional white-collar employment will feel the same effect. Most large corporations have already eliminated several layers of management made redundant by the spread of computers. As technology develops, products do not change as much as the production process, and generally, it takes less labour to produce them. The reduction in employment in the mature production realm is very seldom dramatic but it is continuous. A productive entrepreneurial realm insures that new jobs are being created in new industries to compensate for these losses.

Basic activities which are not characterized by increasing productivity are eventually lost to competition from other regions. Many factors can hamper the search for higher productivity in the production realm.[7] Regulations can have a major impact on costs. Taxes and expensive social programs imposed by governments can increase costs. Supply-side economists have developed the concept of the "wedge" between what an employer pays for labour and what the employee receives. The wedge is the difference between the marginal costs of labour and the marginal return for labour and is fundamentally a tax on labour paid by employers.[8] In North America and Europe, this wedge is now staggering, representing up to 50 per cent of labour costs in some countries. A high level of taxation of labour favours the utilization of machines and equipment, replacing labour, but this is not necessarily the most efficient use of resources. A high wedge hurts the competitiveness of the economic base. In the U.S., the wedge is 40 per cent, versus less than 30 per cent in Japan.

Labour unions and management can also hurt the gains in productivity, by defending the status quo. Unions fight to protect the level of jobs, and thus hinder the necessary adaptation of the production realm to achieve higher productivity. A complacent management is the worst economic enemy of a region. A sluggish production realm is always the result of complacency. Remember what was discovered at the NUMMI plant in Fremont. Japanese management was able to get 50 per cent more output per hour of work than GM management could obtain in similar plants.

CHECKING THE GROWTH OF THE REGION

Growth occurs by the addition of thin layers of demand. Entrepreneurs add new activities and producers expand their present activities. The additional revenues are paid out in wages, dividends, interest, rent, purchases of material and supplies, etc., and get rechannelled in a generalized demand for all kinds of goods and services. This spurs additional local production, and replenishes the basket of imports. Although some products are displaced in the process, there is a net increase in total production as the thin layer of additional demand spreads throughout the economy. Layer by layer, the economic structure evolves and grows, somewhat analogous to the growth rings of a tree.[9]

The expansion of the regional economy puts pressures on the markets for "factors", namely capital and labour. The capital markets respond nearly instantaneously with capital flowing into the region, like water flowing from one pool to another at the pull of gravity. The labour market adjustments are more complex. Pressures are first reflected in additional jobs in the economic base, which rapidly translate into pressures on wages and salaries as the expanding organizations attempt to keep their workers and attract new employees. Immigrants come into the region, young people for the most part, coming from nearby slow growth regions. Illegal and "disfavoured" immigrants also abound in the "land of opportunities", taking the most menial jobs. Thus, immigration checks the rise in labour costs.

The local sector also acts as a sink. Wage pressures from the economic base are diffused in the local economy. In a way, wage pressures in the economic base must also drag along the wages in the local economy. The effects are mutual. Wage increases in the local sector are then reflected in higher prices for the local sector of the economy, further cooling it. Since the local sector of the economy is generally twice as big as the economic base, this dampening effect is substantial.

Wage increases in the economic base are also dampened by the belt economy in the rural areas around the city. Typically, their labour costs are lower because of lower costs of living and because there is usually a surplus of labour. Manufacturing operations capitalizing on lower labour costs, are established in the countryside and challenge the established production realm in the core city, dampening the cost pressures in the economic base.

New England offers a good illustration of that phenomenon. Manufacturing for the high-tech companies of the Boston area is increasingly farmed out to branch plant operations set up in New Hampshire, Maine and Vermont, where wages are lower. A paradoxical consequence of that correction is that manufacturing employment is actually going down in Massachusetts, as its high-technology industries expand.

Higher wages are nevertheless inevitable in growth regions, giving a cost advantage to outside competitors. Large corporations, which dominate the production realm, take a global corporate view and shift production to lower cost areas. The impact of these production shifts are very evident over the long period. The Boston area is now losing its manufacturing activities in electronics, just as it lost its manufacturing activities in textile during the early part of this century, because of pressure in its labour market. As long as a region manages to replace these mature exports by younger activities with a good potential for export, it will not be harmed.

Thus, the exports basket of a region is slowly churning. As other regions make inroads with lower cost products or superior substitutes, the production realm fights back with new products and more efficient operations and structures. The production of some products is expanded, that of others is curtailed. Entrepreneurs bring new firms with new products into the economic base and strengthen it. The old base slowly wears away, but a new one is growing. A growing region manages to win at this game.

To the extent that the value of the export trade increases and puts pressures on the labour market, the level of income per capita will rise. The changes will be slow, dampened by the drag of the local economy and the arrival of immigrants. Changes in real per capita income are of the order of a few percent per year at most. The economic welfare of regions evolves slowly.[10]

FROM REGIONS TO COUNTRIES

The adaptation of a region cannot be properly understood without taking into consideration its belonging to a country. Moving from the regional level to the national level introduces additional considerations. The business cycle, characterized by the periodic occurrence of recessions, is a phenomenon which is beyond the control of the regional economy. But the intensity of its impact will vary between regions, as capital goods industries and durable goods industries are being the hardest hit during a recession.

But in many ways, business cycles are good for the economy. Expansions help the entrepreneurial realm, creating favourable entry conditions. The contractions periodically cleanse the production realm and force it to remain competitive. There are disadvantages to contractions. They are not good times to start a business. Just as it is more difficult to get on a horse than to stay on it, it is also more difficult to start a business than to keep it alive. Because of these factors, the relative duration of boom periods and recessions matters.

Regional growth rates are also affected by the policies of the national government. National policies cannot avoid discriminating against some regions, since not all of them are equal or face the same challenges. Many structural policies end up protecting the status quo and defending entrenched interests. That does not help regions "on the make". In a sense, government is one of the main contributors to social rigidities that some economists say have become the main impediment to growth in advanced economies. Social rigidities hinder the modernization of the production and make it more difficult for the entrepreneurial realm to blossom.[11]

THE SLOW EVOLUTION OF COUNTRIES

Population adjustments are the main regulators of long-term disequilibrium between the regions of a country. People move, especially young people, looking for better job opportunities in high growth regions. Over a period of 10 and 20 years, these movements have a significant impact. In North America, a secular shift is presently under way, from the regions in the centre to regions in the two industrialized sea coasts. Secondary movements toward southern regions complement this.

For instance, from 1950 to 1986, the 12 Mid West States have seen their share of the population of the continental United States fall from 29 per cent to 24 per cent, the nine North Eastern States, from 26% to 21%, while the 16 Southern States went from 31 per cent to 34 per cent, and the eleven Western States from 13 per cent to 20 per cent. Florida and Southern California have been the two fastest growing areas of the United States.

Such shifts reflect in part the relative ability of regions to rejuvenate their economic base. But it also reflects broad changes in prices and in technologies, which had adverse effects on some regions. The difficulties of the regions of central United States can be traced back primarily to the North American retrenchment of basic manufacturing and of grain agriculture in the face of growing international competition. As modern agricultural technology spread throughout the world, and especially in countries such as India and China, world grain production became slowly saturated and prices stagnated. The grain-based and cotton-based agricultural base of central United States went into a secular downfall, despite expensive government programs to prop it up. The world is simply producing too much grain at the moment.

The retrenchment in basic manufacturing industries of the Great Lakes region - smokestack America - is due to increased competition from lower wage countries and from innovative entrants established elsewhere. The spread of manufacturing technology and the secular decrease in transportation costs made inevitable a shift of mass manufacturing to lower cost areas.

These continental movements of workers and populations mask another fundamental recent trend, the migration away from large cities which started sometime in the mid-seventies. Progress in communication technology and better roads have induced a displacement of production activities from large cities to lower cost regions. The creative components of the economy - the entrepreneurial realm and the strategic management of the realm of production - remain largely concentrated in cities, although even there they are slowly spreading from the downtown core to the suburbs. The production realm, especially in tradeable goods, is moving away from the cities in its eternal search for a competitive advantage.

These broad shifts in population can be traced back to the working of the growth process and on the evolution of the broad elements on which it feeds, especially technology, capital investment and external markets. There is not much that can be done to slow down the progress of technology. Indeed, these are huge reservoirs of untapped knowhow waiting to be transformed into more effective products and processes. Capital investments are accumulating at a slow but steady rate. External markets are open fields to every country.

If the nutrients that feed growth are widely available, why do growth rates differ so much between regions? Indeed, is the decline of some regions inevitable? The answer is no. Defensive strategies such as attempting to slow technological progress are futile. But pro-active strategies, which are directed at the growth process, can be effective. Some regions, and some countries, manage to stay in the forefront, despite set-backs in their competitive environment. Are there arid soils and fertile soils?

CHAPTER TEN

ARID SOIL AND THE
DUTCH DISEASE

...Some go in front, some follow;
Some blow hot when others would be
blowing cold,
Some are feeling vigorous just when
others are worn out,
Some are loading just when others are
delivering...

Lao-Tzu

P eople started noting the withering of the maple trees in the summer of 1982. The problem was most severe in the Eastern Townships, south east of Montreal. But the blight spread as far as New England. An exceptionally large number of trees showed signs of decay: dead branches, sick leaves, cracks in the bark. Many were afraid that a new disease, similar to the Dutch Elm disease that is slowly killing those magnificent trees, was attacking maple trees.

When more maple trees died in 1983, a new villain was identified, acid rain, coming from the coal-fired electric plants of the Mid-West. At that time, acid rain was still a little-known phenomenon. The maple tree blight changed that. When the blight continued in 1984 and 1985, a clamour was raised in Canada to do something about acid rain. The maple leaf is Canada's national emblem and the maple is the closest to a national tree in Canada. The acid rain debate became emotional very rapidly. Canadians could not accept that insensitive American utilities could destroy one of the treasures of their natural habitat. A powerful coalition of scientists, environmentalists, farmers and Canadian nationalists joined forces with U.S. environmentalists to bring the U.S. government to force the reduction of emissions (namely sulphur dioxide).

The debate lasted several years. President Reagan, not known for his natural sympathy for trees ("Once you have seen one, you have seen them all") conceded only to earmark more funds to study the problem. Quebec farmers, who were demanding $1 billion, were offered some compensation. Research on the effects of acid rain exploded as governments increased their funding. Acid rain became one of the dominant issues in the 1988 election campaign. Prime Minister Mulroney solemnly promised to negotiate an acid rain treaty with the U.S. government, if reelected.

Then nature, in its own slow way, called everybody to order. Few people listened in 1988 when some scientists mentioned that the situation of the maple was improving rapidly. But in 1989, it was for everybody to see. The forest was flourishing and the maple trees were back in good health.

What had happened? Sulphur dioxide emissions had not been significantly curtailed. Experts went back to their drawing boards. Someone called attention to a surprising thaw which had occurred in February 1981. For 10 days, Eastern Canada and New England were blessed with April-like weather. The maple trees were fooled into their annual spring ritual. Shoots came out and burgeoned, sap flowed and some farmers tapped their trees. But then, winter came back with a vengeance. A brisk frigid week followed, bursting buds and cracking trees. The damage was mostly visible on apple trees. Maple trees were thought to have escaped any damage. The experts also recalled that a similar blight had occurred after winter thaws in 1925 and in 1937. At a scientific conference held in 1989, a consensus rapidly emerged that quirky weather, and not big bad acid rain, had been behind the great maple tree blight.

Acid rain is probably not good for trees. But maple trees can tolerate it. What maple trees really fear are the incredible winter thaws that for a few days have everyone in a state of euphoria. Springtime in February spells disaster for unsuspecting trees which wake up and start a new growing season. Nature can fool itself.

The economy can also fool itself. Take the U.S. dollar. When it surged in value in 1983 and in 1984, many thought that they were better off. European holidays were suddenly cheap. But then the industrial belt that depended on export felt the pressure of cheaper foreign goods overtaking their market. It did not take long to pinpoint the culprit, the strong U.S. dollar. Now that it is back to a lower value, nobody fingers it for the ills of the economy. But what if a good one-third of the economy was fooled by an overvalued dollar, today? What if overvaluation was endemic to most countries, affecting a good part of their economy?

ARID SOIL IN ATLANTIC CANADA

The four Atlantic provinces, with about 8 per cent of Canada's population, constitute the poorest region of Canada. Up to the middle of the nineteenth century, they were as rich as other parts of Canada. But for nearly 100 years, their average income per capita has been significantly lower than the rest of Canada. Output per capita stands roughly at 60 per cent of the Canadian average. Transfer payments have raised their average income per capita to 80 per cent of the Canadian average. Despite significant efforts by governments, all attempts to increase output pere capita have failed. Unless a new recipe is found, Atlantic Canada is condemned to a lower income per capita than the rest of Canada. Why?

Arid soil, conventional wisdom says. Atlantic Canada is too far away from the markets to sustain manufacturing operations. Atlantic Canadians have laid-back attitudes. The climate does not attract dynamic immigrants. Something is missing in Atlantic Canada to allow the economy to flourish.

This line of reasoning reminds me of the acid rain killing the maple trees argument and it doesn't fly either. The economy of Atlantic Canada definitely faces a systemic problem which hampers its development. But it is not because it is far from markets, or because there are no entrepreneurs there. The economic soil is not arid.

In the late seventies, I was invited by several local economic agencies in Atlantic Canada to assist them in developing their strategic plans. This lead me to do a detailed examination of the economic base and of the local economy of several communities. What I observed was an economy with a mature base which did adapt, but which was not dynamic. Its strengths and staying power rested on valuable natural resources. As long as trees grow and people like fish, the economic base of Atlantic Canada will stay on track, albeit behind the rest of Canada. But what surprised me was that few new activities were added to the economic base.

The entrepreneurial realm was fertile. Atlantic Canada has its quota of hairdressers, restaurant owners, lawyers, etc. People started businesses. Furthermore, there were powerful models. Some of the biggest Canadian entrepreneurial families in Canada are based in Atlantic Canada. The Irvings from Saint John are among the richest families in the world, a fortune started only 60 years ago. Then there were the McCain's, the Sobey's, the Aitken's, the Crosbie's, etc. Nobody can say that one cannot make it in Atlantic Canada. Markets were not too distant for the enterprising McCain's, who developed Canada's largest food processing company from a small town in Atlantic Canada. Entrepreneurs can definitely make it in Atlantic Canada. But there are just not enough of them.

I discovered that there were very few young indigenous firms in the economic base of these communities. Recently-established firms were mostly branch plants. Locally-owned firms tended to be old, often second generation. I looked for evidence of the powerful import-substitution mechanism at work. It became evident that the passage from the local economy to the economic base was difficult: only the great entrepreneurs made it. K.C. Irving started as a general merchant, then moved to a string of service stations, then into refining and then into several other areas, including lumber, transportation and publishing. The McCain's started as local potato merchants. But only the best succeeded. Why didn't import-substitution work properly in Atlantic Canada?

It took me several years to get down to a firm diagnosis: the Canadian dollar is greatly overvalued in Atlantic Canada and, as a consequence, the price of imported goods and services is too low, impeding the import-substitution mechanism. In the early sixties, Robert Mundell, then a young radical economist, put forward the concept of optimum currency area, which suggested that it matters very much if two regions with different economic endowment and low labour mobility between them were sharing the same currency and the same monetary policy.[1] It appeared that distortions in the price and cost structures of the Atlantic Canada economy, and the low mobility of Atlantic workers brought about by Canada's extensive social safety net, has made the Canadian currency area less than optimal for the Atlantic Provinces. Jane Jacobs had advanced a similar explanation to explain the problems of the Québec economy. Indeed, in the late seventies, she was sympathetic to Québec independence because it would allow Québec to have its own currency. A devaluated Québec currency for a period of 10 to 20 years would stimulate the import-substitution mechanism, greatly enriching Quebec's aging economic base. (Unfortunately, the proponents of Québec independence propose a monetary union with the rest of Canada.)

The surprising temporary jump in the value of the U.S. dollar from 1982 to 1986 put in sharp focus the role of the value of the currency in shaping the structure of an economy. The high value of the U.S. dollar allowed foreign producers to establish a strong position in the U.S. marketplace. For example, the Japanese automakers captured 25 per cent of the U.S. automobile market. But this jump was just like a one-day thaw in February. The U.S. economy recovered in stride. What if the overvaluation would have lasted several decades? Slowly, the economic base would have retreated to selected sectors where the U.S. advantage is incommensurate. Moreover, it would have been more difficult for U.S. entrepreneurs to compete against importers and to break into foreign markets. This is what has happened to Atlantic Canada. They have been living with an overvalued dollar for more than 100 years.

LUCKY DENMARK, UNFORTUNATE SCHLESWIG-HOLSTEIN

If there was ever a country that deserved to be called a spoiled brat, it was Denmark in the seventies. A small country of five million people, it made all the mistakes that an irresponsible rich country can make, short of declaring war. For Denmark is equipped with a political system which generally saddles it with weak governments. Overspending, high taxes, labour laws which hinder productivity, strikes, inflation — the Danes had it all in the seventies, in a gauche attempt to emulate their Scandinavian cousins with social care from cradle to grave. But on the economic front, they did not have the same Nordic discipline. In the early eighties, they were the sickest country of the European Common Market. Only a radical shift in policies, after much probing by international lenders, stopped the drifting toward economic decadence. But despite all this foolishness, Denmark remained one of the richest countries of Europe.

The Danes were most fortunate to have their economy insulated with their own currency and protected by a movable exchange rate. When the Danes engaged in foolish behaviour, their exchange rate spread the burden to all, and by falling, ensured that the prices that their basic industries faced in their external markets stayed competitive.[2] So their economic base kept on churning and selling its cheeses, pastries and whatever, no matter how bad the skirmishes were in Copenhagen between the tax cutters and the big spenders.

Table 10.1 presents some indication of the performance of the Danish economy from 1970 to 1986, in comparison with the German performance. Their growth rate was slightly higher and their inflation rate much higher. Government was representing a higher share of the national income. Average unemployment was also higher. But in 1986, their GNP per capita income, expressed in U.S. dollars and adjusted for the domestic purchasing power of their currency, was still higher than the German one.

The happy-go-lucky Danes must be the envy of their industrious neighbours to the South. The inhabitants of Schleswig-Holstein, the northern most German state and also the poorest one, are good people, hard working, disciplined, attached to their values, true Germans. Unfortunately, the Smithburgs of Germany are numerous in Schleswig-Holstein. They try hard, but it does not work. What is wrong with their economy?

Schleswig-Holstein is not more distant from the major markets than is Denmark. The climate is as good, and the land as fertile. It belongs to a much bigger country. And the state government receives substantial subsidies from the federal government, something the Danish government does not receive.

Their misfortune is to be stuck with the German mark, the strong German mark, which does marvels for the rich Germans who work, but which is a burden for the citizens of Schleswig-Holstein. The value of the German mark is too high for the economy of Schleswig-Holstein, and it does not allow the economic base to flourish, as it has stymied the import-substitution mechanism. The growth process is choked.

TABLE 10.1
DENMARK, GERMANY AND SCHLESWIG-HOLSTEIN

	Denmark	Germany	Schleswig-Holstein
Population	5,1	61,1	2,6
Inflation (annual average, 1970-1985)	9.1%	4.6%	N.A.
GNP per capita, 1986 ($PPP)	13,030	12,741	11,064
Annual real growth, 81-86	3.3%	1.7%	
Unemployment 1986	6,1%	6,3%	7,3%

Source: OECD, Eurostat (EEC)

This overvaluation is not immediately apparent in their local economy. Who can tell whether the waiters in Kiel, their capital city, are overpaid or not? But thanks to the mighty mark, foreign goods are cheap, and shopping trips to nearby Denmark are worthwhile. On the other hand, the pastries and cheeses and ships and chemical products that were traditionally exported from Schleswig-Holstein are getting expensive because of the high value of the mark: the economic base is under strong pressure.

Same climate, better government, more subsidies, the German market, good people, slightly less distant from major markets. What does Denmark have that Schleswig-Holstein does not have? Mostly its own currency, whose value dances to their own tune, and not to that of a distant, albeit powerful, central economy. Peoples from the Appalachia, New Orleans, the Atlantic provinces, the Great Plains and the Prairies, southern Italy, and Walloony, and from Britany, and Wales should read about the magic of having its own currency and pricing it properly.

"ONE ELEPHANT, THREE SHEEP, TWO PUPPY DOGS AND A RABBIT..."

Jane Jacobs once imagined a weird animal kingdom where animals were branched on giant artificial lungs that cleaned their blood of carbon dioxide. Each machine was servicing several animals, at a rhythm which

165

maintained their average carbon dioxide below a certain threshold. Unfortunately, large animals such as elephants were branched on the same machine as small animals such as rabbits, a significant disservice to the latter especially when rabbits are off running and need much quicker replenishment of oxygen than elephants. When constrained to the rhythm of elephants, they were often on the verge of asphyxia.

The analogy was used by Jane Jacobs to illustrate the predicaments of mismatched regions within a currency area, such as Atlantic Canada and Schleswig- Holstein.[3] A regional economy can be hurt in two ways by a currency whose value is determined by stronger regions of the same currency area. First, given the economic structure of the region, the currency can be overvalued. This is the case of Schleswig- Holstein and Atlantic Canada. The value of a currency is determined by all the international transactions of a country. The regions within the country with the strongest economic base perceive the exchange rate as being low. They are capable exporters and prefer the benefits of a stronger currency. Regions with a weaker economic base prefer a lower valued currency, which would allow them to strengthen their local production realm. In any country, the strong regional economies benefit from what is from their own perspective an undervalued currency, while the weaker regional economies are hurt by what they perceive as a strong currency. "Some are feeling vigorous when others are worn out". As a rule, poor regions should not team up with strong regions for they also get their high price currency. Atlantic Canada is penalized by the stronger dollar whose value is determined by the stronger regions of Canada.

Thus, from 1988 to 1991, the Bank of Canada pursued a tight monetary policy. The unemployment rate in Ontario was below 5% and inflationary pressures were building up throughout Canada. Economists declared that full employment conditions had been reached and that tight money was justified to prevent overheating the economy. For nearly three years, real interest rates hovered above 6%. How unfortunate was Atlantic Canada. It had reached "full employment conditions", when its own unemployment rate was an unacceptable 12%. What it meant was that the best that Atlantic Canada could achieve in the peak of the business cycle was 12% unemployment. (In the previous cycle, it peaked in 1980 at 11%). This is the price of sharing a currency with stronger regions.

Atlantic Canada also suffer from its reliance on a rigid currency. This is the second problem of large currency areas. "Some are loading just when others are delivering". For instance, in 1989, Atlantic Canada suffered a major crisis as overfishing reduced fish stocks in the Grand Banks close to their non-renewal threshold. Fish quotas had to be cut by half. Fishermen stayed at home and fish plants closed. The impact quickly spread to the whole of Atlantic Canada through the multiplier effect. Until fish stock are replenished to their previous levels, which will take several years, the Atlantic Canada economy will remain depressed. I was a Senior Adviser in the Prime Minister's Office in Ottawa at the time. I remember the frantic search for remedies to cushion the shock and diversify the Atlantic economy. Hundreds of millions of dollars of additional "development funds" were committed, on top of the billions of dollars already flowing to the area through various support programs. But there was no quick fix; adjustments are slow to come in Atlantic Canada. Despite all the money channelled in the area, Atlantic Canada was not about to become a fertile land. Oh! did I wish at the time that Atlantic Canada had its own breathing machine.

Let us play Napoleon and declare Atlantic Canada a newly independent country. We assume that the transition from being four Canadian provinces to being an independent country is done under friendly skies, and that Atlantic Canada maintain cordial and extensive economic relations. But wily Atlantic insisted on having its own currency, the Atlantic Cod. Within a month after independence, the I-told-you-so crowd would point out the sinking value of the Cod as a sure sign of the foolishness of carving out such a small country at the tip of northeastern America. Although they still do not realize it, the Atlanticans are just starting to get lucky as the Cod takes a dive. Rapid price adjustments occur, as the prices of goods imported rise suddenly. Atlanticans, which were waiting for the fish to reappear in the Grand Banks to revive their economy, suddenly discovered opportunities at home. The cost of every resource in Atlantic has diminished, relative to the Canadian dollar. Producing locally goods which were previously imported becomes a sound alternative in many fishing villages. The potteries of Fredericton are getting cheaper. Atlanticans barely notice it, for everybody's income has gone down. But visiting Canadians take note. They buy more pottery, more beer and more of everything. What Atlanticans also notice is the rising price of Canadian beer. So they start pushing the locally-made Schooner, whose price hasn't budged.

Economists will now interject that inflationary pressure will build up and that workers will demand higher wages to offset the rising price of imported goods. I'll get back to that point later. Let us assume for the time being that, as in the real world, inflation is less than the devaluation level, improving the price of Atlantic-made goods.

Slowly but surely, more people will be working in the economic base. Unemployment, which had been the highest in Canada for over 125 years, starts coming down, as more people work in the economic base, kicking off the multiplier, shuffling the import basket, etc. Gradually, entrepreneurs root new activities in the economic base. The import-substitution mechanism becomes more productive. Atlanticans become good at developing new exports. A younger rejuvenated production realm slowly emerges, and it is tilted toward sunrise industries. Initially, the new industries rely on lower prices to cut into the market. But over the years, people from all over the world will get to like the new-improved Schooner, just like they did before with Toyota, and a long time ago with Heineken. At first, price is the determining factor; but then quality takes over. After new exports have taken off, the Cod starts to rise in value. Some 15 years after independence, Atlantic could be proud of its strong Cod, which during all those years would have done wonders, namely keeping the cost base of Atlantic Canada at the proper level, a level not dictated by the rest of Canada.

The devaluation of the Cod had two impacts. First, it reduced the costs in the economic base to a lower level, allowing for more exports. Second, it adjusted the costs in the local side of economy to a lower level, an important adjustment that was perceived as an increase in the prices of what was imported. This lowering of domestic costs created opportunities for local substitutes. Taken together, these two impacts had the effects of making everybody a little bit poorer by the same amount, but it also allowed for new basic activities to be rooted, which led to the growth of a younger production realm. Moreover, if a new crisis were to erupt in its economic base, a blight that would destroy its forests, Atlantic could rely on the cooperation of its flexible Cod, which would rapidly cushion the impact by spreading it to the whole economy.

PROPER CURRENCY AREAS

There are costs associated with having its own currency. Every international transaction entails a small additional cost, of the order of 1% or less. There is also the costs of uncertainty about the future value of the currency, which may impact on investment decisions. These costs are greatly annoying to the importers, exporters, bankers and institutions that undertake international transactions. These influential economic agents become strong advocates of large currency areas. Unfortunately, because they are deemed experts on such matters, their counsels are poisonous to say the least. For these costs are less than one half of one per cent of GNP, significantly below the additional growth that in a single year, a properly aligned currency can ensure when labour mobility is not sufficient to ensure full employment.[4]

The benefits for entrepreneurs and for the production realm of a properly aligned costs structure cannot be underestimated. Furthermore, the type of adjustments provided by a lower exchange rate is highly efficient when the economy receives a blow. A devalued currency adjusts prices and real income rapidly throughout the economy. Everybody shoulders the burden of the adjustment, through slightly lower real income (A 10 per cent devaluation will typically lower everybody's real income by 2 to 3 per cent).[5] At the same time, entrepreneurs and producers face a much improved competitive environment, which makes it easier for them to implant new activities and expand employment.

However to be effective, a devaluation must kick start entrepreneurial initiatives by dramatically changing local competitive conditions. The small countries of Europe are good testimonial to the benefit of an independent currency. Whether it is Denmark or the other Scandinavian countries, Switzerland, Austria or the Netherlands, they managed to keep their economy competitive by sporadic and indeed quite infrequent adjustments in the value of their currencies.[6] This does not preclude that most of the time, a fixed value is preferable for their currencies. Indeed, the EMS, the European system to narrow the short-term fluctuations of currencies, is deemed quite a successful structure, as it stabilizes greatly the value of currency. Fortunately, it still allows for realignment when needed. One should be careful to distinguish between a properly aligned currency and devaluation. I am a proponent of the former, not necessarily of the latter.

South American countries routinely devalue their currencies with little success. They are just feeding more inflation in their slow descent to the abyss of economic degradation. Far from curing the problem of chronic inflation, devaluation can merely attenuate temporarily the symptoms and fuel additional inflation. It is also often argued that the chronic devaluation of the British pound in the 1945-1980 period did not greatly help the British economy. Indeed, a properly-valued currency is a necessary - - or facilitating — condition, not a sufficient one to ensure healthy growth.

Furthermore, an undervalued currency imposes a burden on the economy. George Gilder points that the U.S. computer industry was ill-served by the devaluation of the U.S. dollar in the late eighties. Good performance in the computer industry is not driven as much by labour costs as it is by innovation and the ability to lower unit costs through higher volume. Its Japanese competitors benefited from a high yen to buy cheap U.S. technology, allowing them to jump ahead. Gilder argues that sunrise industries are better served by a strong currency whereas old line sunset industries prefer a weaker currency.[7] A properly valued currency is still the best solution.

Devaluation as a policy tool suffers from the image problem of being associated with inflation.[8] But the typecasting is not warranted. Neither devaluation nor appreciation of a currency entails an automatic offsetting inflation or deflation. From a period of parity with the U.S. dollar in the mid-seventies, the Canadian dollar lost about 30% of its value in the next ten years. Inflation was only 11% greater in Canada during the period, not 30% as a simplistic offsetting approach would suggest. Finally, when the U.S. dollar lost 35% of its value from 1985 to 1988, there was little discernable impact on inflation.

A currency should be properly aligned to play its role efficiently. Persistent high unemployment in a region, coupled with an aging economic base, points to a region characterized by low labour mobility and burdened by a non-optimal currency area. Such a region would benefit from a one-time change in its price level, which would lower the cost structure of its tradeable sector relative to that of its domestic sector. Furthermore, a country that is lagging behind or facing negative economic conditions is usually better off with a lower valued currency. Its costs structure would be shifted so that producers and entrepreneurs benefit, while consumers would share the burden with slightly lower real income. On the other hand, a country that has made it or is booming can reap the benefits of its economic success with a strong currency. Its consumers will enjoy a higher real income.

However, having its own currency does not ensure prosperity. Ireland has its own currency, has devalued it often and is still not the most fertile land. But, it has many other problems, which overshadows the advantages of having its costs structure properly aligned.

Whether a region belongs to a larger currency area or has its own money has major consequences on its growth potential and on the distribution of income among its citizens. For a currency is not neutral. It defines a cost structure, which benefits some and hurts others. Thus, a policy which affects the exchange rates and which is good for the country as a whole, is not necessarily appropriate for some regions and vice versa. Furthermore, when economic adversity hits a region, whether the burden is quickly spread throughout the economy and producers are given a break to make up for what has been lost - which a devaluation does - is an important determinant in the speed of recovery. Thirty years ago, Robert Mundell argued that the ability to adjust to economic shocks should be a fundamental criteria in defining such an optimal currency area. Within an over-sized currency area such as Canada, the adjustments of the economy of a region to a shock such as the sudden obsolescence of one of the pillars of its economic base (e.g., fisheries) is slow and relatively crude. Efficient adjustment can be achieved only under conditions of labour mobility which do not exist in the real world. Under conditions of low labour mobility, adjustments are more efficiently done through change in the value of currencies. The existence of non- inflationary full employment conditions with a rate of unemployment above 10%, which is the case of Atlantic Canada, among others, makes the point forcefully.

Dividing a currency area into smaller units, each with its own currency, raises major difficulties and has never been attempted in a modern economy. The weaker residual currency would lose in value, and any financial assets denominated in that currency would also lose some of their value. Initially, there would be a generalized reluctance to store anything of value in such currency. Still, currencies of diverging strength coexist in the real world, without capital flight. For instance, not only is the Canadian dollar weaker than the U.S. dollar, but it is also deemed to be overvalued by 10% to 15% at 85 cents to the U.S. dollar. Yet, there is no capital flight from the Canadian currency area.

Little research has been done on the creation of new currency areas. Conventional wisdom among economists is geared in the opposite direction: joining up existing currency areas into larger units. But this would not be the first time that economists would have been dead wrong.

THE DUTCH DISEASE

Can the exchange rate of a country be systematically above its appropriate value, or below its appropriate value? In the former case, consumers would be better off, while a choke would be gradually applied to the production sector of the economy. In the latter case, consumers would suffer from high prices, thus save more, while the production realm would be expanding on the strength of a dynamic economic base. Doesn't that resemble the respective situation of the United States and Japan in the seventies and early eighties? Let's investigate this question.

Back in the eighteenth century, on the eve of the Industrial Revolution, the Netherlands was the richest country in the world, on a per capita basis. With only a few million in population, the Netherlands was a country of merchants and farmers, and of capitalism. The farmers were progressive, and the land was fertile. The Dutch merchant navy was the most modern in the world and Dutch merchants were running ships on all oceans. The Netherlands was the commercial entrepôt to Europe: a surprisingly high proportion of international trade was moving through the ports of the Netherlands. Why did the Netherlands economic power then wane in the eighteenth century?

The Dutch merchants gradually evolved into international bankers, financing not only trade, but also wars, armies, and princes who were short of cash, despite their huge landholding. In the eighteenth century, Dutch bankers developed a near monopoly on providing credit to the world, supplying what is offered today by the international bankers of London, Frankfurt, New York, Hong Kong, and Singapore.

In many ways, the Dutch had everything needed to start the Industrial Revolution. The Protestant work ethic reigned. The country was under the rule of law and had a fair government, as fair as the seventeenth century ever produced. There were small-scale craftsmanship manufacturing, such as textiles, clothing, breweries, etc., activities which were prevalent throughout Europe at the time. But the Dutch manufacturing activities were strictly local. Although Dutch merchants were the major force in international trade, Dutch goods were not traded.

The Dutch missed their chance at history: the Dutch entrepreneurs did not rise to the challenge of industry and the Netherlands waited a few generations for large- scale industrialization. England took the lead, while the Netherlands economy went into a slow decline.

Several factors contributed to this decline. France and England did not give the Dutch much chance, continually attacking their trade routes. In a quick war in 1782- 1783, the English nearly obliterated the Dutch navy. Historians also invoke what is known as the "climacteric" reason for the woes of the Netherlands. As a country gets rich, its people get soft and lose their drive. The Netherlands succumbed to the trappings of the good life and let other countries, and specifically industrious England, take the lead.

But more important, the Dutch economy became a high cost economy. Being bankers to the world, as other countries have since discovered, tends to maintain the value of the currency at a level higher than it would be if trade was the main determinant of the exchange rate. The foreign investments of Dutch capitalists in 1790 reached three times the size of their domestic product.[9] Too much international money was channelled into florins, inflating their value. This did not create conditions conducive to industrialization. The merchants of the Netherlands became bankers instead of industrial capitalists.

Bankers without strong armies to protect their assets do not fare well in times of war. When the Napoleonic Wars redefined the configurations of Europe, the Dutch bankers' financial assets got lost. There was no significant industrial activity to take over. With a declining economic base, the Netherlands swiftly lost its rank as the richest nation in the world.

Reflecting on this change of fortune, economic historians coined the term Dutch disease to describe the inability of the Dutch economy to switch to industry in the latter part of the eighteenth century. An overvalued currency, maintained as such by prudent and contented bankers and investors, stifled the adaptation of the production realm of the Dutch economy.

The same diagnosis applies to the relative decline of Great Britain in this century. Two world wars saddled it with a huge debt. Its production realm succumbed to a climacteric syndrome, with management becoming unimaginative and overly prudent, and its labour, boisterous, undisciplined and less productive. Great Britain also entered the century as banker to the world and got to savour the advantage of a strong currency. The pound tended to be overvalued, choking the production realm of Great Britain.

How can we tell whether a currency is overvalued or undervalued? Purchasing Power Standards (PPS) were developed to provide an assessment of the relative value of currencies in terms of what they can buy. Foreign exchange rates are not a good comparison basis for assessing the relative value of currencies. Exchange rates represent the relative prices of currencies when small quantities are traded, reflecting current supply and demand conditions. They do not represent the value of currencies, merely their values of exchange in small amounts on a given day. The real value of a currency is given by what it can buy in the country where it is used, and that is not truly reflected in exchange rates.

It has been known for long that using measures based on exchange rates to compare the wealth of various countries is incorrect.[10] Exchange rate fluctuations have no real significant bearing in the wealth of a country, which is what GNP measures based on exchange rate would suggest. When the comparisons are done over a period of time, wide fluctuations in GNP are introduced by exchange rates movement. But personal wealth does not fluctuate this much. In the eighties, the Canadian dollar fell 15% against the U.S. dollar, and then at the end of the decade, bounced back by nearly 20%. Canadians did not feel such dramatic changes in their relative standard of living, although 75% of their trade is with the U.S. This is because most of our income, two-thirds or more, is spent on domestic goods and services which are not traded. That these are theoretically worth more to foreigners is immaterial.

The PPS method provides a better measure of the relative wealth of nations. An international agency, the Paris-based Organization for Economic Cooperation and Development (OECD), has developed sophisticated measures of the value of currencies in terms of their purchasing power. Purchasing Power Standards allow us to convert economic statistics from one currency to another one without distorting their value.[11]

Table 10.2 presents the purchasing power of the foreign currencies in term of the U.S. dollars, for selected years. Any valuation above 100 indicates that the exchange rate undervalues the U.S. dollar, while the opposite holds if the valuation is below 100.

TABLE 10.2
THE PURCHASING POWER OF FOREIGN CURRENCIES
(relative to their exchange value in U.S. dollar)

	selected years		
	80	85	87
Canada	99	89	94
Japan	116	93	148
Germany	150	84	138
France	42	81	123
Great Britain	122	73	95

Sources: OECD

On the whole, the U.S. dollar tends to be undervalued, not overvalued. It is a reserve currency which is widely available. But, as the figure shows clearly, in the mid-eighties, the U.S. dollar had a mild bout of Dutch disease as it suddenly became much dearer in terms of purchasing value. Whereas in 1980, the same basket of goods cost $116 in Japan and $100 in the U.S., in 1985, it cost only $93. The U.S. dollar was powerful. But things went back to normal as the dollar depreciated with respect to the yen, and in 1987, a $100 basket in the U.S. warranted in Japan an expenditure of $148.

A high priced dollar was fine for the U.S. consumer, who was able to buy more goods abroad solely because his earnings were in U.S. dollars. But it made life more difficult for the American producers and entrepreneurs who were paying their wages and interest in U.S. dollars, but were getting paid for their exports in undervalued foreign currencies. So the cards were stacked against the production realm of the United States. The situation has now reversed. Japan is now becoming banker to the world and is exposed to the danger of the Dutch disease.

AVOIDING THE DUTCH DISEASE

Fortunately, the Dutch disease could become a malady of the past. The wide availability of international statistics and the increased awareness of the political and economic costs of a misaligned currency should prevent any country from straying too long from purchasing power parity. The awareness of the costs to be borne by consumers (undervalued currency) or producers (overvalued currency) should keep governments and central banks honest. Moreover, since the overvaluation of one currency results in the undervaluation of others, an international system of checks and balances emerge. Thus, in the future, at least among the Triad economy, countries should be spared serious bouts of Dutch disease.

But it will remain as a regional plague, within currency areas, and where unfortunately, it tends to attack the weaker regions. Regions with older mature economic base are highly vulnerable. The rejuvenation of their economic base is made more difficult by imports priced too low, stifling the import-substitution mechanism and discouraging producers from exporting.

On the other hand, the fast-growth regions perceive their costs as properly lined up, when in fact, they benefit from an undervalued currency which allows their producers to be more competitive abroad. If California,

Southern Ontario, the Greater London area and Lombardi were suddenly given their own currencies, free from that of the U.S., Canada, Great Britain and Italy, their value would rapidly appreciate. Growth regions in large currency areas generally benefit from an undervalued currency. This is partly why their economic base is doing so well.

Countries with disparate regional economies should be envious of multi-currency systems. The Smithburgs of this world are becoming an awfully annoying burden for countries that want to remain at the top of the economic ladder. Unfortunately, just as it was difficult to get a proper diagnosis of the ills of the maple trees of Eastern Township, (remember that it endangered research funding into the effects of acid rain on maple trees), getting countries to fix their structural currency problem will also be difficult. Splitting a currency area has never been done and it is not certain that it can be done.

CHAPTER ELEVEN

STAYING UP THERE

In the long run, a society's strength depends on the way ordinary people voluntarily behave.

James Fallows

T he United States is the numero uno, the richest country in the world. It has the largest GNP of all countries, and the highest GNP per capita. It has held this position for more than one hundred years. In 1989, its GNP per capita was 6.5 per cent higher than that of Canada, the runner-up.

Here are the twenty richest industrial countries according to their wealth, ranked by their GNP per capita.[1] This list deserves careful scrutiny, as it demolishes several myths.

TABLE 11.1
THE TOP TWENTY INDUSTRIALIZED COUNTRIES
(U.S. $ equivalent)

	GNP per capita		GNP
	1970	1989	$ Bil.
	$	$	1989
United States	4,920	20,630	5,132
Canada	3,880	19,315	507
Switzerland	4,770	17,695	119
Luxembourg	3,675	17,240	7
Norway	3,065	16,665	70
Iceland	2,895	15,765	4
Sweden	3,795	15,555	132
Japan	2,765	15,500	1,908
Finland	2,860	15,020	75
Germany (West)	3,380	14,985	929
France	3,275	14,565	818
Denmark	3,440	14,400	74
Great Britain	3,325	14,345	821
Australia	3,390	14,305	240
Italy	2,850	13,900	800
Netherlands	3,460	13,710	204
Belgium	2,950	13,585	135
Austria	2,735	13,405	102
New Zealand	3,305	11,505	38
Spain	2,205	10,265	402

Sources: O.C.D.E.

For instance, the United States is solidly at the top. Herbert Stein, a noted American economist, has calculated that if recent growth rates are indicative of future growth rates, Japan's GNP per capita will not surpass that of the U.S. before the 2020's. This is amazing, given all the misgivings and bad mouthing about the course of the American economy. The United States' position at the top is secured for several decades at least.

What is also amazing is that we do not really know why the United States is so well entrenched in the first place. There is little research on this subject. Indeed, economic research tends to concentrate on the relative growth rates of countries, as opposed to their absolute level of wealth.[2] Thus people marvel at how well Japan is doing on that score, but do not realize that the United States and Canada are well ahead, and not to be overtaken soon.

The fact of the matter is that American and Canadian productivity, although not growing as fast as that of most other advanced economies, is much higher than that of other countries. We are not sure why this is the case. Conventional explanations fail.

The large size of the U.S. economy and the economies of scale it provides, do not constitute a good explanation. Canada, with a GNP a tenth of that of the U.S., is nearly as productive. The stock of real capital, and in particular, the amount of machinery and equipment available to workers, is also not a sufficient explanation. Japan and Germany also have a lot of equipment. The same applies to the educational level of the labour force. Western Europe and Japan are as well endowed. Natural resources and food, which are abundant and relatively cheap in North America, cannot explain the large difference. Finally, one cannot really argue that U.S. corporations are more efficient organizations than those of Western Europe and Japan.

Three factors (which apply also to Canada) could explain a large part of the gap. First, a highly efficient local economy, mainly the service sector, ensures low cost availability of a wide array of goods and services. Japan and Germany may be efficient in the export industries, but their local economies is much less efficient. North America's domestic industries are highly productive, in particular, in distribution and services. Since the local economy accounts for about 75% of domestic consumption, it has an important impact on the standard of living. Domestic cartels and barriers to entry abound in Europe and Japan. The highly inefficient distribution system of Japan is costing them dearly in terms of cost of living. The unabashed competitive environment that pervades the North American domestic economy cannot be found anywhere else in the world. It yields cheap housing, cheap gas, cheap food, cheap clothing, and overall, a superior standard of living.

The second factor is the high level of entrepreneurial fertility in the North American economy. Canada and the United States lead all other advanced economies in terms of new business formation. The North American economy is highly open to new entrants. There is little restriction compared with the barriers faced by entrepreneurs in Western Europe and in Japan. A continuous flow of new businesses keep the production realm in good shape.

Finally, North America is well endowed in infrastructures. Land transportation is efficient, thanks to the extensive networks of roads and railroads. Energy is relatively cheap, given the low costs of fossil fuels and high level of investments in productive capacity.

Let us go back to the list for a second surprise: all these small countries cuddled near the top. Most of them are not even in the Common Market, and they have little pretension as rain-dancers. Still, they are ahead of the giant economies of France, Germany and Japan! What is tiny Iceland doing there, maintaining its lead ahead of Japan for twenty years? Such a superior performance by small countries goes against conventional wisdom. Furthermore, their success is not due to their prowess at economic management.[3] Their record in terms of macro-economic management is generally poor. With the exception of Switzerland, all have suffered from severe inflation. Many have large budgetary deficits. Taxes are high in most of them. Economists do not offer satisfactory explanations for their overall performance. Some argue that small countries can generate the social consensus needed to sustain enlightened economic policies more easily. But this argument does not explain their inability to contain inflation, except in Switzerland, the least homogeneous of the small countries.

One important feature common to all these small countries is the fact that they each have their own currency. Although they are all pegged to that of a large neighbouring economy, they are also the object of occasional devaluations, which ensure that they tend to be properly valued. That greatly helps their economies. Otherwise, their overall good performance hasn't found a satisfactory explanation. But they surely demonstrate that bigger is not necessarily better.

Finally, the table indicates that the star performers of the rain-dancing community, staid hard-working Japan and Germany, are not really doing much better than eccentric France, cranky Great Britain and carefree Italy. They appear to be locked together in that second tier for several decades.

What this table tells us is that explaining the overall economic performance of a country is not as easy as it seems. Policies, whether they are structural policies or stabilization policies, do not explain everything. Other factors, not related to government, matter. Indeed they may matter more than government policies.

But then one should ask: how significant are these differences between countries. Indeed, to the casual observer, the differences between these national averages are getting difficult to notice. For the differences in income between regions of the same country are much more significant than the differences between countries. For instance, the difference between the five richest states and the five lowest income states in the U.S. is about 70%. That is also roughly the difference in average income per capita between Newfoundland and Alberta, which define the Canadian extremes. In Germany, the Schleswig-Holstein per capita income is nearly half that of nearby Hamburg, the richest region. Differences between countries are generally smaller than these interregional differences.

THE TRIAD ECONOMY

This situation reflects the great level of integration of the industrial economies. Indeed, one can talk now of the Triad economy, the integrated economy of the advanced industrial countries.[4] This economy is structured around three poles: Europe, North America and Western Pacific rim. About 20 countries form the Triad economy.[5] With a combined population of 700 million, these countries represent 14 per cent of the world's population and 80 per cent of its economic output. Among the Triad countries, the United States has the most important national economy, followed by the Common Market as a whole, and then by Japan.

The Triad countries share fairly homogeneous economic characteristics. Their income per capita is comparable. They share the same technologies, they consume similar products, they lend to each other and they trade mostly among themselves. Moreover, their consumers are becoming increasingly indifferent to the national origins of what they purchase, to the despair of their own governments. Fashions and fads are more and more the same. When a new product becomes a hit in one country, it often spreads very rapidly to the other countries.

Walk into kitchens of houses in Melbourne, Chicago, Toulouse or Guttenberg, and you will see the same appliances, very nearly the same models, and many of the same brand names. The Triad countries are countries of the middle-class, where people work mostly in services (70%) and in manufacturing (20%). Their governments are all democratic, oscillating from left-of-centre to right-of-centre. They all provide a pervasive social safety net that ensures a minimum level of security to all their citizens.

On the production side of the Triad Economy, the same homogeneity is encountered. Production technologies are similar. Automation is highly advanced. A limited number of multinationals — the IBMs, Toyotas and the Exxons of this world - - are present in most, if not all, of these countries, spreading their management and production know-how. The workers are all well-educated, and are fairly well paid by world standards. For tradeable goods and services, competition is international. Much has been said about the globalization of the economy, that is the integration of competition in a world-wide scale. The integration is pervasive, from the neighborhood restaurant (e.g. McDonalds) to designer labels. What is superior is traded, licenced, copied, improved upon within months by the marketplace. Innovativeness is the basis of competition. Moreover, laws and regulations, despite significant national differences, provide a fairly homogeneous business environment.

LIFE AT THE TOP

Switzerland is up there, close to the top, indeed, numero uno in Europe, with a GNP per capita equal to 87 per cent of the U.S. one, in terms of the purchasing power of the Swiss franc. How does Switzerland manage to stay near the top? It is isolated by mountains. It is not well endowed in natural resources. There is no oil, and most of its land is not suitable for agriculture. It does not belong to the Common Market. It is a small country, with only six million citizens. Moreover, in recent years, some of its exports have faced intense competition from the Japanese, the type of competition that crippled some U.S. industry. Think of Japanese watches.

Yet, the Swiss manage to make it to the number one position in Europe, and to stay up there. Not only is it one of the richest countries in the world, but both unemployment and inflation are below one per cent. And no oil. How do they do it?

Several factors have put Switzerland on the top. First, over the years, Swiss entrepreneurs have rooted a fairly diversified economy. What has grown in the production realm are international specialties highly adapted to a rich country: precision machining, from watches to optical instruments; sophisticated equipment, such as machine tools; aluminum, which uses Switzerland's low cost hydroelectric power; international financial services to individuals, a small niche about one-tenth the size of the London financial market, but highly profitable; hosting of international organizations and conferences; and upscale tourism. The relatively high value of these exports is what propelled the Swiss to the top of the pile.

At the same time, the Swiss government is frugal, minimizing the social cost to be borne by the production realm. The wedge, that tax on labour, is the lowest in Europe, which probably accounts for the fact that they have the lowest unemployment rate in Europe. Switzerland has also managed to avoid war, an easy way of saving on infrastructure expenditures, although it spends about 3 per cent of its GNP on defence, roughly the same as Canada. Finally, the Swiss have bourgeois values, and believe in hard work. So they are up there, among the best, despite severe handicaps.

But being rich brings problems. The Swiss francs appreciated. This made imports cheaper, which is nice for the consumers. But exports got more difficult to sell on the foreign markets, and exports represent half of their GNP. Furthermore, in the eighties, Swiss watchmakers were hit not only by a soaring currency, but also by a technological revolution. The low ends of the product lines were abandoned, the weakest firms left. But their watch industry adapted and restructured. So did exporters in other industries. The Swiss production realm showed great flexibility, a sure sign that the growth process is in a healthy environment in Switzerland. New technologies were harvested. Capital investments were made. New markets were developed. Organizations were also restructured. That is the price of getting rich. As is any structural change, it was painful for some. But the whole country gained.

The changing value of their currency played a big role in this adjustment process. The changing value of the currency is what basically distinguishes the adjustment process of a region and that of a country. From 1970 to 1987, the Swiss franc appreciated by 36 per cent against the German mark, and 174 per cent against the U.S. dollar. This appreciation in value was due to the increased attractiveness of the goods and services that Switzerland was exporting and to the role of the franc as a reserve currency for the well-to-do. As a consequence, the Swiss had to completely restructure their export basket. As the Swiss franc appreciated, some exports were dropped and replaced by others with a higher value added. But this revamped export basket gave another push upward to the Swiss franc, demanding further restructuring.

The reevaluation of the currency created a paradox. The Swiss GNP physically increased at barely one per cent per year in real terms, one of the lowest growth rates in Europe. Growth in wealth is due essentially to currency appreciation. But because such a large part of what the Swiss purchase is imported, the Swiss have felt a significant real increase in income.

Switzerland's wealth creates tremendous pressures on its labour market. Wealthier people consume more. In the seventies, the pressure on wages was partly solved by bringing in guest workers. When the guest workers came to represent over one-fourth of the labour force in the early eighties, restrictions were imposed. As a consequence, wages increased and more labour saving technology had to be used. There was also gradual adjustment of wages in the local economy and domestic prices went up, compensating for falling prices on imported goods. Inflation was checked by this offsetting trend.

It is tough to stay on top. The Swiss' production realm must remain competitive in its international specialties. Cheap copycat imports from lower cost countries undercut them — cheap Hong Kong watches, cheap Japanese machine tools, cheap Colorado mountains, etc. Switzerland will lose some. Thus, its entrepreneurial realm has to stay productive and keep adding new products into the economic base. That is tough.

A major challenge of Switzerland is also one of keeping everything under control. It cannot let the Swiss franc rise too much or fall too rapidly without creating havoc in the 50 per cent of the economy which relies on external trade. On the other hand, labour market pressures will have to be solved not by importing guest workers, but by letting wages rise. That is the type of problems that Geneva, Basel and Zurich have.

HOW DIFFERENT IT IS IN BOSTON

If Boston were the capital of New England, an independent country with its own currency, it would face the same type of problems. New England would be the richest country in the world, significantly ahead of the United States. Table 11.2 presents statistics on per capita personal income by regions. for international comparisons, this data can be used in conjunction with Table 11.1.

TABLE 11.2
PER CAPITA PERSONAL INCOME BY REGIONS
(U.S. $1989)

	$	Index
New England	21,598	123
Mid West	20,401	116
Far West	19,251	109
Great Lakes	17,282	98
Plains	16,353	93
South East	15,409	88
Rocky Mountains	15,397	88
South West	15,247	87
United States	17,594	100

Source: Survey of Current Business

What propelled New England into this position? On the one hand the Boston region exports a lot of high technology products, financial services and universities services, all highly-valued products and services. Its southwest area is adjacent to New York and it constitutes its richest suburb. But more importantly, New England has successfully managed to adapt its economy to changing conditions.

The New England situation is also very different from that of Switzerland.[6] As the richest and most productive area of the United States, New England's production realm benefits from what is a relatively low value of the U.S. dollar, very much a situation similar to Toronto in Canada. If it had its own currency, the New England Cod, it would appreciate strongly, increasing the prices of their exports on foreign markets. The basic industries would have to lower their dollar price because of the high value of the Cod. But with a low U.S. dollar, Boston's basic industries can charge higher prices. Their shareholders and their workers gain from this situation. All the other workers and the New England consumers lose somewhat. A high valued Cod would allow them to buy cheaper New

York products. Now they are penalized, because they must use the cheaper U.S. dollar.

Boston's labour situation is also different from that of Switzerland. Boston solves its labour market problems by importing labour from the rest of the United States, a luxury which is socially and culturally expensive for Switzerland. Wages tend to stay low in New England, as it draws labour from the rest of the United States.

So here we have two of the richest regions in the world. They are rich because they have higher value basic activities and their basic industries have remained highly competitive. Luxuriant areas in the garden, blessed with fertile soil, good watering and a good mix of species. But because of different institutional framework, the respective situations of New England and Switzerland are worlds apart. In Boston, basic industry owners and workers profit from the high U.S. prices of their products. Boston consumers do not get as many benefits. Furthermore, Boston shares its wealth with incoming workers. In Switzerland, the consumer benefits. That is why one is much better off being a waiter in Geneva than in Boston, although they could do the same job. The Geneva waiter is paid in Swiss francs, the Boston one in U.S. dollars, and job security is higher in Geneva as the labour market is much tighter.

These institutional differences have strong implications. Belonging to the U.S. currency area implies that Boston will share the wealth of its basic sector with all the United States. Through the adjustment of the exchange rates, regions share with other regions in its country. Policies which are good for countries are not necessarily appropriate for regions and vice versa. This complicates the art of gardening.

INTERNATIONAL ADJUSTMENTS

The major difference between the adjustment process of a region and that of a country lies with exchange rates, which are fixed for a region and which fluctuate for a country. The relative values of currencies in terms of their international purchasing power are always changing, depending on the supply and demand for them. Over the long-run, the fluctuations depend primarily on the balance of trade of the country, which is the aggregation of the trade of all regions, with the inter-regional trade cancelling out. (Throughout the following discussion, services such as transportation and tourism are included in the definition of trade. In official statistics, trade is often restricted to goods; services are treated separately.).

A country exports the products that are produced most efficiently, just like a region does. The international value of these exports determines the value of imports the country can buy. This difference between "what" and "how much it is worth" is crucial. All countries export, even the most unproductive ones. What their exports are worth depends on how good they are at producing them.

Take a Chevrolet Cavalier produced in Detroit, and a Toyota Corolla, produced in Japan. Assume that consumers all over the world estimate that these two cars are roughly equal in value and are ready to pay the same price for them, whether it is in dollars, yen or francs. Assume that it takes 20 hours of work in America to assemble the Cavalier and only 15 hours in Japan.[7] Moreover, let us assume that every time they manufacture 1,000 cars, General Motors and Toyota throw a party for the workers that built the cars. At the end of the banquet, a huge cake is offered to the workers, a cake of the same size in each country. Ah ha, the pieces are bigger in Japan. Because there are fewer workers at the Japanese party. The Japanese have an absolute advantage over the Detroit workers. This is why some countries are richer than others. They use fewer resources to produce certain goods and services; therefore they price them cheaper and sell more. They get a bigger piece of the cake.

At the level of a country, productivity defines income. In the nineteenth century, the British were the most productive workers, and they were also the richest. Then the Americans took over. Now the Japanese are about to give the Americans a run for their money. They are far from overcoming them, as the Japanese local economy is far from being as productive as the U.S. local economy. But they are slowly gaining.

Japan's post-war development is characterized by a steady increase in its exports to the United States. As the lower cost country in the duo, Japan could count on competitive advantages in a broad range of products. Thus, over the period, Japan was in the position of increasing its exports to the United States by continually targeting new industries with a low cost-strategy.

Figure 11.1 shows some of the resulting adjustment in the prices and exchange rates. Over the years, the unit prices in U.S. dollars of what they were exporting grew, as Japanese packed more value into what they were exporting. The ever rising yen dampened Japan's relative cost advantage. To compensate, Japan exported more highly valued goods. The average unit price of their exports increased in dollar value at the same rate as the yen. Initially, their exports were dominated by textiles and by low price products, (giving rise in the 1950s to the belief that "Made in Japan" meant cheap goods). Then as the yen increased in value, the Japanese moved into steel and basic consumer goods, then into cars, electronic products and computers. To persist in the strategy, they will have to move into producers' services.

FIGURE 11.3
JAPAN: VALUE OF THE YEN
AND UNIT PRICES OF EXPORTS ($)

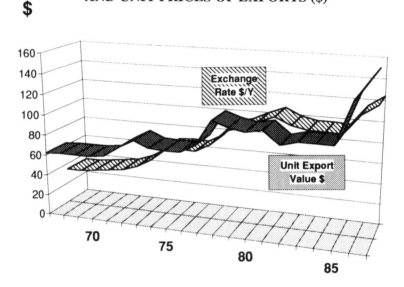

Source: International Financial Statisitcs: UNO

Meanwhile, they also upgraded what they were importing. Indeed, as the yen increased in value, the unit price of their import increased at the same rate. Japan moved into high-priced imports at the same rate as they moved into high-priced exports. The rich live rich.

As long as it takes fewer Japanese workers than American workers to produce the same product, the yen will inch upward to reflect the higher productivity. The Japanese standard of living will also improve, the higher valued yen allowing them to buy more abroad.

The Japanese may have given the Americans a run for their money in tradeable goods. But the local sector of the Japanese economy, which produces housing, sells fast-food, runs stores and produces TV programs, is much less productive than the U.S. local economy. A highly productive local economy makes the Americans much wealthier. Japan still has a lot of catching up to do. Moreover, they will find that it is much easier to improve the competitiveness of car manufacturing activities than to improve the productivity of their retailing structure and of their housing stock.

Furthermore, the international adjustment process is slow and somewhat amorphous, despite rapid movements in exchange rates. Consumption patterns evolve slowly. Moreover, the local side of the economy, where two-thirds of GNP can be found, is shielded from direct international pressures and it adjusts much slower than the basic sector of the economy. There is also a lot of interference muddling the short- term in futile attempts to delay changes: tariffs and quotas on imports, export subsidies, exchange controls, etc. Thus it will take time for the Japanese to catch up.

Nevertheless, international comparisons, even when they are done on the basis of a purchasing parity standards, are becoming less meaningful. The differences between countries are no more significant than the differences that we are accustomed to inside the countries. There is slightly more difference in wealth between New England and the Deep South than there is, on the average, between the United States and Japan (28 per cent versus 25 per cent in 1988). This is the essence of the Triad economy.

STAYING UP THERE

Still there is widespread concern in the United States and Canada that, over time, they could fall behind other countries of the Triad, as Britain did, in a secular decline. Should we be concerned that the United States and Canada will gradually achieve lower growth rate than the rest of the Triad countries and over the long term, end up perennial losers? I do not think that such concerns are founded. Several factors can bring an economy to a lower position on the list of the richest countries. Let us analyze the case of Canada and the United States.

First, the productivity of the production realm could fall in relative terms. The NUMMI plant illustrates such a situation. It would take fewer workers to build cars in other countries than it would in the United States. Such a widening discrepancy would be due to managerial decisions, the U.S. production realm being less effectively managed than that of Japan or of European countries. That major differences in management practices and effectiveness can last is doubtful. Managerial technology is one of the most easily exported technologies. No matter what is being written about the national character, it is difficult for North American managers and business schools to accept a permanent laggard situation. Even Great Britain is now vigorously fighting back, beginning to climb from its lagging position. There is no mystery in good management, and countries learn from each other. Management techniques and performance will tend to be competitive within the Triad economy, equalizing the chances.

Second, North America could end up with a portfolio of mature and declining industries. This would result in a fall in the value of its exports, making them increasingly vulnerable to competition from cheap labour countries. This can be caused only by a systemic failure of its entrepreneurial realm. North America is gifted with a dynamic entrepreneurial realm. It is easy to start a business and the entrepreneurial route is highly prized for social success. The abundance of large cities provides numerous proving grounds for import-substitution. Moreover, the productivity of the entrepreneurial realm can be monitored and its drying-up can be prevented by proper policies, such as a properly valued dollar and a fiscal incentive for entrepreneurs whose role is to rejuvenate the production realm.

Thirdly, North America could be the victim of its own follies, a high-tax society with not only a low value return in the taxes paid to government, but also with strong disincentives as a corollary. Sweden and Denmark demonstrate that high taxes are not necessarily the kiss of death for an economy. But the revenues generated by governments can be spent in a highly unproductive manner. For instance, health and education now represent between 15 per cent and 20 per cent of the demand on the resources of most Triad countries. Whether these resources are marshalled through the public sector, as it is in most countries, or through the market mechanism, as it is mostly in the United States, does not appear to be critical. What counts is the productivity of these two large sectors of the economy. Different levels of productivity can make a difference. But here again, I doubt very much that North America will accept for long (e.g., a few decades) an inefficient health maintenance sector or an inefficient education sector.

Finally, the U.S. could catch the Dutch disease, choking its economy with a systematically overvalued exchange rate. Such a situation could result from the role of the dollar as a reserve currency and by a superior appeal of United States financial assets to foreigners, a consequence of large government deficits or tight monetary policies. Fortunately, this is a disease that can be easily diagnosed and cured. Since an overvalued currency pleases mostly investors and bankers, fighting the Dutch disease is also politically popular in most democracies.

THE LIMITS TO GROWTH

Are there any limits to the overall growth of the Triad economy? If nothing seems to prevent the U.S. from staying up there, does it mean that the Triad economy will just keep on growing? The answer is yes, pending the absence of a war or of a major ecological disaster which would change the physical parameters of the earth. For the next 20 years, the consensus among economists calls for an annual average growth of the order of 2 per cent to 3 per cent per year, for the advanced economies. If one assumes that population will grow at 1 per cent per year, a generous assumption, we will witness increases in average GNP per capita of the order of 15 per cent to 25 per cent per decade.

Some countries will do better than others. Countries on the verge of joining the Triad, Spain, Portugal, Ireland, Greece, Turkey and much of Eastern Europe, should continue to experience "catch-up" growth rates. So will Korea, Singapore, Taiwan and Thailand.

But, within the Triad as presently defined, the post-Second World War catch-up is completed, foreclosing a return of the miracle growth rate of 7 per cent to 15 per cent that some countries sustained for a while. Growth is now driven by productivity increases and entrepreneurial creativity. Throughout the Triad Economy, fast-growing regions, anchored around dynamic cities, are growing at brisk rates (4 per cent to 6 per cent a year), pulling the rest of the economy along through diffusion of technology and improved managerial methods.

Increasing the number of these fast-growing regions could have an impact on the growth rate of the Triad economy. We know something about the secret formula of the fast-growing regions, the Jacobsvilles of this world. First, their entrepreneurs frantically add new activities, new products and services, in response to local needs, and once in a while, come up with a better mousetrap which is exported. Second, they are driven to improve the competitiveness of their production realm, and as a result, their exports increase. Both sets of activities lead to more exports from the growing regions, but also to more imports of everything else.

This acts as a stimulus to all other regions, which are more passive and wait until demand pulls the expansion of their production realm.

There will be obstacles to growth. There is a school of thought which maintains that the world will reach some physical limits very soon. I have strong reservations about this view of the world. Technology, that is, know-how, has now become the basic fuel for economic growth. It is no more steel, nor energy, nor food. Indeed, the world has plenty of resources. The limits to growth, to the extent that they exist, are now man-made. Governments are able to erect obstacles to international trade, and slow down the growth in the exchange of goods and services. I will also pass "sous silence" the supreme folly of governments, war, which not only commands scarce resources and talent, but destroys physical capital and ruins the production realm.

There is also a pessimistic school among social scientists. They argue that increased social rigidities are slowly choking the forces of change that are fundamental to economic growth.[8] In a wealthy society, too many interest groups are at risk from economic growth. Through the political process, these interest groups ensure that laws protect their turf and that economic growth does not perturb their own little world. Indeed, these social scientists maintain that the slowdown of the U.S. economy since the fifties is mainly due to these increasing social rigidities, just as the decline of Great Britain was brought about by the conservative attitudes of a society more interested in protecting its individual turf than in expanding what was available to all.

Responding to such an argument is difficult because nobody denies the existence of social forces that strengthen the status quo. The valid question is whether the forces of change, just as widely distributed in the economy, are more powerful. The present performance of the Triad economies indicates that the forces of change manage to expand the economy by 4 per cent to 6 per cent a year, mainly by building better and more productive organizations and by tapping the potential of technological progress. Whether the forces of the status quo could eventually dominate is pure speculation.

Moreover, the forces of change, the entrepreneurs who root new activities and the managers who increase the competitiveness of the production realm, do not rely only on the new technologies and on the availability of capital for investment. If that would be, there would not be such sharp difference between regions and growth would be much more evenly distributed across regions. In fact, both proper local conditions and enlightened policies can foster the creativity of the entrepreneurial realm and the competitiveness of the production realm. Moreover, policies directly aimed at stimulating entrepreneurs and managers in doing their tasks are most likely more effective than policies aimed at stimulating technological research and capital investments. In other words, dollar for dollar, a better treatment of capital gains, which rewards entrepreneurs, is more effective than an investment tax credit, which subsidizes capital.

Curing the economies of laggard regions, the Smithburgs of this world, could also have a major impact on the average growth rate. The large financial and social investments of the population of Smithburg, in housing, local businesses, friendship ties, etc., led them to measures of despair, like demanding huge subsidies for obsolete plants or preaching for tariff. The economy of Smithburg somehow has to be revitalized. Growing a new production realm, out of an entrepreneurial realm, is the generic way out. This is one of two major issues underlying this book; maintaining the good health of a Jacobsville is the other one. This is what public policies on economic growth should be all about. In the remainder of the book, we will explore good gardening techniques.

POLICY CONSIDERATIONS

CHAPTER TWELVE

FOOLISH SPENDING AND SNAKE OIL

God gave me my money

John D. Rockefeller

One hundred and twenty-five years ago, doctors were leeching blood in the hope of curing the sick. Phlebotomy was part of official dogma. Since then, medicine has progressed tremendously. Some old remedies still work, but in different doses. Others are known to be harmless and not very effective. Dangerous remedies were abandoned. No doubt, 100 years from now, some of today's remedies and medical practices will also look strange, ineffectual or dangerous. That is progress.

The official dogma in economic development is fairly eclectic. Since our knowledge about economic development is about at the same stage as medicine was in the nineteenth century, there is much room for snake oil vendors who capitalize on our ignorance. Let us reexamine some generally-accepted policies, whose efficiency is highly questionable, although generally harmless. In certain circumstances, some of these policies are surprisingly effective and therefore justifiable. But in most circumstances, they promote foolish spending, an expensive way of getting at times, something, at other times, nothing. Moreover, the snake oil vendors in the development crowd are also in it for themselves, selling illusions, which is a cruel game. Let us first look at current techniques to promote entrepreneurship.

GROWING CORN IN FLOWER POTS: SMALL BUSINESS INCUBATORS*

There are two types of incubators: the real ones, businesses where entrepreneurs work and learn their trade before starting their own business, and artificial ones, which are the latest fad in economic development. Artificial incubators* are small business malls targeted toward start-up business and offering subsidized rent and various other business services. No decent industrial commission can be without one. Large corporations are doing their civic duty by converting old plants into incubator* space. Industrial and office building developers are offering incubator* space in their buildings.

But it is foolish spending. Look at what an entrepreneur gets. Rent and other office expenditures are not important for a business start-up. Many entrepreneurs start in their basement. A rule of thumb is that rent costs less than 10 per cent of wages and start-up entrepreneurs have problems much bigger than rent. Moreover, any entrepreneur worth his salt knows that if he is tight for cash, rent can wait. The same applies to other services subsidized by incubators*, such as cleaning, conference room facilities, secretary, etc. These expenditures are seldom essential and can be compressed.

Thus, the amenities provided by a small business incubator* are not really critical to a typical new business. If they are offered at very low cost, the entrepreneur will take them, and in fact will tend to use more than he needs. But if they are not available, he will manage without them. There are three other reasons why good entrepreneurs avoid incubators*.

First, incubators* get clogged with losers and with businesses with no growth potential. It is very difficult to identify among new businesses the rising stars of tomorrow at the budding stage. The operators of incubators* may have a higher batting average than most at detecting new businesses with high growth potential, but they are defeated by the law of large numbers. The majority of new businesses that survive stay small, for reasons that an incubator* cannot influence. Thus, incubators* typically get filled with small businesses that become sturdy survivors. Many depend on the life support system provided by the incubator*. The few fast-track companies that the incubators* nurture leave and are replaced by low potential firms. Fairly soon, the place is filled with smalltimers that need the life support systems, the break on rent and a cheap telephone-answering service.

A visit to a mature incubator*, one that has been in existence for at least five years, is most instructive. What one sees is mostly businesses that will remain small and dreamers who pursue fantasy at the taxpayers' expense. Incubator* managers will argue that they have an exit policy: after five years, they demand that a tenant leaves. But that is usually a white lie. Tenants do not leave. Managers do not disconnect the life line that will kill a small business. Moreover, incubators* have empty space. The managers rationalize that it does not hurt to keep the placid small businesses.

Second, incubators* are not very good at providing higher level services, the "business inputs" that a new business really needs: advice, contacts, partners, funding, market information, pep talks, etc. If these services were provided, they could make an important contribution to a start-up. But incubators* are not run by hot-shot advisers, they are run by dull, efficient office managers, who are not qualified to provide business inputs. In the first few years of operations, an incubator* can rely on local businessmen to serve on the Board and to provide free advice. The initial manager of the incubator* is typically a true believer who can spend nights assisting a struggling entrepreneur. But as the years go by, the incubator* changes. The businessmen get bored with the losers and delegate their assistants, who have fewer business contacts. The steady tenants, the placid small businesses that pay their rent, do not really care about business inputs, contacts, business plans, great ideas, etc. What they want is the corridor painted, an efficient receptionist, a clean conference room, and that the place not be run like a madhouse. The initial manager who was the true believer is long gone, exhausted after vainly trying to save a few start-ups that unfortunately did not make it. A plain office manager who can run an office has replaced him. Unfortunately, office managers are generally of little help to new entrepreneurs. End of the experiment.

Third, incubators* do not attract healthy Heffalumps. An entrepreneur projects himself in his business. While not saying it explicitly, his business is a strong social statement: he is telling the world, "Look at me, I am making it". Real estate developers know that. They provide corner offices. They provide direct entry. They provide reserved parking spaces for the entrepreneur and visitors. Lawns are mowed regularly, and the entrepreneur can hang his shingle outside for everybody to see. Incubators* typically miss that point. They do not provide social recognition. They rely on what I call Russian architecture: long dull corridors, office neighbours who are not proud, who tape handwritten notes to their door saying "back in two days". This is not the company that a "real" entrepreneur wants to keep.

Many incubators* have empty space. The two oldest incubators* are the Business and technology Centre (BTC), in the Minnesota Technology Corridor in downtown Minneapolis, and the University Science Centre right next to the University of Pennsylvania, in downtown Philadelphia. Two good locations, particularly for high-tech start-ups. Both were founded by true believers, Bill Norris of Control Data in Minneapolis, and Dr. Edward Tenan in Philadelphia. Both were properly funded. In fact, the two are good pilot tests. But both have empty space and have not been very productive at generating fast-track companies. In fact, they did poorly.[1]

There is a niche for incubators*. Industrial and office park developers should routinely provide such space, as a lower cost option in their developments. In many small communities, a business incubator* can be a rallying point when such a rallying point is needed, and that also can be useful. But take a walk through BTC in Minneapolis and through University Science Centre before buying snake oil. Learn to differentiate between incubators, the real ones, and incubators*, the artificial concoctions. Real incubators, models, sponsors: this is what matters. A few corn plants in flower pots on the back porch does not make one a corn farmer. Foolish expenditures.

GARDENING IN BARREN SOIL:
UNIVERSITIES AND SCIENCE PARKS

It makes sense for a community to harness the unused potential of its university to foster economic development. Universities are willing partners, especially if it results in added funding for R&D. It is often love at first sight. Deans tell communities that terrific research is being done in their labs and that universities have a lot of brain power to offer the local business community. Professors serving on blue ribbon committees make good impressions. They know so much, they speak well, they know what it is all about.

These marriages often produce development centres and scientific parks, two of the most barren amenities in economic development. A development centre intervenes at the pre-start-up phase, when researchers test the idea and assist the entrepreneur with prototypes and market research. Heavily subsidized, development centres also provide financing for joint R&D projects. Business schools also join, to assist local businesses with market research, organizational analyses, etc.

Not much economic development comes out of these experiments. Great reports get written, putting the talent of professors and graduate students to use. New channels of funding are opened for university projects. Students are exposed to the entrepreneurial spirit, a very important contribution. Professors see how businesses are run, and this might improve their teaching. But the soil is pretty barren around universities when it comes time to cultivate entrepreneurs.

A good incubator organization is exposed to the marketplace and to the discipline of the market. Strike one against universities. Entrepreneurs at the pre-start-up stage really need business inputs, contacts, money, practical advice. Strike two against universities. Third, commercial technology does not come from university labs; it comes from the marketplace, from competitors, from meeting deadlines, from designing a better mousetrap that costs less and has bells and whistles. Strike three against universities. Finally, universities are not in the sponsorship business. They do not give commercial contracts to entrepreneurs. Strike four.

But what about Stanford and M.I.T., and their respective association with the Silicon Valley and Route 128? Their success cannot be luck. True. But let's see what was done.

Dean Fred Terman was an exceptional leader, a champion. While not many deans and college presidents can be expected to do as well as he did, we all can learn about what universities can do for promoting regional economic development by observing the priorities of Dean Terman. First, he developed the Electrical Engineering Department at Stanford to be among the best in North America. That helped him attract the best and brightest among the ten of thousands high school graduates who choose electrical engineering in North America every year. The students who made it to the corner building in the Quad on the Stanford campus knew that they were among the best. And they worked accordingly, like champions. Top rate education was the number 1 priority of Dean Tarman. Second, Terman instilled entrepreneurial values among the students — electronics would save America, great engineers can build great businesses, etc. Entrepreneurial-minded EE students were not only encouraged at Stanford, they were supercharged. (This is back in the forties, when the Harvard Business School did not even have a course on entrepreneurship.) Terman's number two priority was to transmit entrepreneurial values to his students.

Third, Dean Terman spotted the entrepreneurial talent and nurtured it, becoming a mentor to many of Silicon Valley's great entrepreneurs. He made models of them, setting them up next door, in the Stanford Industrial Park, and use them as examples for his students to emulate.

The later successes of Silicon Valley were achieved by the process of economic growth described earlier. Start-ups became incubators. Fast-track firms became sponsors. Models multiplied. This is where the action was. Lockheed came to the area in 1948 because Alan and Malcolm Lockheed were from nearby Los Gatos and because Stanford was producing first-rate graduates.[2] Shockley brought his seven bright boys to Palo Alto and then managed to blow his business to pieces in less than a year. But out of this came Fairchild, which led to the semiconductor industries. Hewlett-Packard grew, from a few hundred employees around 1950 to the multinational that we know today. Good engineering, everybody will tell you.

Very few technological discoveries were actually transferred from Stanford laboratories to fast-track companies. (Genetech, a biotechnology firm, was a major exception.) What Stanford transferred to Silicon Valley was mostly students, the best. It also contributed to the emergence of a network of people who believed in building businesses and in being the best, (and in bitching about those anti-business Stanford professors).

A similar story can be woven around M.I.T. — being the best, offering the best graduating engineers in North America, promoting pro-entrepreneurial values among students, developing local models, such as Polaroid. Then Ken Olsen, who graduated in engineering, showed the MBAs of the world how engineers built a great company, Digital Equipment. M.I.T. presidents Karl Compton and James Killian not only maintained close contacts with big high-tech businesses, but also were concerned with the new ones. In 1947, before Silicon Valley and before Route 128, when venture capital was still a dream, Killian was one of the major promoters of American Research Development.

Universities have a most important mission in any community: education. If they do it very well, and promote entrepreneurial values among their students using every trick in the book, they will have made 90 per cent of their contribution to economic development. Beyond this educational mission, universities can provide leadership to mobilize support for entrepreneurs and new ventures, capitalizing on their moral authority. Tangible demonstrations of support can be provided by outreach programs aimed at entrepreneurs. By their mere existence, these programs stress publicly the solid commitment of universities to entrepreneurial ventures. This is what Dean Terman at Stanford and the various presidents at M.I.T. have done successfully over the years.

But what about the Research Triangle Park in North America, the hottest development concept in the United States. A 1,500 square mile industrial park catering primarily to research and development organizations, the Triangle is defined by three nearby universities, Duke in Durham, North Carolina State in Chapel Hill and the University of North Carolina in Chapel Hill. Over 27,000 people had jobs in the Park in 1987. Several thousand jobs in nearby manufacturing plants were also generated by activities in the park. Many government officials, in search of ideas for economic development, have visited the Research Triangle Park and have come away impressed. But museums are always impressive.

Let's look at the facts. It took 30 years to get to this point. In 1987, two employers, Northern Telecom and IBM, account for half of the jobs, and a good part of these jobs are in manufacturing, not research. Three other employers account for 6,000 jobs. And about 50 smaller ones generate another 6,000 jobs. Facilities supported by government research funds account for about 5,000 jobs.

From the perspective of employment, the Research Triangle is a big success. For the most part, the jobs pay above-average wages and the park has created numerous opportunities for graduates of nearby universities. Indeed, the Research Triangle Park is a genuine real estate success, one of a kind. More than 150 similar parks associated with universities have been established since the early 1960s. The majority are outright failures, a testimonial to the problems of the concept. M.I.T. tried hard in Boston with the M.I.T. Technology Square. Although a large number of high-technology companies were established in the Cambridge area, most did not go in the M.I.T. Technology Square. The concept was also tried in Philadelphia, around the University Science Centre. But research and development establishments were located in the suburbs, not in the University Science Centre. Indeed, if the Research Triangle Park had not landed IBM and Northern Telecom, its success would be modest.

Economic development should not be confused with a real estate operation[3], of which the Research Triangle Park is first and foremost a brilliant demonstration. No other planned industrial park in the world approaches its success. It now has a critical mass of establishments, sufficient to be an attraction in itself. But it took a good 30 years and several million dollars in public funds to establish it. Despite this success, it did not create a Route 128 or a Silicon Valley. It attracted fairly sterile establishments, which were not good incubators, sponsors, or models. It has not created a self-generating cluster of high-technology industries. Few spin-offs have been generated. The Park relies mostly on branch plants, on faraway head offices, and on federal government funding. It does not rely on the dynamism of local establishments.

No doubt high-technology start-ups will increase in the area and a few fast-track high-technology companies will appear. This will be the Park's real economic contribution. But will that be sufficient to compensate for the barren research establishments? This is the important question. Future growth will have to come from dynamic establishments. The barren establishments will age. Like the General Paper mill in Smithburg, these establishments will move out of the limelight. New ones in other regions of the country, with younger scientists and newer technologies will take over the frontier of high-technology. Research centres pass. In 1986, General Electric gave away the old Thomas Edison Laboratory in Princeton, one of the past high-tech meccas of the United States. Big corporations give away their museum pieces, not the building blocks of their future.

And that is what the research laboratories of the Triangle Research Park will be in a few decades, old labs.

Research laboratories do not add new activities to the economic fabric: they do research. Research is an important function in the production realm, particularly for large corporations. But research is not at the core of the economic growth process. This does not mean that new ventures will not emerge from the Research Triangle Park. Good engineers can build great companies in good settings. But if new high-technology ventures are sought, there are more fertile environments than the rolling wooded hills of North Carolina.

I am not biased against research conducted at universities. On the contrary, I am a strong supporter of public financing of basic research conducted at universities. But we should not have any illusions. Basic research is an international commodity, widely diffused in scientific journals. The flowering of research in genetic engineering in the late seventies and of superconductivity research in the past few years testifies to the wide diffusion of basic research. Furthermore, the rapid pace of basic research in these two areas was not brought about by a Manhattan project, the application of megabucks to a scientific challenge. Like most periods of rapid progress in knowledge, these rapid advances were due to breakthroughs in equipment and techniques, which themselves reflected the slow but sure pace of scientific progress in all areas. If the installation of a telescope is delayed five years or a cyclotron ten years, the human condition will barely be affected by it.

Basic research at universities should be vigorously pursued, for this is one of their purposes. Whoever pays should ensure that it is frontier research, and that it is tied in strongly with education. Good education à la Dean Terman; to produce seeds for tomorrow's development. But financing basic research is essentially a country's contribution to the advancement of humanity, and the fostering of growth throughout the world. Let's not expect a direct tie-in between growth and basic research. It does not work that way.

LARGE PUBLIC WORK PROJECTS: HORSES, MULES OR JUST PLAIN FUN?

Governments, or more specifically, politicians, love public work projects. The bigger, the better. Politicians read public opinion polls. Job creation is the prime concern of voters. Politicians are thus in the job business. More and more, public expenditure projects tend to be presented as job creation projects. For instance, politicians do not finance the construction of a library anymore; they invest $700,000 to create 45 construction jobs and 7 permanent jobs, and, incidentally, provide books to a neighbourhood.

Such representation is misleading. Any expenditure sustains, while it lasts, a specific demand and therefore, is a job-creation activity. The sign on a government construction project that says it creates 150 jobs is just cheap bragging. I could say the same when I buy jelly beans, as long as I buy enough of them. But this is not the issue. First, demand is fundamental. Beyond the market economy, it is easy to err. When the political system decides that the demand for a project is sufficient, it often errs. It hides its error by making the service free. But the economic contribution of the project remains limited. Politicians have overpaid for a service of less value than expected.

Some also argue that public expenditures are anticyclical tool, to dampen the effects of recession. But the long lead time of most government projects does not allow this, although politicians often get away with this argument. The economic impact to assess is the dynamic effect on the economy, beyond the direct impact of the project.

In the seventies, Hydro-Québec built a $15 billion hydroelectric project in Northern Quebec, generating as much electricity as seven nuclear plants. It was a financially sound project: the cost of the electric power is lower than if it had been produced by coal or nuclear plants. The government was very proud of itself because it was creating quite a few jobs. But with $15 billion, it could not miss. The relevant question is whether something was left behind in the economy, other than a large, efficient electrical generating system. The answer turns out to be no. A little town of 3,000 people, solely dependent on the dam was created. Local suppliers who expanded during the construction phase shrank their operations when the construction ceased and are now clamouring for additional work. The engineering firms are in a similar situation.

It could have been different. New firms could have started in the boom. As the project came to an end, these new firms could have diversified into products or services demanded by the market economy. The old circular flow in Chapter Two would have taken over as these companies injected a demand equivalent to what they were selling. But this is not what happened. Hydro-Québec is a well managed utility; it went to trusted suppliers, already in business. These suppliers expanded like a balloon for the duration of the job. When the project was over, they did not diversify into new products. They shrank back, leaving nothing dynamic in the economy.

Jane Jacobs tackles this problem in Cities and the Wealth of Nations, when she takes to task the Tennessee Valley Authority, a utility which has spent billions in one of the most disadvantaged regions of the United States. Unfortunately, it has left little as an economic legacy, except a string of power-hungry sterile branch plants totally dependent on an electrical life-line. Public expenditures on big projects do not have the same dynamic effects as private expenditures. If one million consumers were to spend a thousand dollars each of government money, for a total of one billion, we would buy products and services that, after our binge, people would keep on consuming. We would allow new activities to get woven into the economic fabric. When the Tennessee Valley Authority spent its billion, it did not cause any new permanent activities to get started in the Tennessee Valley. Outsiders came, built and went. They did not think about staying and going into import-substitution. The local people fed them, worked for them while it lasted, and went looking for work afterwards.

Not all public expenditures are sterile. Around Boston, the Department of Defence's procurement expenditures were critical for the development of the high-technology industry, which capitalized on this business to diversify into new areas. Through the entrepreneurial process (incubation, models and sponsors), new activities were generated. Defence contractors also managed to find civilian uses, or should I say circular flow uses, for products developed under defence contracts.

So where does that leave public works projects as development tools? Let's divide the issue into two components: the original expenditure, and its dynamic effects. In an egotistical world, where all regions are competing against each other for handouts from higher level governments, the winning regions are the ones that get the government spending, at least in the short term. No matter what it is for, public expenditures stimulate the local economy. It is even better than local government spending, which merely churns local demand. What counts is attracting out-of-town public spending.[4]

Thus, Seattle should be commended for landing a new $300 million naval base in the late eighties: not only has it obtained construction spending that could have gone to San Francisco or San Diego, but it has permanently turned on the federal money spigot in Puget Sound. Every year, more than $350 million of taxpayers money will flow into Seattle, and sustain the local economy. Our Seattle readers will say that makes sense.

There are two problems with that. First, Seattle has to support a 600-ship U.S. Navy in return for the base, a moral concession that did not please all local residents. Getting government projects usually demands hard work and ideological sacrifices. But that is the minor problem.

The bigger problem is what to do for an encore. The base will shrink over time, as it becomes more efficient. And so will its suppliers. With the years, the base will become old work and eventually, the old mule will die, without any family. The problem with a naval base is that it is relatively barren. It will not generate new activities. Thus, Seattle's economy will have to rely on something else to rejuvenate it. Either other components of the economy will make up for that hard-working mule by the seaside, or it is back to Washington. What does the United States need that it doesn't have and that Seattle can provide? Seattle politicians are back in business.

GIVING MONEY TO THE RICH: SUBSIDIZING CAPITAL AND R&D

In 1985, Domtar, a large Canadian pulp and paper company, demanded $200 million from government to assist it in building a new paper plant in Canada. The plant, budgeted at $1 billion, was to create 500 jobs. Domtar had sales of $2.4 billion, and after paying its workers, suppliers and bankers, its cash flow was $200 million. Although it was in good financial shape, Domtar argued that the project was large and risky. Without the grant, it would build a smaller plant, most likely in the U.S. The government blinked and wrote a cheque. Did that make sense?

The calculations underlying such a large project are complex. Sophisticated computer analyses are made, generating piles of computer printouts. But as many readers probably suspect, what counts in these analyses are the assumptions — that is what is fed into the computer. The fact that many of these assumptions have to hold for 30 years and deal with such fickle factors as profits and exchange rates makes such exercises somewhat artistic endeavours where creativity counts and where reliability is never taken for granted.

Let us assume that Domtar's model required an investment of $1 billion which was to yield an annual cash flow of $270 million, a yield of

27 per cent. The $200 million grant reduced the required investment to $800 million and increased the expected return on investment to 34 per cent. To obtain such a return,Domtar fought for the $200 million, probably spending a few million dollars in the process, in management time, consultants, colour slide presentations and the likes.

There are two issues involved here. The first is whether Domtar would have invested elsewhere if the $200 million bribe had not been paid. This is possible, but the bribe was stiff, $400,000 per job, to move them from point A to point B. (Politicians will try to throw in indirect benefits, multipliers effects, suppliers, etc., to lower this figure, but we can cut them off. Most activities have indirect effects. Very seldom do they matter.).

A more important issue is whether Domtar would have expanded without the grants. The answer is yes. Organizations seldom petrify and CEOs are fired if they let this happen. If one avenue of expansion is not interesting, another one is immediately investigated. Let us go back to the annual return sought by Domtar: 34%. Why does it have to be so high, given that Domtar's cost for external funds was about 14%?

The major difference between the returns sought and the cost of external funds is accounted by risk. For the 34% was a highly uncertain return. The sophisticated assumptions that took 50 pages of computer print-outs to lay out were only assumptions, loaded with uncertainties. Nobody can be sure about the future. So the calculations are padded, thickly. High discount rates are used. Indeed, it does not matter how sophisticated the assumptions are. What really counts is how thick the pad is. A discount rate of 25 per cent before taxes is comfortable. A 30 per cent rate is better. And 40 per cent is good management.

These thick buffers are well justified. In 1991, the Canadian dollar hit 87 cents, against 70 cents that was assumed in the model. The increase wiped out all the benefits of the $200 million grant and more. Fortunately, Domtar's buffer was thick.

Grants can have a major impact on location, but little impact on the decision to expand. CEOs do not have the choice. They have to expand their organization to please the shareholders and maintain their stock price. In theory, stockholders are supposed to underwrite the risk. But CEOs will take the money where it is easiest to obtain. Spending $2 million to obtain $200 million was a good move for Domtar. This is also why half the lobbyists in Washington hang around the tax committees.

More or less the same argumentation applies to R&D subsidies. Applied research is essential for corporations to maintain the competitiveness of their product line, and in the case of technology-intensive products, to develop the next generation of products. R&D in the most capital intensive of corporations can represent up to 15 per cent of total revenue. Such a high number is startling until one realizes that competitors also spent about the same amount and that the price structure of these industries allows for high margins that make sufficient room for these large R&D budgets.

Governments throughout the Triad economy are subsidizing a significant amount of corporate R&D, through various programs and fiscal breaks. In Canada, a typical break is a subsidy that amounts to 25 per cent of total cost or roughly 1 per cent to 2 per cent of the revenue of the corporation. Should government subsidize corporate R&D, under the aegis of a stimulant to economic growth? The answer is no, just like it was no for capital investments.

What would happen if such subsidies were phased out. At first, the corporations affected would howl. No manager likes to lose free money. Corporations would pare their R&D levels to account for the higher costs, but probably not by much. The R&D budget in a corporation stems from a complex decision process. It is not resource-driven. Does a 2 per cent reduction in the cash flow bring a corporation to curtail its R & D programs significantly and adjust its growth objectives? No. Once the bad initial feelings subside, adjustments are made in the overall budget. The growth imperative of a large corporation does not depend on government subsidies and is not affected by 2 per cent change in net revenue. The available cash flow of the corporation after paying dividends is allocated by a political exercise which takes into account a high level of uncertainty about the future. R&D is an insurance policy which will be maintained.

The U.S. semiconductor industry convinced the Reagan administration to put up $125 million per year for five years to subsidize 50 per cent of the budget of Sematech, a research consortium for the industry. The promoters argued that Sematech could be a critical element of a U.S. strategy to win the semiconductor race against the Japanese. Without subsidies, the industry would have not proceeded with Sematech and, according to the promoters, would have been doomed. Surprisingly, the Administration succumbed to this blackmail. But $125 million represents 1 per cent out of the revenue of the industry, and no industry will be threatened by a revenue shortfall of 1 per cent. This suggests another motive behind Sematech, a more strategic one for its promoters. The subsidy was used to pressure some key members of the industry to join the consortium. The recalcitrant companies were the best managed ones, in an industry where many of the largest companies are not necessarily well-managed.[5] The second tier companies that pushed for Sematech were institutionalizing sharing of applied R&D, not a bad strategy for laggard corporations.

Subsidies for capital and for R&D can sometimes be justified in small corporations, where this cash flow arbitrage does not occur because the meagre resources of the corporation make the idea preposterous. In such instances, subsidies can be likened to injections of equity capital and they can represent a large amount of the equity of the company. To the extent that the equity market is relatively inefficient for these small corporations, subsidies supplement "loose change". But even such programs could be scrapped if there were ways of making the equity market for small businesses more efficient.

TARGETING INDUSTRIES: WHAT IS THE BATTING AVERAGE?

Korea has become the largest shipbuilding country in the world. Here is how it started.[6] In the early seventies, General Park, who headed the government, called the CEO of Hyundai and asked him to start building large ships, like Japan was doing. A few days later, the CEO declined the offer, stating that Hyundai did not know much about building ships and that the industry was highly competitive. Park was quite annoyed. Politely, he thanked the Hyundai's CEO. If Hyundai wanted to do only the easy things, this was fine with him. However, the Korean government would find other partners to do the difficult things, he added. The CEO got the message. A year later, Hyundai's first ship rolled off into a glutted world market. Fortunately, the Korean government supported Hyundai while it learned its trade, underpricing the competition. Now Hyundai is a major force in international shipbuilding.

That is targeting — unsophisticated style. The government identifies a promising industrial sector for exports. It then gets the private sector to enter into it. The government picks up the tab, subsidising the risk while the domestic producers learn the business. A few years later, the country can be on top of the pile, if it is cost-competitive.

Japan's industrial strategy has used targeting extensively, in a more sophisticated way, as long as Japan was catching up. Indeed, this is what gave rise to the expression "Japan Inc.". The Ministry of International

Trade and Industry (MITI) identified promising sectors and got the major companies in the industry around a table. Various subsidy schemes were concocted. And the big moves were undertaken. Textiles, steel, shipbuilding, automobiles, consumer electronics, machine tools, construction equipment, semiconductors and superconductors were all targeted over the years. The question is whether targeting is what built the Japanese economy. Or is it the lower cost advantages that it held until the mid-seventies. Or are the Japanese simply more efficient manufacturers, as they demonstrated clearly in Fremont using good old American UAW workers. The right answer is definitely not "targeting".

Critics of the "targeting hypothesis" say that MITI's batting average is far from good. It made quite a few mistakes in the past. Targeting implies deciding "who" will do "what". Honda was once told by MITI that it was in the motorcycle business, not in the car business. Honda said baloney, went on to build cars and became a world-wide car manufacturer. Targeting was not much of a factor there.[7]

Targeting is easy when a country has a significant labour cost advantage, and in fact is a valuable strategy for a developing country. Such a country cannot err as the initial risks are borne by government subsidies while the companies learn their new trade. Once they learn it, they will be able to sell their product in the export markets with a low price strategy. This is what Hyundai did in North America. The Hyundai cars are fine cars, well-designed and well-built. But they sell in North America mainly because of their low price, made possible by their lower labour costs. Japan was a low price competitor when it was targeting, up until recently. Now the yen has risen in value, and the Japanese cannot count on low cost labour anymore. They find targeting much more difficult. This is the problem with targeting throughout the Triad economy, where cost advantages are minimal.

Targeting policies are also proposed for sunrise industries, the industries of tomorrow. Government picks up the tab for research and development expenditures. But since these industries are emerging throughout the Triad economy, targeting strategies are being reduced to picking the winners in worldwide competition. This is like betting a huge amount of money on the Kentucky Derby winner in January when nobody knows yet which horses will run.

The targeting game is played with a few major tools, all involving some sort of subsidy. Cost-plus procurement is used by the Pentagon to subsidize industrial R&D, as military products such as aeroplanes and telecommunications equipment are later knocked off as civilian products. Indeed, one of the star companies of the U.S. high-technology establishment, Digital Equipment, started in this fashion, commercializing a civilian version of a military minicomputer. The U.S. government is often accused of unfairly subsidizing the American aircraft and semiconductor industries, through these cost-plus Pentagon R&D contracts.

Because they do not have a huge defence procurement budget, most countries use other tools. They sometimes play crudely, as Japan does by closing its domestic markets. Other policies are sometimes more sophisticated, such as export credits and special tax-treatment for R&D.

The fact is that all Triad countries subsidize some industries that they judge to be critical. But they also monitor other countries. Accusations of cheating on the GATT rules on unfair subsidization is a sort of check-and-balance mechanism. My prognosis is that low-scale targeting will go on forever. In Canada, there are 10 provinces which are all doing it, trying to outdo each other without being caught. State governments in the U.S. are discovering it. Influential politicians in Washington have been playing the game for decades. I do not see how the practice can be stopped.

But does it matter? Of course not, except for the taxpayers. Politicians will always be attracted by sunrise industries. But it is difficult to pick the winners in sunrise industries. The batting average of politicians is fairly low. Looking back on the promises of industrial targeting, Canadians were supposed to have the best nuclear reactor in the world, the best 1960 jet fighter, the best 1976 corporate jet. Canadians were supposed to have cornered the teletext business, which was supposed to be a multi-billion dollar business by now. Canadians were supposed to be a major force in personal computers, in software, in movies, in records, in this and in that. Blessed are the politicians, for their electors have short memories.

It all boils down to having a local cluster of companies on the top of the pile in a world industry. That is not easily done. Money helps, whether it comes from stockholders or from governments. But that is not the most important thing. Being in the right industry at the right time with the right technology is what matters. Finding the right combination is easier ex-post then ex-ante, in particular because the winning technology is often not known in advance. It is like the Kentucky Derby. First, one's horse has to be invited to enter the race. Then the horse has to run in the money. For a corporation, the right combination can get it in the race. But it still has to place among the winners; something which only a few do. The entrepreneur and the right organization matter a lot at that stage. Even then, the uncertainty is very high. Winners must make the right moves at the right time, benefitting from the lucky breaks before the others. To foresee the winner is quite a challenge.

For Hyundai in Korea, the game is simpler. Because of lower labour costs, it knows that it will be among the winners. Thus, Hyundai can make a few mistakes along the way, and still make it on the basis of lower prices. But the Triad countries have roughly the same labour costs. The winners are more difficult to pick: skills, wisdom and stamina are what matter.

Venture capitalists, with several billion dollars at their disposal, are always looking for winners. Their batting average is said to be that of baseball players. The stock market is also looking for winners, and also has a lot of money. It bets on a lot of horses in January. In comparison, the government resources allocated for targeting sunrise industries are peanuts. Foolish spending, but politicians love it.

PROTECTIONISM: PASSING THE BUCK

A subtle form of subsidizing, which unfortunately is also the most inefficient, is protectionism. Government tinkering has been a plague accompanying international trade. In the old days, governments used tariffs to raise revenues. In pre-industrial Europe, tariffs represented over 50 per cent of government revenues. Even today, in some small developing countries, taxes on imported goods still generate a significant proportion of government income. But in the Triad countries, governments derive less than one per cent of their income from tariffs.

Nevertheless, protectionism is still very much part of the agenda. Tariffs are not high anymore, having been reduced significantly since the Second World War, and representing much less of an expenditure than transportation costs in the Triad economy. Quotas, voluntary restraints and regulatory constraints have replaced them, by prohibiting or restraining, directly or indirectly, the importation of foreign products. Consumers get hurt, through higher prices. For instance, the voluntary restraint program on the export of Japanese cars to the U.S. cost car buyers of America something like $1 billion a year (or $100 per car) in the mid-eighties. This money was pocketed by the car companies, including the foreign ones, in proportion to their market share. Thanks to the government, stockholders got a little help from car buyers.

The overall direct costs of trade restrictions are less than commonly assumed. They cost Canadians, who are among the most "protected" consumers in the Triad economy, about 3 per cent of their aggregate income in purchasing power. For the U.S., the estimates are about 1 per cent, or a few months of economic growth.[8] These direct costs, although important, are not outrageous.

Indirect costs, the "what if" costs, are more significant. Protected industries are passing the buck to other industries, which feel more international competitive heat as a consequence. The problems can be illustrated by the following example. "Dinosaur" manufacturers, a declining industry, has serious competitive problems because of outrageous work practices imposed by the unions. They obtain from the government a "voluntary" import restrictions program. Imports of dinosaurs decline, to the delight of the domestic dinosaur industry. But as a consequence, the exchange rate rises slightly. All other industries competing with imports feel more competitive pressure from abroad. Exporters also suffer a loss of profits. The buck has been successfully passed: the slight rise in the exchange rate has caused exports to fall and imports other than dinosaurs to increase. Everybody's worse off, except for the dinosaur manufacturers and their workers, who smile all the way to the bank having passed their problems to others.[9]

What is worse is that protectionist measures usually provide only temporary relief in the Triad economy. The production realm in the competitive countries will continue their drive toward lower costs. Moreover, the market will try to circumvent the artificial barriers. Voluntary restraints against the Japanese did not work. Japanese car manufacturers upgraded their car export mix, and indeed, made more profits on each car sold. Moreover, they moved onto the higher margin, middle-line American models and, as expected, clobbered them.

The story of the Chrysler revival is justifiably used to defend the benefits of quotas.[10] But several factors were more important in the rebirth of Chrysler. Compared to the leadership of Iaccoca, the quality of the new management, the loan guarantee, the cuts in wages and in employment, the break consented to by suppliers and banks, the decentralization of components and parts production to suppliers, and the timely arrivals of the K-cars, the benefits given by the voluntary restraint program (which cost $1 billion a year) seem relatively minor. Moreover, its continuation several years later illustrates a basic flaw of temporary protectionist relief: it tends to be institutionalized as a permanent fixture. Once a crutch is given to an industry, the industry comes to depend on it.

In Triad countries, protectionist measures are mainly used to protect mature industries, from which growth cannot be expected. If worst comes to worst, a region is better off biting the bullet, kissing the protectionist measures goodbye, and concentrating on recharging its production realm with industries that have growth potential. The costs to other industries and to consumers seldom warrant quotas. A region which depends on them should assume that reason will eventually triumph and that quotas will disappear. It should concentrate on generating new industries.[11]

GETTING THE PRIORITIES STRAIGHT

I am often dazzled by the policies and the twists to existing policies which are suggested in the pursuit of economic growth. It often reminds me of an old poster by Norman Rockwell: "Angling". Two people are coming back from fishing. There is a middle-aged man, fully equipped with the latest high-tech fishing wizardry: long boots, two fancy rods, a net, several flies, a Swiss army knife, a genuine fish bag, etc. But no fish. And there is a barefoot kid, his head half-hidden under an old straw hat, with a wooden rod and five fish tied to a string. Good fishing does not start with the equipment.

Growth is elusive. Too often, governments fall for the latest fad. Small business incubators are typical. It is definitely the most written about concept of the past five years in the development literature. Sacred cows roam as free in the economic arena as in the backward villages of India.

With government spending at such a high level and with regulations all pervasive, I do not really care if the producers of running shoes get a little protection, and if scientists working on the strength of the chemical bondage in propylene under high pressure and low temperature get a little bit more funding. What is worrisome is that so many interest groups wanting a piece of government pie appropriate the promise of economic growth as a potential benefit. It is not that some growth will not come out of it. Spending money generates jobs, whether the money is spent on jelly beans or on a new mathematical theorem. But buying snake oil merely eases the conscience of politicians.

Many things can be done to spur economic growth. Most of them cost little money. But they need attention and leadership. They should be at the top of the list of priorities. Snake oil vendors can do whatever they want as long as they do not interfere with these priorities.

216

CHAPTER THIRTEEN

REFORESTING

"Roger Smith, General Motors made $4.7 billion last year. You did not have the right to close that plant."

Michael Moore, author of Roger & Me

Rage. And despair. The plant that was the lifeblood of the community is being closed. What will this community do? How about our houses? Generally, nobody wanted to believe that it was coming. But the plant was obsolete. It was badly located. Workers were older, cranky. And highly paid. The plant ranked among the lowest in quality. Padlocking was inevitable. This year, or next year. No, it is not the fault of "some big bad guy on the thirty-eight floor who cares only about profits".

Plant closures are a rite of economic life. Most "deaths" go unnoticed. But the spectacular ones create the shocks and the misunderstandings. In 1989, film maker Michael Moore drew America's attention to the plight of Flint, Michigan, where General Motors closed two large plants. But before, there had been the steel plants, the coal mines, the rail yards, the stock yards, the textile mills, etc. The list is endless. Indeed, one day, computer plants will join the list.

"The guy on the fourteenth floor" did his job. He is not to blame. Change is relentless, and sometimes, it occurs in burst. But what about the communities, the people that have houses and those who run small commerces. Is there life after the padlock on the gate? Is there anything that could be done to rejuvenate the Smithburg economies, short of continuing the subsidies or giving the area its own currency? The answer is a definite yes. Indeed, Smithburg can provide a good illustration of reforesting techniques, how the conditions conducive to the development of a younger economic base can be influenced by local policies. Smithburg can be "saved". Old trees take years to die. The chances of revitalizing Smithburg are far from being zero, under the canopy of the old General Paper plant.

The diagnosis is classic: the Smithburg economy is overly dependent on a single industry which has entered a state of decline, a region with a tired production realm. Over the years, the General has sterilized the entrepreneurial soil of Smithburg. There is nothing in Smithburg but an aging plant and people. But there are a few years left to grow new activities, before that old tree, the General Paper plant, dies for good. Meanwhile, Smithburg could use its potential as a sponsor, to rejuvenate the economic base.

A first move would be to take a very close look at the old tree, working closely with the plant authorities to reopen it and with the political heavyweights in the area to find out how long the plant should stay open, and to ensure that its cutting rights would not be transferred to another plant in the near future. Then, an industrial commission should be formed with fresh faces, to harness the local leadership needed to pull the community in the right direction. On the Commission would sit representatives of the present economy: the plant manager, the union steward, somebody from City Hall, and four or five of the most dynamic and concerned local businessmen. Out of this group would emerge the leaders of the revival of the Smithburg economy.

I would propose a simple reforesting strategy. We would assume that Smithburg has 10 years to grow new basic activities under the canopy of the dying tree. Initially, the strategy would establish conditions leading to the growth of wild grass, that is, small local initiatives creating a positive entrepreneurial climate. Phase Two would translate this early entrepreneurial activism into more solid small basic firms. The community would remain on the watch, with the fertilizer, the water, the shade, and whatever it takes to get it to grow. The General Paper plant should also be an asset to use as a sponsor. Within 10 years, given a good climate, five to ten medium-size basic firms could emerge, employing in the 10th year, several hundred people. Such a base would be strong enough to sustain the local economy when the old paper plant dies. Properly nurtured, there is nothing that prevents that new base from growing by itself into an economic base with more than 1,000 employees in a generation. New houses would be built in Smithburg!

WILD GRASS

Phase One of the strategy aims at getting some momentum in the Smithburg entrepreneurial realm, small successes that build confidence and get local people to attempt entrepreneurial activities. The revitalized Commission would be the starting point. It should investigate any little opportunity that can be turned into a development success: uplifting Main Street (even if it means only sprucing up a few stores), an improvement in the camp grounds, a major repair contract at General Paper awarded to a local firm, etc. The purpose is to send a broad signal to the whole community that something is happening in Smithburg.

A first impact will be achieved by the self-confidence and the drive of the leaders. The local weekly paper, an important feature in a small community, can be an important tool in that regard. Week after week, a "business" story should be found on the front page. No entrepreneurial gesture should be too modest to go unreported in positive terms.

The challenge is to instill a sense of "can-do" in the community. An

219

incubator* will most likely be proposed by a well-intentioned promoter. If a building is available and required funds are modest, it could be set up, provided that sufficient assurances are given that it will not remain empty and that its first tenants would not be failing firms. Smithburg can do without a symbol of failure.

THE FIRST SHOOTS

One follows a loose script in order to grow wild grass. It helps to be an opportunist. Occasions should be pursued as they arise, and if the climate is positive, some will arise. On the other hand, expectations should remain realistic. Nobody should be chasing the President of ADAMCO to get him to set up a branch plant in Smithburg.

One day, the first shoot will appear. It could happen in many ways. It could be an electrician who works in one of the area's paper mills, looking for assistance to start his business. He wants to team up with his brother-in-law who lives in Jacobsville to establish a motor rewinding business in his father's old garage. They have "contacts" and feel that they can get some contracts from the paper mills. But they are still short of money to buy their machinery. They want to know what the Commission can do for them.

The commissioner might lose this one. Anything can happen. The brother-in- law may not exist, or have no money. The electrician could be a procrastinator who will never quit his job. But eventually, another entrepreneur will succeed. On the other hand, this first venture may succeed. The brother-in-law may turn out to be a high-powered ideal partner. The word will get around, they will obtain the General Paper contract, and then the work for the local trucking firm, etc.

Then, a "If this guy can do it..." thought will set a housewife to thinking about her meat pie project. She already sells her meat pies to a cafeteria at a paper plant. Maybe she could get into the school system if she had a little push, and then, buy a small truck, etc. And thus, entrepreneurial seeds will slowly germinate throughout the small Smithburg economy.

Jacobsville will be important to Smithburg's economic rebirth. The ties between the two cities are numerous. But more important, Smithburg knows Jacobsville and its market. As a depressed area, Smithburg also has a cost advantage over Jacobsville. Most likely, the first new basic businesses in Smithburg will "export" to Jacobsville.

220

Offering business support to these struggling ventures is critical. The commissioner must be their business agent, assisted by members of the Commission. They will weave development networks, first in Smithburg, then in Jacobsville. The General Paper plant manager will learn that he can give contracts to local firms and not only get away with it, but feel mighty proud of it. He will pass the message to his underlings, with whom local entrepreneurs are most likely to be in contact. He will also pinch hit with other plant managers in the area, to get local guys through the door. In Jacobsville, the transplanted sons and daughters of Smithburg will start being proud of their hometown. "Something is happening in Smithburg, I can't believe it!" They will also pitch in when asked, making phone calls, giving references, using their influence, passing a tip, etc.

This sounds artificial, and indeed, the way it is done is purposely artificial, for the strategy is based on growing new development networks in barren Smithburg. Development networks are very active in healthy cities. Business people regularly call each other to exchange information and introduce acquaintances. Names are continually dropped. Informal business propositions are made at social meetings, ushering in permanent business relationships. Reputations are constructed through inoffensive luncheon comments ("Hey, these guys did a super job..."). Entrepreneurs cultivate these development networks. They try to meet the right people. They keep their ears open. They spend hours thinking of strategies to meet important people, etc. In Smithburg, where doing business is not a common activity, this has to be done artificially.

TOOLS FOR GROWING BUSINESS

After a few years, some fast-track firms will turn up in Smithburg. They will have good management, good products and the will to expand.[1] A development agency can support these fast-track firms which feel the strain of rapid growth. They can count on a wide range of tools, as governments multiply development programs to mid-size business.

Indeed, the proliferation of programs to assist small- and medium-size basic businesses is a key feature of the recent evolution of industrial policies. Governments have discovered the potential contribution of small- and medium-size businesses to employment and have introduced a large variety of programs aimed specifically at stimulating their growth and increasing their competitiveness. These programs form the core of states' and provincial industrial strategies. Several of these measures and policies were criticized in Chapter Eleven as being inefficient. But, under appropriate circumstances, efficient programs can be implemented.

Thus, we have regional industrial policies in force throughout North America. The focus is on mid-size firms, with a special emphasis on manufacturing. Programs range from financial assistance for expansion, exports and R&D to management assistance and technological assistance. But how can one tell whether these programs are worth their costs? Three broad principles can help to assess them.

First, any program that supplements the equity of start-ups and rapidly growing firms has some positive effects. To the extent that they provide money to cash-hungry growing businesses, these programs correct major imperfections in the equity markets for small firms and fast-growing private firms. Subsidies also compensate for the unwillingness of entrepreneurs to share ownership of their firms, which deters them from selling equity to outsiders. Whether subsidies are correctly channelled to firms with good potential is something else. Indeed, many programs are inefficient in that respect. Picking the winners is tough. Emphasizing bureaucratic or "expert" approaches is surely not the right way. Tax-oriented measures, which let investors pick the winners, are preferable in that regard.

Second, financial inducements can encourage entrepreneurial businesses to undertake "growth strategies". The status quo is often the least risky route for the owner of a small business. Programs tilted toward riskier decisions can change their attitudes. Grants increase the profits of firms that take "preferred" paths. Such programs can be fairly effective. For many years, the Montreal garment industry was thought to be impervious to change and to modernization. Faced with foreign competition, many owners preferred to quit rather than reinvest. A special modernization program administered by a government supported productivity centre for the garment industry was highly effective for the modernization to the industry, reducing costs, improving productivity and increasing flexibility.

Third, policies and measures whose main effective thrust is to reduce the costs of capital are generally of doubtful effectiveness. This is the case of financial assistance programs targeted to large, well capitalized businesses. There are few justifications for such subsidies, other than to bribe them to select a particular location for a new establishment. Large organizations do not have the option to quit, when faced with the dilemma of modernization. They must modernize. An organization that does not do it when there is a need for it, or expand when the opportunities are there, has deep managerial problems. Change of leadership is more warranted than financial assistance. An exception to this blanket condemnation can be made for temporary relief: financial assistance can be warranted to meet an unexpected challenge that might destroy an organization.[2]

There are additional ways to assist fast-track firms. In their early years, shortage of equity and lack of contact with dense development networks are common. The standard policy response is to create venture capital institutions, which can be privately owned. The Small Business Investment Corporations (SBIC), which have access to low cost funds guaranteed by the Small Business Administration, are typical. Impatient governments have also created state-owned venture capital institutions. But the institutional route has its limits. When one counts the number of investments they make in a single year, compared to the number of fast-track firms in their region, it becomes clear that they provide a very porous sieve. Most fast-track entrepreneurs do not connect with venture capital institutions, no matter how solicitous they are.

Loose change or informal venture capital remains by far the major source of equity for most fast-track corporations during their early states. Thus, the provision of loose change should be encouraged. The province of Ontario has set up an imaginative program which supplements by a 33 per cent grant, equity investments by outside investors in small businesses active in manufacturing, research and tourism.[3] The province of Quebec has set up the Quebec Stock Saving Plan, a fiscal measure which strongly encourages Initial Public Offerings which in turn stimulate private investments in companies which have the potential to eventually go public.[4]

GROWTH STRATEGY FOR SMALL CITIES

With time, Smithburg's development challenge should become that of a small city with a diversified economic base, with a population anywhere between 20,000 and 200,000 people in its trade area. Small towns, where the business community is fairly close, can be a good breeding ground for entrepreneurs.

Local development agencies can have a significant impact on local economic development. The first step in the implementation of a successful strategy is learning about the trees in the forest, namely the business in the economic base. The idea is to identify the firms in the economic base which have a good potential for expansion. The number of basic firms will vary, typically 30 to 50 in the small towns, up to 300 in the larger secondary cities.[5]

A clinical analysis of the economic base of a small town can reveal its strengths and weaknesses and potential sources of dynamism. The level of entrepreneurship is reflected in the birth rate of new basic firms. Models, incubators, and potential sponsors are identified. Scenarios are developed for declining establishments. The causes of growth for the fast-track firms, usually the comparative advantages of the region, are also identified.

Generically, a development strategy aims at increasing the number of dynamic firms in the economic base, by accelerating the number of new firms and by creating stimulative conditions for existing firms. The objective is to get a well-balanced production realm, a proper mix of sunrise, noon and sunset industries. A dynamic entrepreneurial realm will yield such a structure over the years. Models, institutionalized sponsorship and weaving development networks into the business community are used to make the entrepreneurial realm more dynamic.

Table 13.1 presents guidelines for the elaboration of a local development strategy. Local attitudes of entrepreneurs and managers are what count the most. Successful development is highly opportunistic. The business leadership should be in position to intervene rapidly, with such diverse interventions as preventing a plant closure and assisting a firm to get a contract. The agency has to learn to use the local business community, as ultimately, the ones who matter most are the business leaders. Healthy cities can usually count on their elite and their institutions to intervene when the common good demands it. Their ability to work together efficiently is often critical to the success of local development efforts.

Small cities have many advantages in that regard, as their business communities are typically close-knit. For instance, the local media tend to be much more cooperative in promoting local businesses. An added advantage is the small size of their economic base. A few success stories, either in fast-track firms or branch plants, can translate into a significant growth rate. Finally, economic growth is a lot more visible in smaller cities, creating much stronger models. Large metropolitan areas tend to grow in faraway suburbs. The expansion of housing in smaller cities is more visible to the residents. So is the transformation of the commercial sector. That has a major impact on attitudes.

However, there are disadvantages in being a small city. A few

TABLE 13.1
GUIDELINES FOR THE ELABORATION
OF A DEVELOPMENT STRATEGY

1- The agency should concentrate its intervention on a limited number of firms in the economic base. The local sector of the economy takes care of itself, as there is a high level of entrepreneurship. In the economic base, many firms have limited growth potential, although they are quite resilient. This reduces the scope of work of the agency to less than half the firms in the economic base and to new basic firms.

2- The agency should not play the entrepreneur. It should concentrate on creating stimulative conditions and on assisting firms. Entrepreneurs will identify opportunities.

3- Five-year objectives should be determined, in terms of jobs, for each category of existing firms and for new firms in the economic firms. The staff of the agency should be assessed mainly on the performance of the region on these indicators.

4- Job creation will be accelerated mostly by providing all possible assistance to the fast-track firms, which should create over half of the new jobs, and to new firms, the second most important source of new jobs.

5- Build momentum, that is, a local business climate where expansion and development is valued. Success stories among fast-track firms and the establishment of new firms should be publicized in the business community.

6- The business community that matters is small, from 50 persons to not more than several hundred persons, depending on the size of the region. Half of these people are typically in the producer services sector — lawyers, accountants, brokers, etc. They are part of the peer group whose opinions matter to entrepreneurs and managers.

7- In some regions, attracting out-of-town branch plants can be a productive avenue of growth. These regions are relatively few. Success at attracting such plants, either in the region or in a surrounding region is the best indicator of the potential of this avenue. If the past experience is bleak, forget about it.

8- A regular survey of jobs in all the basic firms should be conducted. The survey should allow the agency to identify early any problem or opportunity. (Such survey takes only a few hours in the plane)

9- Infrastructures do not matter that much. Other local agencies are usually better suited to promote infrastructure development. The agency should also leave the incubator business to real estate developers and to grassroots groups.

10- Very often, many agencies compete over the responsibility of local development. The quality of the private sector leadership should determine which agency will prevail.

declining establishments can not only represent a significant dead weight, but may cancel any gain in basic employment elsewhere, preventing an expansion of the local economy.

Defeatist attitudes can be solidly ingrained in a community, and they are tough to change. Leadership may be absent. Good intentions do not necessarily make strong leadership. Political interference and suburb versus core city squabbles can poison the whole process. Finally, poor execution is often a problem, as development agencies in smaller cities do not always have good staff, and replacing staff often meets with strong resistance.

A strategy is not essential to the growth of these cities. Indeed, all the large cities of today were once in the position of being smaller, and they grew naturally out of that situation. But smaller cities do not benefit from the advantages of the larger cities: extensive development networks, large local markets, institutions, etc. A hands-on strategy, of the type described in Table 13.1, compensates for these weaknesses and helps smaller cities grow faster.

THERE ARE NO BAND LEADER
IN LARGE METROPOLITAN AREAS

The fact is that most economic growth originates in larger cities. They provide a rich milieu for entrepreneurial initiatives, especially for innovative import-substitution products with high potential. The large corporations are also anchored in large cities and are not about to let their strategic decision centres leave these dense nodes of development networks.

Most large cities of the Triad economies are now actively involved in promoting their economic development. Much of their efforts bear on attracting branch plants, a zero-sum Peter-rob-Paul game with little overall economic consequences. But there have been more ambitious attempts at stimulating growth. Boston, Atlanta, Montreal, New York come to mind in North America.

But large metropolitan areas have a particular problem when it comes to articulating a development strategy. What do you do when there are no band leader to coordinate the efforts of the players? This is a challenge faced by most metropolitan areas. The numerous players, in the business community, in the political realm and among institutions, all have their own agenda and timetable when it comes to promoting economic growth.

Indeed, in big cities, not only is there no band leader, but there is also no place for one. Job creation and economic development are political issues in the public domain, up for grabs by anybody, and fairly high on the agendas of many local groups, some of which have widely divergent interests. Fortunately, a natural division of labour occurs, without too much consultation; it reduces the potential friction, although there remains many opportunities for divergent action.

Local politicians have a four-year electoral planning horizon. Anything that risks spoiling the last year of that horizon is crossed off the agenda. Politicians are interested in visible activities. External promotion is one of them; city halls rarely hesitate to finance external promotion. As long as the electorate believe that branch plants play an important role in economic growth, promoting the area to "outside investors" will be looked after. What they also do is to compete against each other, core city against suburbs, and suburbs between themselves, for industrial and commercial real estate. Much energy is spent on such efforts, but the net regional effect is minor.

An important contribution of local politicians is to run a good government. Unfortunately, contrary to popular belief, police, street cleanliness, local taxes, and good schools are not prime contributors to growth. Indeed, good city life is negatively correlated to economic growth.[6] The best cities are not necessarily the fastest growing ones: cities become genteel when they stop growing. But good government creates conditions which sustain positive attitudes, attract immigrants, and make the place a nice place to live, although the link between good local government and economic growth is not that strong.[7]

State (or provincial) politicians often have a different agenda than local politicians. Large metropolitan areas are either the largest or the second largest cities in most regional jurisdictions. Their growth has a major impact at the state level. Thus, their development matters to the politicians at the state level. In terms of economic growth, state politicians tend to concentrate on infrastructure and taxes as chief areas of concern. Knowing what to ask for is also very important. In most state houses, large cities compete with small towns and rural areas for government largesse. Targeting the political capital of a city can bring important dividends or useless "pork". What politicians deliver over their terms of office matters. A city can end up with a covered stadium and a brand new "government building" while its economic base rots due to a crippling tax structure.

The business community is fragmented into numerous groups with widely divergent interests, from suburban Chambers of Commerce to local chapters of national business associations. Generally, one association, typically the main Chamber of Commerce, represents the interests of the business community at the regional level. This group interacts with local and regional politicians on development issues. Its prime asset is its political clout, if it can mobilize its membership. It has the resources to study issues and to prepare well-documented briefs. However, much of the energy of Chambers of Commerce is spent on the local sector of the economy, and not on the economic base. They end up promoting major civic infra-structure projects, such as a domed stadium, convention centre or urban transportation systems, all things which are important for the community, but only loosely related to economic growth.

However important the Chamber is, it seldom reaches the big boys, the most prestigious members of the business community, the CEOs of the largest local corporations. They tend to stick with their own. They are often found on ad-hoc groups formed by one of their peers to tackle a specific issue. In general, sustained participation from these people is not to be expected. The community has to accept their underlings as representatives of large local corporations.[8]

Many other groups are to be found within the business community. Trade associations, such as High Technology Councils, and ethnic associations, are very much concerned with local economic growth conditions. Real estate developers are in the growth business full-time, and on some projects, they can be at cross-purposes with the rest of the business community. Universities also want to join the in-crowd, something new in many cities. They have the prestige and numerous resources. Their main objective is to multiply their links with the business community and diversify their sources of research funding. Finally, churches are now frequent participants in policy debates on growth and must be taken into account.

Given this wide cast of characters, implementing a development strategy is a complex exercise in a metropolitan area. Knowing what counts matters. But more importantly, developing private leadership is fundamental. This is the only way to ensure the continuity of vision needed over the long term to influence the course of economic development. Moreover, private leadership can influence the political realm, and maintain the actions of government within a broad pre-determined course. Often this leadership is scattered in many organizations which loosely cooperate. However, looking back at successful experiences, one often finds that a few individuals have mattered most, by providing a unifying vision of what the future can be. These individuals are typically found at the head of local universities or local corporations. They have a strong influence within the business community. They rally the community around a vision of what the city could be and lead the way to this future.

WHAT MAKE CITIES GROW

The recipe is simple: a dynamic and diversified production realm, coupled with a fertile entrepreneurial realm, providing a continuous stream of new activities in sunrise sectors. Sunrise activities are now most often related to the information economy. More and more, growth rests on the ability of organizations to deal with ideas and information and to establish new links between people and organizations. The ability to usher change and assist organizations to change will become growth activities. Planning, creative research and communication are functions growing in importance. So are the research and development activities which characterize new industries.

Conversely, manufacturing is becoming less important as an engine of growth in large cities. The development of communication and transportation and the trend toward smaller scale production lead to decentralized manufacturing. Cities which have traditionally relied on a strong manufacturing base, and particularly on large scale manufacturing, have serious growth problems.

Government towns also face problems. Government employment also hit a plateau several years ago. The continuous growth of employment in government- related activities has masked this phenomenon in most capital cities. Modern communications allow government relations to be decentralized. Government cities will have increasing difficulty growing on their traditional base. Diversifying will also be a challenge for these cities.

What can a city do to master its own development? Three generic strategic thrusts can form the core of a growth strategy.

Entrepreneurial development - Strategies to multiply entrepreneurs concentrate on models, sponsors, enrichment of the business inputs (through development networks) and strong social support. Entrepreneurs naturally drift toward activities with high potential, such as sunrise industries.

Promoting high growth activities - Strategies to promote local development of activities which are growing more rapidly because of secular demand trends or because of technological progress. This is done by supporting the development of technological inputs, attracting potential incubators, selectively supporting some industries, etc.

Development of the communications and planning functions - Strategies to promote the local establishment of head office functions and of producer services functions. Strategic producer service industries such as financing can be targeted for special attention.

Winning strategies typically include a combination of these three thrusts, although one tends to dominate. As expected, these thrusts can be obscured by the usual noise that passes for development in most cities, squabbles to attract manufacturing plants, infrastructure developments, high profile but ineffectual government programs, etc. They can also be masked by high profile "targeting" strategy, aimed at specific sectors. But a targeting strategy must adhere to the mechanisms which shape the development of industries in a region. Whether it is the development of high technology, financial services, cinema, or tourism, the rules are the same. The entrepreneurial seedbed has to be fertilized. Technological expertise in the targeted sectors has to be built, to attract the best and the brightest. If the ingredients are present, the clustering mechanism will take hold and the sector will develop rapidly. However, most targeting strategies are more naive. They rest on the proposition that money can solve the problem. Great sums are spent to transplant mature organizations into an area. What they usually get are low technology assembly plants and sterile research laboratories. Industries grow in regions, they are not purchased.

INDUSTRIAL POLICIES

The emergence of industrial policies spearheaded by regional government is one of the most intriguing developments in the area of economic development in recent decades. Extensive experimentation has led to a variety of regional programs and policies aimed at stimulating growth of regional firms.[9] But this plethora of assistance programs for businesses boils down for the most part to various ways of channelling money to firms, to induce them to develop in a specific preferred direction.

I will not come back to the various policies discussed in Chapter Eleven. Foolish spending does not do much damage. But some assistance programs can be worthwhile. What works and what does not work demands a detailed analysis. What is clear however is that the most successful programs are directed at fast-track firms and start-ups, and supplement their equity capital. But more experimentation must be done to find ways to reach effectively both the entrepreneurs and the firms that can respond positively to a "development" bride.

Economic development relies very much on attitudes. Policy makers have discovered that entrepreneurs love the money, but find the process of asking for it somewhat distasteful. States and provinces that package their industrial policies in comprehensive programs aimed at demonstrating an understanding of entrepreneurs are on the right track. Positioning the government's efforts as a dynamic partnership between a government that has funds and entrepreneurs that have ideas, creates a climate of cooperation.

On the other hand, programs that attempt to change the policies and orientation of mature firms are less commendable. "Bribing" might work with small- and medium- size businesses. Money can also lengthen the economic life of an aging plant. But financial inducements will not affect the strategic behaviour of large organizations significantly, other than moving a plant from point A to point B. Large organizations will grab all the money offered, and will rationalize the gesture in a very convincing manner. But if the money was not there, they would most likely pursue the same course of action. Large organizations generally immunize their development from the vagaries of government programs.

Procurement policies have never been too successful, within the framework of an industrial strategy. There have been circumstances where government purchases were critical in nurturing the development of new products or firms. For instance, the Japanese government was instrumental in the birth of the Japanese supercomputer industry, channelling its purchases of supercomputers to three emerging Japanese producers. Governments and government-supported institutions are the main buyers of super-computers. Some defence related spending in the United States has also had some positive industrial pay-off. But there are not many examples of such impact. One of the major problems with government procurement is the prevalence of special government specifications. The more customized the purchase, the less efficient is the sponsor.

There is also a major administrative challenge in fitting a procurement policy within an industrial policy. Sponsorship implies positive discrimination, something that procurement policies are supposed to prevent. It is also difficult to prevent it from degenerating into disguised and expensive pork barrel procurement. Tough choices are made by sponsors: who should make it, what premium should be paid for the development, which specifications should be established, what should be done with the inevitable delays, etc. Governments seldom have the structure to make these tough choices; compromises are much more common, and they greatly reduce the efficiency of governments as sponsors.

Should state governments join the international "seek and find" game, with overseas offices and extensive promotion programs? This presently-fashionable trend is not necessarily very effective, although politicians take the credit for any external activity that locates in their jurisdiction. Promotion can enhance the attractiveness of some areas. In that light, promotional programs are justified on a purely defensive basis, as competition for branch plants intensifies. But the priorities should be clear. The action starts at home. Foreign corporations will generally be attracted foremost to areas demonstrating growth. Thus "growing your own" should be a priority even in areas which depend on foreign branches for a large part of their growth. The development of local basic business should be the dominant thrust. Prospecting abroad should be a secondary thrust.

IDEOLOGICAL QUALMS

Many readers are probably wincing at my pragmatic approach toward government intervention in economic development. To what extent should governments be in the business of subsidizing the growth of the private sector? Most economists cringe at such subsidies, for they represent an inefficient allocation of scarce resources. But economists tend to concentrate solely on allocative efficiency, which is concerned with the allocation of capital that will yield the lowest prices. Entrepreneurs and innovation are not considered in their models. Selectively encouraging innovators to reduce the cost of uncertainty has no place in their paradigm.

But in the defence of economists, it should be said that a region can grow without the government pumping money into the private sector through various assistance programs. Indeed, I am not certain whether in the long run, such programs really matter, as the private economy would organize itself accordingly in their absence. Nevertheless, over the years, I lost many of my ideological reservations toward government interventions designed to stimulate growth, for two fundamental reasons.

First, governments will intervene anyway, whether one likes it or not. As long as economic growth is important to voters, politicians will respond with highly visible interventions. There is not much one can do about this except try to find ways of improving the effectiveness of the interventions.

Second, governments and businesses are now in such a symbiotic financial relationship that it is most difficult to consider governments as neutral. Taxes are not neutral. Some firms pay more taxes than others. The 1982 Reagan tax cut included a multi-billion dollar transfer to old line manufacturing firms. In 1986, the reverse happened, with a major increase in business taxes. The expenditure budget is also far from neutral. The budget of the Department of Defence is a major instrument for industrial policy (albeit an inefficient one), channelling several billion a year in the development of advanced technologies. Economic neutrality is a fiction as far as modern governments are concerned.

Thus, I stopped long ago to worry about the principle. However, I believe that interventions can be greatly improved upon. Indeed, the bulk of the funds spent by government for the purpose of stimulating economic growth are ineffective. Most of the funds go for infrastructure and to large organizations, two inefficient avenues. Financial assistance given to any corporation with equity in excess of say, $25 million could be stopped immediately with little real impact on the economy. (This includes all programs, from employee training and export financing to revenue bonds and R&D subsidies.) Large organizations have a growth dynamic of their own. The lack of subsidies is seldom a factor hindering their growth.

Sometimes, organization-threatening crises can justify government intervention, Chrysler being a good example. However, before intervening, government should ensure that a new CEO is at the helm and that the stockholders, creditors and employees also give up something. If the major constituencies of the organization are ready to make sacrifices, government assistance can soothe the wounds. Otherwise, no deal.

Smaller growing companies are in a different situation. They are short of equity, and the equity market for small firms is far from perfect. Investments by outsiders in small businesses have low liquidity and information is costly. The smaller the organization, the higher is the risk represented by expansion. Expansion moves tend to be big steps. A plan to double total capacity is totally unrealistic in a large corporation, but is common for small ones. Thus, there are generally more risks to expansion in smaller organizations than in larger ones. Whether the specific programs are for R&D, expansion, or developing new markets, the effect is the same on a small firm: grants increase the cash flow often significantly because of the relative size of the company. Because of the high level of uncertainty, the company cannot always obtain the funds elsewhere, or does not take the risk. Government funds can make a difference. I can live with these subsidy programs for firms in the economic base.

CREATING CONDITIONS

The economic growth of an area reflects its present and past entrepreneurial successes at rooting growing activities. Given the state of technology and the overall level of development, there are always activities for which there would be an additional demand. There are others which could be done more efficiently. The idea behind good micro-gardening is to ensure that entrepreneurs and managers attempt to do it. This entails risk and rewards. But the equation can be improved by creating better conditions. Surprisingly, most of these conditions are locally defined.

Thus we should worry more about these conditions than about the ability of the entrepreneurs and managers to do their jobs. Take the entrepreneur. The human genius generates a constant stream of new products and service ideas. This is not done only in the laboratories and research centres. New combinations of old technology are always being discovered. The Club Med concept does not rely on any new technology: air transportation, comfort and amenities in warm climates, people management and telecommunications. An entrepreneur mixed these old elements into a new product. An organization was built to develop its potential and in the process, perfected it and lowered its costs. Copycats multiplied. Club Med has been a great incubator. Other types of vacation products are now hitting the marketplace. But Club Med can withstand the competition.

A community can influence this process. For instance, it can make the profession of entrepreneur more socially and economically desirable. But a community should not seek the opportunities. The entrepreneurs will do it much better than communities can ever do it.

A great economic experiment is under way in Eastern Europe. Long suppressed economic forces are being unshackled in thousands of communities as these countries revert to a market economy. Wild grass is already spreading like prairie fire. Midsize organizations are multiplying, announcing the large corporations that will eventually dominate their production realm.

Market economies are emerging. For the next twenty years or so they should grow rapidly, catching up on the better organized economies of the Triad countries, benefiting from the technological advances and commercial ideas which have been successfully experimented with. But there will be areas where growth will be faster and areas where growth will be slower, drawing out attention to the complexities of the growth process.

Politicians will call for a new Marshall plan. Ambitious programs will be launched. There will be numerous get-togethers of experts, bankers and policies makers. Some good will result, for good policies count even for catching up. Indeed, this will become evident as some countries will do better than other. The critical policies are easy to identify: keeping inflation under control, ensuring a properly valued exchange rate, providing a basic financial system, enforcing property rights, etc. Entrepreneurship should be allowed to flourish and large firms should be subjected to the discipline of competition.

But local conditions will also matter. How dynamic is the entrepreneurial process in a community: incubators, sponsors, models? How strong is the competitive drive of large locally based organizations? Is organized labour allowing corporations to be flexible?

Dynamic entrepreneurs and managers will tackle the challenge of producing, distributing and selling their output. They will find raw materials, parts and equipments. They will meet delivery schedules. They will get customers. However, only as long as they are able to get organized and as long as the inefficient ones are removed by competition.

Not all countries have succeeded in providing these basic conditions of a market economy. The world provided numerous examples of missed opportunities. South America always had problems with market economies, and its political leaders have developed a long tradition of undermining its mechanisms. Most of Africa wasted thirty years of post-colonial independence. India and Pakistan are also testimonial to bad policies. But countries can get it right. Germany, Japan and Italy showed how rapidly countries could catch up after World War II. More recently, Spain, Turkey, Korea, Taiwan and others have successfully caught up.

If they do not "blow it" with stupid policies, Eastern Europe countries will also catch up rapidly with the Triad economy. If China can grow at 10% a year for ten years, so can Easter Europe, even tripling their GNP in the process. Indeed, their GNP in the year 2010 could be 6 times as large today, if history repeat itself. They will develop a work ethic, just like Spaniards, Turks and Italians die when they faced the challenge of growth a few decades ago.

Eastern Europe has several cards up its sleeves, compared to the fast-track countries of the fifties, sixties and seventies. International trade is more developed. Not only are there fewer barriers, but buyers from Triad countries will swarm over Eastern Europe. Credit is much more developed. They will be able to count on tourism as a source of hard currency. Technology is more advanced and more readily available.

Indeed, their rate of growth will be constrained by the fertility of their entrepreneurial realm and the ability of their private sector to grow, to organize itself better and develop larger organizations. The first indications coming out of Eastern Europe are that their private sector is off to a good start. Entrepreneurship abounds. It will move from small-scale to large-scale rapidly. There will be setbacks, from major strikes to financial crisis and bankruptcies. But the numbers will win eventually, as entrepreneurs simply multiply. Indeed, they will demonstrate that catching up with the Triad economy is relatively easy. The Triad countries, pushing against the "technological" envelope, cannot run as fast.

FINDING OPPORTUNITIES

Every age provides opportunities for new activities. The overall state of development of the economy defines a sort of frontier where new activities appear. The coming years could be those of what was called the "second divide": flexible production, custom high-quality products, highly automated and interactive processes that capitalize on the information technology, etc. This would replace the giant mass production manufacturing plant as the epitome of the age of the economy, just like this one replaced the old textile plant, when the first industrial divide occurred at the turn of the century.

The second industrial divide rests essentially on the unleashing of the power of what George Gilder has called the microcosm,[10] the conquest of the electron structure on which electronic technology rests. The giant technological leap that humanity is presently taking is yet to be fully visualized. The harnessing of analytical power on a chip is progressing at a very rapid rhythm. Next year's achievement will completely overshadow the remarkable achievement of this year. Indeed, it is very difficult to imagine today how "smart" the machines, equipment and products of tomorrow will be. The contribution to economic growth of the mechanical engine, from the water mills of the 14th century to the sophisticated turbine of the twentieth century, will pale in comparison to the analytical power that the chips of tomorrow will provide us.

One recent example can give us a hint of the progress to come. For the past fifty years, tinkerers have been working, in laboratories of large corporations and in garages of would-be Steve Jobs, on developing "silence machine". The theory is straight-forward. A generator produces sound waves which are out-of-phase with the incoming noise and thus which cancel it. Advances in computer technology have allowed the development of sensitive noise analyzers and powerful wave generators. Silence machines are about to break out of the laboratories as hundreds of research teams are zeroing in on the technology. The impact will be felt in numerous applications: in cars, in the kitchen, on the shop floor, along the highways, etc. Twenty- five years from now, this achievement of the 1990's will be taken for granted, as mundane as the achievements of the year 1965 now appear to be in 1990.

The second industrial divide will open up terrific opportunities for entrepreneurs and managers. Telecommunications, low cost transportation, capital equipment, new smart products and a growing fragmentation of demand are broad trends which favour a complete "overhaul" of the manufacturing systems of advanced economies. Smaller flexible production units will multiply, putting a premium on innovation and quality.

Smaller cities, the Jacobsvilles of this world, could be greatly favoured, as agglomeration economies lose some importance. But our Jacobsville is a twentieth century success story. Mining, wood products and machineries testify to what is now an old industrial base. But changes and innovations are the essence of its economic development. On that basis, Jacobsville is ready for the twenty-first century. Its entrepreneurs are continually searching the economic fabric to find places to patch new ventures. They will use the technology of tomorrow to serve the needs of tomorrow. Telecommunications and cheap transportation will keep it competitive with faraway towns.

Managing their growth rate offers people the opportunity to decide on the type of community they want. Some communities will be choosy, constraining their growth in narrow corridors. This is their choice. Others will be unbridled, aiming at being much bigger, keeping the growth machine turning at high speed. This is also a valid choice. The important point is to keep the local economy in good health, continually renewed. Reforesting starts at home.

CHAPTER FOURTEEN

ADVICE TO PRESIDENTS, KINGS AND PRIME MINISTERS

When experts can promise nothing more arresting than doubt, uncertainty, and incremental minor improvements, others will not fear to tread. There are no popular quack cures for polio and broken bones, but quack cures abound for cancer, arthritis and the common cold.

Lawrence H. Summers

Economists belongs to an unusual profession where being articulate is often more important than being right. Nothing illustrates this better than the forecasting performance of economists. Every month, fifty prominent American economists are canvassed for their forecasts on the outlook of the U.S. economy: real growth, inflation, interest rates, unemployment, exchange rates, etc. Looking back over their forecasting record over the years yields a sobering lesson. The graph below presents their performance for short-term interest rates, one of the most important economic indicators. Plotted on the graph, against the actual behaviour of the market, are their average forecasts at various times in the past ten years.

FIGURE 14.1

CONSENSUS FORECASTS OF U.S. SHORT-TERM INTEREST RATES

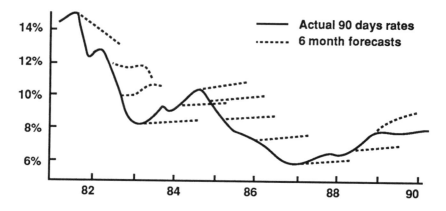

Source: Blue Chip Economic Indicator

Their performance suggests a strong herd effect. Playing it safe, economists tend to forecast "more of the same". Thus, they generally miss the turning points, which are basically what people would like to know. Surprisingly, despite this dismal record, their forecasts are still in demand. Such impunity encourages a free flow of advice. And as long as our anxieties about the future directions of the economy flourish, economists will find an eager audience.

Offering advice on national policies is big game for economists. So far, our tour of the garden has led us into modest areas of the economy, where entrepreneurship flourishes, small and medium size firms grow and corporations compete and innovate. This, I strongly believe, is where economic growth is rooted and where most of our attention should be focused. Still, national policies do matter. It is our turn to deal with the big picture.

There is a crowded field of pitchers offering advice to Presidents, Prime Ministers and other helmsmen. Moreover, a lot of the advice is well-thought out and impressive indeed. In the early eighties, a Royal Commission appointed by the government of Canada, spent three years and $20 million to chart a course for the Canadian economy.[1] Such Commissions of inquiry pop up regularly when governments are short of solutions.[2] Private efforts are also frequent. In 1986, the Massachusetts Institute of Technology set up a Task Force on Productivity staffed by some of its most prestigious professors, including a Nobel laureate. Their report, published in 1989, proposed a detailed road map for the U.S. economy.[3] Across the Charles river, Michael Porter, one of the better known professors at the Harvard Business School, headed, for two years, a group of over 20 researchers, investigating ten advanced industrial economies, to find the keys that would unlock the gates to sustained growth. His recommendations were the subject of an 855-page book published in 1990.[4] He then went on to do a special study of the Canadian economies, financed jointly by business and government.

ADVICE REFLECTS ONE'S PERSPECTIVE

Some advice makes the leap into policy. The Canadian Royal Commission proposed the Free Trade treaty which was successfully negotiated between Canada and the United States. In the late seventies, conservative economists proposed a "renewal agenda" which had as its central element, a significant reduction in the personal income tax rate. Embraced by President Reagan, this conservative agenda became as influential as the New Deal had been fifty years earlier, and it spread to most OECD countries.[5]

But most advice is lost in the wind, for good reasons. For it is generally simplistic and incomplete. There is no magic formula, a sort of "Magicgro" that could be sprinkled over the economy and turn it green. Yet charlatans regularly pop up, with "the" solution to our economic woes. The problem is not with them, it is with us the people, who just as regularly fall into the trap and get intrigued by the magic formula. It makes for best-sellers, overnight reputation and bad advice which, fortunately, is seldom taken up.

Tending the economy is tedious. There are no cure-all solution. Good advice is multi-facetted and somewhat boring. Thus, do not look in this book for a central policy proposal. There are no such easy ways out.

Good advisers also tend to be somewhat predictable, very much like good gardeners. Good advice generally reflects the analytical perspective of the adviser. Take the reports from blue-ribbon commissions made up of representatives of labour, business and academic circles. These groups have to wrestle with the need for consensus among their ranks. Thus, they tend to recommend tinkering at the edge and correcting widely acknowledged malpractices, such as reducing the deficit. Professors approach their inquiry on a much stronger theoretical footing and tend to be bolder, but also have the luxury of being less practical.

Still, behind any analyses, and consequently, behind the recommendations that evolve from them, there stands a particular view of how the economy works. This creates a lot of opportunities for divergent opinions and conflicting advices.

My initial interest in economic development can be traced back to the mining community where I grew up in northern Quebec. It was spurred by attempts to diversify the local economy into forestry products. I then went to study economics in Pittsburg, at a time when it was going through an industrial transformation, shedding its old steel heritage. Later on, I was hired as a consultant by local development organizations, first in small towns such as St-Georges, and then, in large cities such as Montreal and Minneapolis.

While writing this book, I was a senior aide, first to the Premier of Quebec, then to the Prime Minister of Canada. The analytical perspective which emerged from this diversified experience was rooted in practical considerations and in beliefs about the workings of the economy. The paradigm which frames them, and which is captured by the garden analogy, forms the basis for most of the policy proposals which I set forth in this chapter.

Growth occurs at the local and corporate levels, in the realm of entrepreneurs and in the realm of production. National policies do not reach these areas easily. Nevertheless, overall business conditions can influence growth. Although I am quite sceptical of the ability of governments to command rain or sunshine, still national policies have an impact.

Indeed, some policies can be disastrous and just avoiding them is a positive contribution. Governments also regulate many gardening practices, what can be done and what cannot be done. Their performance can generally be improved.

The diversity of economic situations, from one country to another and from one year to another, often calls for specific responses. Nevertheless, there are universal principles which can ensure better climatic conditions for entrepreneurs as well as an environment conducive to growth and innovation in the production realm. Here are seven important ones. They are not new and not original. But they remain the essence of good economic policy.

PRINCIPLE NO. 1: AVOID DROUGHTS AND FLOODS

All economies are subjected to business cycles. Ups and downs in aggregate demand and supply are inherent in any dynamic system. Because of their control over the central bank and the large impact on their budgets, central governments can potentially soothe these fluctuations in business conditions. This is what monetary and fiscal policies attempt to do. But soothing business conditions is not necessarily stimulating growth.

To what extent is growth influenced by business conditions — the "local weather conditions" of the economy — defined by interest rates, inflation, backlogs, capacity utilization, etc.? Less than commonly assumed. As long as business conditions stay within an acceptable range, the historical evidence shows that "business conditions" are not critical to the determination of the economy's long-term rate of growth. To use a gardening analogy, the plants will adapt to weather conditions, as long as the weather remains within reasonable limits. Neither flooding the garden nor a drought will be good. But too much water or a dry spell are acceptable, as long as they do not last.

Beside, the business cycle is slowly getting tamed. Simply because there are more economic stabilizers imbedded in the economy, recessions are getting less severe and less frequent. Over the past 30 years, the U.S. economy has been in recessionary periods 20 per cent of the time, versus 45 per cent of the time between 1870 and 1919.[6] Minor recessions, slow-downs that last six months to a year, still appear unavoidable, an unfortunate side-effect of anti-inflationary monetary policy. Recessions can be seen as temporary dry spells which are barely noticeable over the ten to twenty year perspective that interests us.

Moreover, enough is now known to avoid a catastrophic 1930-type depression. Never again will governments tolerate the triple-whammy that hit the industrial economies around 1930: a shrinking money supply, rising barriers to international trade and foolish governments that reduced their expenditures in a period of economic contraction. Since the Second World War, no industrialized country has fallen into a depression, despite a wide variety of shocks and difficulties, some quite severe. We can safely assume that long dry spells will be avoided in the future.

We can also be moderately hopeful that governments will avoid flooding the economy with too much water, creating spiralling inflation. For a while, in the seventies, there were causes for concern, as double-digit inflation spread to most industrial countries. Fuelled by the short-term monetary policies of governments, inflation spiralled until it became evident that only drastic action could flush it out of the economy.

Thus the industrial world witnessed in 1981-82, the first bona fide policy- induced world-wide recession, and a severe one at that. In North America, a sharp tightening of credit by the U.S. Federal Reserve Bank precipitated a major recession which cooled the inflationary pressures that were sustaining double-digit inflation.

Most future recessions are likely to be policy-induced, although not necessarily intentionally. Governments have not yet found a better way than tight money to prevent creeping inflation from degenerating into spiralling inflation. The last 40 years have demonstrated clearly that industrial economies cannot avoid creeping inflation, slow but highly-diffused increases in prices. Keynes observed justly that prices fall less easily than they rise. In the decentralized economy, that phenomenon results, thanks to the law of the average, in rising prices. As economic agents learn about inflation and try to catch up, they add inflationary pressures. Thus creeping inflation has a natural tendency to accelerate. When the rate of inflation becomes disquieting to policy makers, they resort to the only known effective tool at their disposal, restrictive monetary policy. As interest rates creep up, the demand side of the economy starts to cool down. Sales of houses and of durables, which depend on credit, usually fall first. The currency appreciates, exports fall, imports surge, also cooling domestic production. A reverse multiplier effect goes into action, slowly cooling down inflationary pressures.

Tight money is the most practical way of cooling off inflationary pressures, with a monetary induced recession as the ultimate remedy.

Periodic cleansing of inflationary pressures used to be done naturally by the business cycle. Policy makers have taken over. What we can ask of them is that they do not overdo it. Cool the economy when it is getting too hot. But more importantly, don't let it get too hot, as it did in the late seventies. Or unnecessarily cold.[7] Prudent monetary policy is probably the best route to achieve this objective.

But this is easier said than done. For any attempt to keep the internal economy in balance can spill over and affect the external equilibrium. Prudent monetary policy usually brings an increase in exchange rates as well as that dreaded condition, the "Dutch disease".

PRINCIPLE NO. 2: BEWARE OF THE DUTCH DISEASE

In the world of theoretical economics, freely fluctuating exchange rates behave like automatic pilots, rising and cooling the economy when it is too hot, falling and stimulating the economy when it slows down. Yet, the industrial world has generally developed under fixed exchange rates. Gold has long been the standard and governments fixed the value of their currency in terms of gold. For much of the nineteenth century and up to the second World War, exchange rates between major currencies were stable. Changes were infrequent and when occurring, were made over-night to limit speculation.

After World War Two, the raindancers met in Bretton Woods, a mountain resort in New Hampshire. They designed a fixed rate system, built and set the price of gold at $35.00. The next twenty-five years was a period of impressive growth worldwide, the golden age according to English economist Angus Maddison, who is the foremost expert on economic growth around the world and across centuries.

But, as mentioned earlier, that system broke down in 1971, when the United States became unable to hold the price of gold at $35.00. Since then, currencies' values have fluctuated with supply and demand. Capital flows amounting to billions of dollars a day, dictate the direction of changes. Professional traders handle portfolios and move them between currencies, depending on market conditions and their expectations about future directions and the needs of their clients. They create the supply and they create the demand.

Central banks are important actors in this game. By buying and selling treasury bills, they have a significant impact on short term interest rates. Whenever the differentials between domestic rates and foreign rates change, international capital flows and affects the value of the currencies. When a central bank maintains significant interest rate differentials for long periods, the impact of the higher (or lower) exchange rates on the economy of a country can be significant.

This happened in the early 1980's in the United States. The large unexpected deficit of the federal government, coming on the tail end of the restrictive monetary policy of 1981-1982, created a growing divergence between U.S. interest rates and foreign ones, resulting in an unprecedented inflow of foreign capital. Its conversion into U.S. dollars pushed up the exchange rate. Exports fell. Moreover, Americans used their strong dollars to finance a shopping spree of cheaper imported goods, prompting a further deterioration in the balance of trade and services. Pressures on the exchange rate finally relaxed in 1985, as the need for foreign capital softened. The exchange rate fell back, and starting in 1987, the balance of trade started to improve.[8]

Some people did not find this episode at all amusing. Exporters suddenly lost their foreign markets, as their overseas prices increased by 90 per cent from 1980 to 1984. The U.S. market was also flooded with cheaper imported goods. For instance, the Japanese yen fell by 23 per cent. There was a heavy price, borne mainly by selected manufacturing industries dealing in goods traded internationally, while the rest of the American people were sipping beer in their backyards, enjoying the double treat of a marvellous tax-cut and a strong dollar. The involuntary price jolts to which these industries were submitted, flooded their garden.

Another major cost went unrecorded. The import substitution mechanism dried up. The high exchange rates made it more difficult for entrepreneurs to start businesses competing with imported goods and services. Throughout the economy, there were fewer new businesses started in areas with an international trade potential.

In hindsight, letting the dollar surge was a policy blunder. Who are the culprits? Supply-side economists blame the Federal Reserve Bank, which did not print enough money, allowing interest rates to rise, and Congress, which did not cut expenditures. Keynesian economists say hogwash to that: the problem was an irresponsible tax-cut which created the huge deficit and discouraged domestic savings.

But that is not the real issue. Was it proper to let the dollar surge in value, inflicting a major trauma to the supply side of the U.S. economy? Wherever a central bank raises interest rates to cool the demand side of the economy, it also chokes the supply side of the economy, which only adds up to inflationary pressure. Flexible exchange rates turn the tables against an efficient monetary policy.

The purchasing power of the Canadian dollar is estimated to below 80¢ in 1991. Yet, a restrictive monetary policy started in 1988 has maintained the value of the Canadian dollar above $0.85 for 1990 and 1991. High short term interest rates made the Canadian dollar highly attractive, generating large inflows of capital. Meanwhile, attempts by Canadians to develop new exports markets and profit from the Canada-US Free Trade Agreement are defeated by an overvalued currency.

Central bankers should try to stabilize the values of their currency close to its purchasing power parity. Unless they participate in a system of fixed exchange rates, such as within Western Europe, they find the task very difficult.[9] The system is the culprit, that is, the acceptance of flexible exchange rates. Western European countries, led by Germany and France, never accepted that their currencies fluctuated widely against each other. Since 1979 they have managed to maintain an internal system of fixed exchange rates. This has called for significant coordination of monetary policies. Germany calls the tune, and the other countries play along. The results are impressive. Not only did the countries participating in the European Monetary System (EMS) manage to control inflation even better than the United States, they kept the relative values of their currencies stable.

The EMS was the result of several years of closer and closer integration of monetary and exchange policies. A return to a system of fixed exchange rates among the large trading block cannot be achieved quickly. Stating clearly the intention of achieving exchange rate stability and taking practical steps to achieve it would be a major change in global economic policy. Countries would be immunized against the Dutch disease. We also could do away with raindancers.

The next logical step beyond the EMS is a single European currency. But creating a European currency area is a dangerous step which should be avoided, and most likely will be. A single currency area would just increase regional disparities over time. The pressures toward homogenized price and cost structures will build up faster than labour mobility, creating increasing regional discrepancies in productivities and structural pockets of unemployment. As a consequence, political pressures will build up for equalization transfers, from the rich regions to the poorer ones, entrenching the disparities.

Furthermore, devaluation is a policy tool which should not be forsaken for ever by any country. Those who berate devaluation generally forget that prices and wages do not fall easily in periods of excess supply. In certain circumstances, adjusting the value of the currency is a very efficient remedy to line up properly domestic and tradeable prices. Keeping national currencies under a system of fixed exchange rates ensures the availability of that option, if it is ever needed.

Finally, a system of fixed exchange rates would also impose tighter discipline on national governments. For to maintain a currency's value, it is much better if the government does not live dangerously back home. Considerable concerns have been raised about the large government deficits in the U.S., Canada and Italy. These concerns are well-justified. Large deficits result in ever increasing financial needs, and the impact of these is far from positive. Servicing the debt now represents 35 per cent of the taxes collected by the Canadian government. The emergence of large deficits in the United States in the early eighties contributed to the surge of the dollar. Italy is lucky to be able to count on a high domestic saving rate to soak up its huge government deficit. But no individual or institution, including government, can get away permanently with mere promises to its stakeholders. This is the premise behind chronic deficit financing. The party will eventually end, with a terrible hangover for all concerned. In trying to maintain the illusion, governments must live dangerously, and this increases the risk of major spillovers.[10]

PRINCIPLE NO. 3: AN EFFICIENT GOVERNMENT IS BETTER

It would be nice if there were a strong negative correlation between big government and long-term economic growth. Unfortunately, the real world is pulling a neat trick on economists and politicians: it refuses to settle the issue. There is only a weak correlation between the level of government spending and economic growth. Figure 14.2 presents the evidence, which is not very conclusive. Japan is a low-tax country, the U.S. a mid-level one, and Western Europe and Canada, high-tax countries. The latter two manage to do more or less as well if not better than the U.S. in terms of economic growth. Since it joined the Triad Economy around 1970, Japan's growth is no longer at the catching-up level of the sixties, despite the fact that it maintained its low taxes. In fact, although Japan has half the tax level of Europe, it is now in the same league with respect to growth.

"Supply-siders" have developed compelling theoretical arguments to illustrate the pernicious effects of big government on economic growth. The vision presented in this book does not contradict their views. The dynamism of the entrepreneurial realm is affected by high taxes and regulations, but several other factors influence the process by which new firms emerge and are successful. In a similar vein, the international competitiveness of the production realm is affected by the so-called "wedge", the slice of the economic pie that the government confiscates. But as Toyota showed at NUMMI, there is more to competitiveness than factor costs. Indeed, innovation and not factor costs is the critical variable in the production realm. However, supply side economics is much more than taxation. Other factors are far more important to the good health of the supply side of the economy.

FIGURE 14.2
TAXES AND ECONOMIC GROWTH

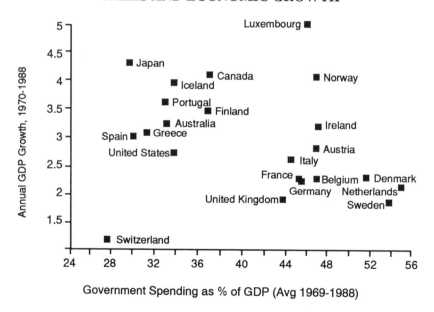

Government Spending as % of GDP (Avg 1969-1988)

Source: OECD, National Accounts Statistics

249

But the supply-side viewpoint on big government is still valid. Nothing illustrates better the pernicious effects of high taxes than the positive impact of cuts in income tax rates. Beyond their impact on individual entrepreneurial behaviour, they bring about a surge in consumer demand, which is highly stimulative in the entrepreneurial realm. The evidence of the 1964 and 1982 U.S. tax cuts strongly suggests that, of all ways to stimulate the economy, reducing broad-based taxes seems to be the most effective in reaching deep into the fibres of the economy. The resulting surge in demand opens seams throughout the economic fabric, onto which entrepreneurs immediately patch new activities. Thus periodic tax cuts, which purge the economy of the effects of the inevitable creeping upward of our taxation systems, can send entrepreneurial pulses throughout the economy. In other words, a tax cut, rather than low taxes, is a good tonic for the supply side of the economy.

Furthermore, the viewpoint of supply-siders on the perniciousness of big government is highly valid. One can demand a smaller and more efficient government for reasons other than the impact of taxes on growth rates. Government should minimize what Jane Jacobs calls "transactions of decline". Defence expenditures might be necessary for the security of the country. But their long-term economic impact is dubious: they are sterile elements in the circular flow. Taxing highly productive regions to subsidize low productivity regions can be good social policy, but it is bad economic policy and in the long-term, reduces the growth potential of all regions.

Finally, the bureaucratic monopolies that governments create in order to deliver the services they appropriate do not come close to meeting the standards of efficiency that competition imposes on the private sector. The spread of government bureaucracies can have a significant impact on long-term growth. Shielded from competitive pressures, they are high-cost elements in the production realm. If 20 per cent of the production realm is located in high-cost government bureaucracies, the net cost to consumers is clear.

Privatization of state-owned corporations and of government services is well underway.[11] Great Britain pioneered it. Canada, France, and numerous other countries have jumped on the bandwagon. The dismantlement of the huge monopolistic bureaucracies in Eastern Europe is the ultimate privatization exercise. In Western democracies, the impact of privatization on public finance is generally small. The major gains lie in increased flexibility of the economy and better service to customers.

Privatized corporations sharply improve their performance. There are no shareholders more benevolent than governments. There is no management more inert than large government bureaucracies.

Privatization also educates the public in the merit of owning shares. A large, diffused ownership of the production realm is a preferable outcome, because it enlarges the equity market and associates the population's interest with that of the production realm. Privatization also sends strong signals to the business community. The government is telling it that from now on, the respective roles of governments and corporations will be more sharply defined. To the financial community which finances government deficits, the message is twofold. Not only is the government reducing its indebtedness, it is also restraining its domain. Since financing government activities rests on a finite tax base, any restriction in its domain of activities is akin to enlarging its equity base and strengthening the position of the debt holders.

From an economic perspective, the primary role of government is to run its shop efficiently. Which basic services will be provided to all and how national income will be redistributed are political choices. Once these choices are made, the responsibility of government is to realize them in the most efficient manner. That generally does not mean a bigger government. Efficiency is seldom associated with the government as a provider of goods and services. The better this is understood, the more efficient is the overall production realm.

PRINCIPLE NO. 4: THE PROPER GOVERNANCE OF CORPORATIONS MATTERS

The legal framework defines the rights and obligations of corporations and shareholders, and regulates investment practices. Its efficiency can have a major impact on economic growth. Corporate behaviour is highly influenced by the legal framework. How intensively corporations strive for increased competitiveness depends very much on the rules of the game, on how competition is unshackled, and how welcome change is in the production realm.Cameron

The legal framework is less constraining to entrepreneurs. Their entrepreneurial goals lead them to fight the status quo, and that involves the system. Confiscatory taxation of entrepreneurial gains, the high costs of regulations, the security of the welfare state and regulatory barriers to entry, may not be conducive to venturing. But the entrepreneur can cope with these irritants. Entrepreneurship is not less prevalent in countries such as Canada, the Netherlands and Sweden, where taxes are higher, the safety net cushier, and regulations more prevalent. The entrepreneur is highly adaptive and will put up with any situation, as long as local conditions are good.

Things are different in the production realm, especially in large corporations that do not have the flexibility of the entrepreneurs. The issue of the governance of corporations is absolutely fundamental. In the absence of a controlling shareholder, management has effective control of the Board of Directors, and therefore, of the direction of the corporation. But there is a price to pay for this control. The rules of the game force management to pay inordinate attention to short-term performance on the stock market. Maintaining the value of the stock is important to avoid take-over attempts or negative reviews by analysts. As a consequence, the values and attitudes of shareholders are tilted toward short-term performance, particularly in North America.

Given their objective of remaining independent, this behaviour is to be expected. These corporations are highly vulnerable to hostile take-overs if the market value of their stock falls below the break-up value of the corporation. A winner can do anything it wants with the corporation, including dismemberment to recover the purchase price. Corporations tend to be undervalued on the stock market because they respond to multiple constituencies. Many diversified corporations do not benefit from their diversity and the aggregate value of the components is higher than the value of the whole, putting them also in a danger zone. By breaking implicit contracts with other stakeholders of a corporation, sharp raiders can make significant profits in carving up a corporation. Thus, public corporations are swimming in a sea of sharks, and not even the largest corporations are immune from attack. Raiders and investment bankers put 10% of Fortune 500 firms "into play" during the 1980's.

The positive side of such an environment is that corporations tend to be slimmer and in better health. Moreover, there is growing evidence that restructured corporations are doing better since their transformation.[12] Unfortunately, the negatives are numerous. In such a hostile environment, a short-term focus is essential to survival. Thus, corporations tend to shy away from projects with high uncertainty but long-term pay-offs. Also, indebtedness tends to be higher, increasing the vulnerability of corporations in recessionary periods.

Finally, shareholders are treated as preeminent stakeholders, the "owners" of the organization. Unfortunately, this notion flies in the face of reality. Organizations are not "owned" by anybody. They are webbed together by a complex set of contractual arrangements, most of them implicit. The providers of the capital are one class of stakeholders among many, and no less or more essential than other classes of stakeholders. But securities laws are still based on 1900s know-how, when the reality of modern organization was still little known. This creates a most dysfunctional legal environment.

The situation is somewhat different in Japan and continental Europe. Management controls their boards, even more than in the United States. But corporations are less dependent on the stock market for raising capital. Not only are shareholders less central, but institutional shareholders tend to side with management against intruding raiders. Thus, the performance of the corporation on the stock market has little influence on senior management. Issuing new capital stock is not an important source of financing and hostile takeovers are rare. Friendly bankers generally control a major proportion of the stock. Management can focus on the long term, which is in its own best interest and also in the best interest of the corporation.

The critical governance issue is how can management be kept alert without becoming myopic? There are three broad avenues that could lead to a solution of this quandary. A first avenue is to increase the influence of the major institutional shareholders on the board. This avenue requires a fundamental change in attitudes, from the current "exit" posture (sell if one is not happy) to a "voice" posture (make one's influence felt if one is unhappy). This would represent a major transformation of the way markets operate. Peter Drucker has been a strong advocate of active institutional shareholders. In fact, large pension funds have already started to voice their opinions.[13] The major institutional holders of General Motors stocks demanded to be heard when the Board selected a new Chief Executive Officer in 1990. But there are some negative aspects to this approach. Some will argue that the pensioners and holders of mutual fund shares will be poorly served by the divided loyalty of the money managers. Others will argue that the financial community already has sufficient influence, especially since its focus is mainly on returns to stockholders and it cares little about other stakeholders, namely workers and the communities where the corporation is present. Nevertheless, this avenue seems the most promising, given the limits of other avenues.

A second avenue relies on legislative and regulatory measures to make corporations more immune to hostile takeovers, a return to the sixties and seventies when hostile take-overs were unheard of. It was not the best situation. Unfortunately, many recent legislative and regulatory proposals are heading in that direction. Restrictions on take-over practices and more discretionary power to boards of directors can significantly tilt the balance of power. The negative side to these proposed changes is the risk of more complacent management and a significant loss of "corporate wealth."

The third avenue is to increase the prevalence of "controlling" shareholders. This is the route which will be taken if nothing else is done. Controlling shareholders and shareholders whose holdings are sufficiently large to discourage hostile take-overs, are slowly spreading among the largest corporations. This situation is already found in Canada, where all but a few of the largest corporations have controlling shareholders. This is also the case in Germany where that role is played mostly by the three largest banks. In both countries, hostile take-overs are rare, and controlling shareholders are locked in for the long term. Thus, management is free to concentrate on the long-term development of the corporation. It may help the governance of the major Canadian and German corporations, but not to the point of making this superior performance self-evident. Moreover, I am somewhat worried about the long term, when combinations of complacent controlling shareholders and complacent management could become common. That would not bode well for the competitiveness of the production realm, but this is where the U.S. corporate system could be heading.

The governance of large corporations is a complex issue. Several problems are involved: corporate efficiency, concentration of power, shareholders' rights, etc. The present rules, which force corporations to swim among myopic and hungry sharks, are not healthy. A corporation is first and above all a multi-constituency organization. The present practices on Wall Street reduce it to a set of assets to be disposed of to the highest bidders by shareholders. No matter what one's views of what a corporation is, they will always be organizations responding to multiple constituencies. If Wall Street does not recognize it, the organizations will adapt to this new environment, most likely by taking the third avenue described above, which has its share of negatives, not the least of which is the tendency of controlling shareholders to short-change minority shareholders. Governments should think about the issue because it will soon be on their doorsteps. Institutions, and in particular pension funds, could greatly improve the situation by becoming more active "owners".

PRINCIPLE NO. 5: FLEXIBILITY IS CRITICAL FOR GROWTH

Mancur Olson is the economist who argues that advanced economies are slowly choked by entrenched interests fighting against changes and gradually ossifying the economy. Marshalling an impressive array of statistics, Olson develops a strong case for an entropic vision of the world, where egoistical interests slowly spread throughout the fibres of the economy and strengthen the forces of the status quo. Government is one of the main instruments used by entrenched interests in their mischievous undertakings. Policies claimed to be in the national interest serve the purpose of entrenching the present claims of certain groups, with the hidden cost of preventing changes.

I do not share Olson's pessimistic outlook on the pernicious march of ossifying institutions, leading to the triumph of mediocrity. Entrepreneurs are continually assaulting the status quo. So does competition. No matter how strong the institutions are, they cannot avoid being affected by new ideas, new products, and new technology. But Olson has a point. The institutional structure tends to resist change and the political arena is where the status quo finds its protectors. We should be concerned about it. Protecting the status quo is a corollary of a significant proportion of government interventions in the economy, either as a voluntary or as an unintended effect.

The competitiveness of the production realm is highly correlated with its ability to adapt. Corporations adapt by investing in equipment and improving their products and their methods of production. But changes typically hurt some as much as they benefit others. The losers demand the protection of the government. Out of these demands come regulations which hinder change. Nothing illustrates this quandary better than labour regulations, which are warranted to ensure that workers can exercise their rights of collective bargaining and protection against unfair practices. But labour also uses the leverage offered by labour regulations to protect the status quo and to trade off changes against an improvement in their own situation. Indeed, it is difficult to prevent such use of the leverage provided by labour laws, something which is recognized and accepted by both labour and management.

But such attitudes create complacency. The NUMMI situation is the perfect example. Why did management and labour practices at the shop floor level at GM evolve over the years to the point where Japanese methods were 50 per cent more productive than U.S. methods? Highly intelligent managers fully dedicated to improving efficiency were working at GM. Workers were also dedicated, as they proved later when they worked for Toyota. Nevertheless, the American "system" channelled production practices into highly inefficient patterns. A complex covenant of laws, regulations, and contracts regulated that system. Over the years, the cumulative impact of the resulting trade-offs between management and labour was a major loss of productivity.

This example illustrates the importance of ensuring that flexibility is not hindered by the legal framework which structures the environment and practices of organizations. Improving the flexibility and fluidity of the production realm should be as much of a concern to the lawmakers as are the rights of workers. For flexibility and fluidity are insurance against the obsolescence of these organizations that are locked in a continuous search for competitiveness.

Labour regulations are not the only culprits. Environmental and product safety regulations also constrain flexibility. Ensuring that regulations allow the production realm to change, as opposed to locking it into a particular technology or process, should be a principle underlying any new regulation.

Demanding that governments pay attention to ensuring flexibility in the production realm is a vague demand. Modern political science theory tells us that politicians react to specific demands much more spiritedly than to grand demands in the name of the public good. How to restrain politicians in their continual quest to protect well-established constituents against changes brought about by the marketplace is one of the important challenges to our modern political system.

PRINCIPLE NO 6.: COMPETITION POLICY: INNOVATIVE-NESS SHOULD PREVAIL OVER EFFICIENCY.

Adam Smith's most famous admonition is that business people should not be allowed to conspire against the interest of consumers by agreeing among themselves to restrict competition and artificially lift prices. One of the government's major economic roles, according to Smith, was to be the watchdog of competition throughout the economy.

Adam Smith was mostly concerned about market power, whereby a producer, or several of them conspiring together, get a sufficient market share to be able to artificially raise prices, or attempt to restrict the number of competitors. Smith's mistrust of business and of the potential abuse of market power is at the root of the comprehensive competition (anti-trust) legislation in place in all advanced industrial countries. Since abusing market power can be done in quite subtle fashions, competition legislation has developed into a fairly comprehensive code of conduct for business. Not only are practices associated with abuse of market power illegal, such as price fixing and unduly restricting distributors and retailers, but the mere fact of having excessive market power is frowned upon. A company such as IBM, which had a two- third share of the computer market in the sixties and seventies, was the object of a massive anti-trust suit by the U.S. government throughout most of the seventies.

But then come the Europeans and the Japanese. While recognizing the virtues of competition and the risks of undue concentration of market power, they have taken a benign view of the danger of collusion between competitors and have allowed extensive cooperation between them. Furthermore, Europeans have tolerated mergers and acquisitions creating large corporations with complete dominance of their domestic market.

Their rationale: in order to face international competition, cooperation among domestic competitors and large size are important assets. This logic dominates European industrial policy: the pursuit of economic growth overshadows concerns about market power abuses and the potential costs to consumers. Such thinking has led the Japanese government to be the catalyst behind the formation of numerous research consortia in several Japanese industrial sectors, with the stated objective of pooling resources and talents to design the next generation of products. In Europe, governments have concluded that the best approach to meet the competition from U.S. and Japanese giants was to authorize mergers that created huge, world-class European firms.

The same industrial policy rationale has been used to criticize U.S. anti-trust legislation as being too rigid and not responding effectively to international competition by allowing cooperation and alliances between American competitors. It is better, the argument goes, to accept some risk of collusion by letting competitors cooperate on product development and on sales abroad rather than risk their long term disappearance under the pressures of foreign competitors.

The argument has been heard. Since 1980, the U.S. antitrust policies have been somewhat relaxed, although less under President Bush than under President Reagan. In Canada, the 1986 legislation on competition instructs the court to specifically take into account foreign competition and the need to be more competitive in export markets in assessing the risks resulting from undue concentration of market power. What we are witnessing is the slow triumph of the argument of economic efficiency. Bigger size provides the economies of scale that allows producers to reduce their costs and their prices. Furthermore, by exchanging ideas and pooling R&D resources, new products appear faster on the market and domestic producers benefits from a competitive advantage. Export sales also benefit, allowing further cost reductions. Thus, consumers benefit from economies of scale. The risk of abuse of market power is a problem that the pursuit of economic efficiency in the face of international competition overshadows.

But along come the traditionalists, with Michael Porter, the Harvard professor, as their latest champion. They argue that the maintenance of domestic competition is essential to the long-term competitiveness of an industry. Porter, in particular, put forward an "industrial policy" argument, not a "market power" argument, to defend tough competitive legislation. Intense competition in their primary market, the domestic one, forces firms to innovate and thus, it prevents any complacency that is fatal in the long run. Competition keeps them in good competitive shape and they are better equipped to face international competition. For innovation, Porter argues, is the ultimate source of competitiveness, much more than economies of scale can ever be. Furthermore, it is the domestic market that counts, for it is close to head office and it is where new products are tested. Corporations cannot afford to lose in their home market.

Porter draws a parallel between the innovativeness of the Japanese automobile industry, where eight domestic firms bitterly dispute the domestic market, with the stodginess of North America's "Big Three" automobile manufacturers, who during the sixties and seventies, tamed their rivalry and were happy to divide among themselves the big North American domestic market, without having to innovate significantly. Strangely, anti-trust legislation, the bane of industrial policy advocates, is being rescued by another branch of industrial policy.

But no legislation can cure the appetite of corporations for growth. The team at the top, led by the CEO, has to tackle new challenges. A bigger firm, whether it is achieved by internal expansion or by mergers or acquisitions, is the most likely outcome of this imperative. Knocking out the competition is also part of the game. If strategic alliances provide an advantage, they will be sought. And if such actions reduce the pressure on prices, so much the better.

Governments are sometimes asked to pursue conflicting objectives. Creating conditions conducive to economic growth can clash with the interests of the consumers. What should it do in the specific case of competition policy in industries facing intense international competition?

The debate opposes concerns for innovativeness and concerns for efficiency. Should the pursuit of efficiency, and short-term competitiveness, have priority over the pursuit of innovativeness and long term competitiveness. The debate consigns the market power argument to a secondary role, the danger of abuses in that regard being seen as an unfortunate side effect from the search of efficiency. The major drawback, and a very costly one, in this search for greater efficiency, is large corporate size and its sequels, complacency, lack of innovativeness and gradual demise.

Dilemmas over short-term costs and long-term benefits are common in public policy. They are usually resolved in favour of the long-term benefits. In this vein, competitive policies should be construed in a way to ensure long-term innovativeness, even at the expense of short-term efficiency. Such a principle calls for prudence in loosening anti-trust laws.

It will always be difficult to demonstrate, in specific situations, that a merger creating a large size corporation will hinder future innovativeness, just like ex-post studies of mergers does not indicate clearly that there are automatic gains in effectiveness. But as the advanced economies move from the age of mass-production to that of flexibility, it will become increasingly important that more attention be paid to the flexibility and innovativeness of the production realm.

Such a preference for innovativeness over efficiency should not preclude, automatically, cooperation between competitors. Large size is the enemy. In areas where they do not compete, competitors can strike alliance. Pre-competitive research, to lay the technological ground for product development, can be done in consortia. So is developing joint-suppliers. This is quite different from buying up a competitor in order to be in better shape to compete on foreign markets, an argument which has all the smell of market power abuse, and not much else.

Competitive policies should heed to sound principles about keeping the markets honest. They should also heed to similar concern about the long-term health of the production side of the economy, and in particular about its long-term ability to innovate. Concerns about its efficiency should also be heard, but not at the expense of innovativeness.[14]

PRINCIPLE NO. 7: TAKE IT EASY SUBSIDIZING MOTHER-HOOD AND APPLE PIE

Conventional economic analysis has more or less decreed that capital, education and R&D are paramount in the growth process. That contention has not fallen on deaf ears in the political realm. A major amount of public money earmarked for growth ends up in the kitties of citizens and corporations that make large capital expenditures, are in the education business or are involved in R&D. I have already discussed these issues in Chapter Eleven, but would like to return to them briefly.

Subsidizing capital can be done in many ways, and indeed, taxation of income has become so pervasive and complex that it is often difficult to determine whether a measure is a subsidy. What often appears as a subsidy is a legitimate lower level of taxation. A strong argument can be made that taxing both capital gains and dividends is double taxation. But I do not want to get into these arguments, which often boil down to how much the rich should be taxed, a totally different issue. What is more germane to our discussion is the use of discriminatory taxation in the form of investment tax credits and accelerated depreciation allowances. The econometric analyses of these tax measures have tended to be inconclusive with respect to their impact on economic growth. There is no doubt that these tax breaks lead to cheaper and thus to more intensive use of capital. But growth is fundamentally driven by opportunities in the entrepreneurial realm and by the need to stay competitive in the production realm. The rental cost of capital plays a minor role in the critical decisions affecting entrepreneurial and corporate behaviour in these two areas. Thus, more generous tax allowances on capital are really extraneous to these motives.

The same can be said about expenditures on education. Proponents of more government spending on education should find other justification than economic growth to demand government largesse. Additional expenditure on education does not significantly affect the economy's growth potential. The causal links between spending on education and economic growth in advanced economies have never been proven, despite the numerous learned treatises on the subject. Indeed, that education is a factor "on the critical path" toward higher growth is dubious at best.[15] The production realm most likely gets workers who are sufficiently educated, although better educated workers are always preferred. The problems of the production realm are of a different order. Attention to quality,

260

dedication, and initiative, all important factors, are most unlikely to be correlated with the budget of the Department of Education.

Moreover, better education can probably be attained by means other than emphasizing spending. Not that more money would not be useful. But money is perhaps not the whole problem. Indeed, many empirical analysis suggests a low social return for public spending on educatin, specially at the higher level.[16] Attitudes toward learning and attention and care in the act of communicating values and knowledge is probably more important. Japan, whose educational system has obviously something going for it, spends less per capita on education than does the U.S.. So does Germany. Justifying more education expenditures on the basis of economic growth reminds me of that suburban mayor who argued for a new neighbourhood library on the basis of the jobs it would create.

The R&D issue differs from the education issue. R&D has two facets, basic research and applied research. Basic research is a public good. If government does not subsidize it, not enough basic research will be done for the common good. Thus, there are sound economic reasons for subsidizing basic research. But one should keep in mind that the benefits of basic research know no boundary. The Japanese benefit as much from the results of North American basic research as do the Americans. Thus, all Triad countries should do their share. Furthermore, it is not certain that the present level of basic research is not beyond the optimal level.

The prescription is different for applied R&D, which translates technology into new products and new processes. Over 90 per cent of the $110 billion spent in the U.S. in 1986 was in applied R&D, and about 40 per cent of that amount was contributed by the federal government. Military research accounts for a large proportion of U.S. government funding (70 per cent).[17] I will not question whether the R&D that the government is buying is worth it; that is beyond the scope of this book. The relevant question is whether government subsidies to applied R&D have anything to do with economic growth.

The answer is no. There are no significant benefits in subsidizing the cash-flows of technology intensive corporations, which is what subsidies for R&D do. The fact that applied military research finds its way into the civilian economy is also irrelevant. Most new civilian planes and aircraft engines have military lineage. But this is a rather circuitous road to take and a non-efficient one at that. The non-military applied research (not related to public goods) finds its way into corporate budgets, as a source of income to finance applied research. If corporations were deprived of these funds, they would restructure their budgetary decisions and find the money elsewhere. The non-military applied research funds that find their way into the private sector represent a few tenths of one per cent of the GNP. Corporate treasurers, who have the task of managing corporate finance, have bigger challenges.[18]

Investment, education and research & development are "growth" icons. They should not be. More public spending to subsidize them will not speed up economic growth. Innovative corporations will budget sufficient funds for R&D and for capital investments. They will train their workers. They can also find in the labour market skilled technicians, engineers and managers. There are no indications from labour market data that there is a shortage of highly skilled workers in advanced economy.

I am not arguing here that funds to education and to basic research should be cut, or not increased. But the pursuit and diffusion of knowledge do not require justification by the promise of more economic growth.

GOOD GROWTH POLICIES

Patience and modesty are virtues that governments should pay heed to in pursuing economic growth. The key actors in the growth process are entrepreneurs and corporations; governments are mere stage hands. Economic growth has its own rhythm, associated with the ability of thousands of firms and entrepreneurs to expand their activities and add new ones. All the intensity of government policies cannot do much to accelerate that highly diffused process.

But bad policies can slow it down, and indeed, at the limit, grind it to a halt. This is what has to be avoided. On the other hand, good policies can ensure that the growth process tracks its optimal path. Unfortunately, once it is along its optimal growth path, good policies are quite boring, and politically dull.

Furthermore, the basic "good" policies are few. Proper macro-economic management matters, but mostly to the extent that the extreme are avoided. Corporations and entrepreneurs can cope fairly well with the middle-ground. What is also important is a properly-valued currency, so that the economic base stay in a healthy shape and the import-substitution mechanism keep on functioning properly. Thus, the value of the exchange rate is critical, and subject to a proper valuation, fixed exchange rates are superior to flexible exchange rates. Indeed, central banks should have their priorities straight: a properly priced currency is more important than fine-tuning the aggregate demand.

The most important policy area is the institutional framework, which defines the conditions under which business is conducted. A good framework facilitates change and rewards success. It favours flexibility over brute force, quality over quantity, the long run over the short-term. It does not encourage the entrenchment of management and the development of an implicit "cozy pact" between management and labour.

Governments should also be worried about the cost of doing business. Ultimately, all government revenues are borne by the production side of the economy. A tax is a share of some revenues generated by the production of goods and services. How much is that share and which revenues are taxed are critical to the growth performance of the economy. The good growth performance of high-tax countries suggests that the size of the government take-out matters probably less than the way it is taken out. Taxes on risk, taxes on success, taxes on changes, taxes on flexibility, taxes on the long term, are the worst taxes. Taxes on consumption and taxes on the local economy, hurt the least.

Politicians always think of new policies to spur economic growth. Comptemporary politics is biased toward activism. Thus politicians are bound to be generous with subsidies. Economic growth has political sex-appeal and is a good excuse to buy political support. But most of these policies, were it not for their costs, are largely harmless and irrelevant to growth. Educators, scientists, corporate chieftains and promoters of all types and colour drape themselves in the mantle of economic growth to hide their blushes when they accept government largesse. But let us hope that politicians frown away from bad policies that hurt growth, such as tariff barriers, nationalization of sick industries, encouragement of labour rigidity, etc.

As corporations expand their reach globally and the development of communications blur the traditional frontiers, national governments will see their freedom of choice severely curtailed. This process serves as a good filter to eliminate bad policies. The nation-state as a national policy unit will slowly fade out. Countries that depend on the economy to glue themselves together will start feeling loose.

LOOKING AHEAD

CHAPTER FIFTEEN

THE FADING OF THE NATION STATE

If I had my way, I'd pay a third of my taxes to an international fund dedicated to solving world problems, such as the environment and famine. A third to my community, where my children are educated and my family lives. And then, a last third to my country, which each year does less and less for me in terms of security and well-being, and instead subsidizes special interests.

Kenichi Ohmae

I taly is a land of paradox. The chronic problem child of Europe, it is also one of the most livable European countries. A fragmented political realm, the result of a cranky electoral system, has saddled the Italians with a succession of minority governments of short duration. What has emerged is a bloated bureaucracy, an inefficient welfare state, and erratic political leadership. Moreover, it has been running a chronic budgetary deficit whose size makes the U.S. and Canadian federal deficits look tame.

But all this seems to have been good for the Italian economy, which has been one of the most dynamic of Europe. Thus, Italy has slowly been catching up with its more affluent European neighbours. Over the years, despite the inefficiencies of its government, its economy kept on growing at one of the highest rates among the large European countries. It has numerous dynamic cities. Its GNP per capita has now surpassed that of Great Britain, and is slowly overtaking France.

What lessons can be drawn from the Italian paradox? First, solid economic performance can occur while governments are busy at something else. The Italian experience demonstrates that within a broad range of policies and institutions, any government can ride an economic boom. The Italian bureaucracy provides such a reasonable government. The Italian economy did not need a firm hand at the tiller to achieve record growth.

Second, in the one area where it tried to stimulate growth, southern Italy, the government failed abysmally. In economic terms, the south remains an arid land. Despite the best efforts of the Italian government, the best advice of the experts from the European Economic Market and the quadrillion liras which have been poured into its economy, southern Italy's GNP per capita is still two-thirds that of the north. Governments are not very good growth catalysts.

Kenichi Ohmae, the influential Japanese economist who coined the term "*The Triad Economy*", has been arguing recently that such a paradox is not surprising. In his latest book, *The Borderless World*, Ohmae argues that governments are gradually becoming irrelevant in the economic realm, as "globalization" takes over.[1] As the industrial economies integrate on a global scale, national governments lose much of their ability to influence the course of economic growth. They are being superseded at one end, by multinational corporations and by a body of supra-national regulations (best illustrated by the GATT agreement), and at the other end, by the toiling entrepreneurs and by demanding consumers who show little respect for government edicts. This argument had been made in the past. Daniel Bell, who is best known for its work on the post industrial society, have said of national governments that "they are too big to take care of the small things, and too small to take care of the big things." Thomas Courchesne, a noted Canadian economist, has argued along similar lines that Canada's federal structures are now under pressure as much by the forces of globalization as by Quebec nationalism.[2]

This growing lack of relevance of national governments also explains the strong economic performance of the small countries of Europe, whose governments have abdicated any pretence of influencing the broad economic variables. By gearing their policies mostly at making their economy more adaptable, they are achieving a remarkable success.

THE SLOW DEMISE OF THE NATION STATE

The national government is at the core of the modern industrial economy. Through taxation and public spending, it churns between 25% to 40% of national income and plays a major redistributive role, ensuring that minimum standards are met and providing public services to all citizens. The national government defines the rules of the economy, from the labelling of food products all the way to the terms and conditions of private pension plans. The national government is also held responsible for the performance of the economy, being blamed for unemployment, inflation, high interest rates, recessions and the unfortunate situation of chronically depressed areas. We live in the age of the Keynesian government which has created an expectation of full employment and rising income. Unfortunately, other than getting the economy out of the ditches where it sometimes lands, governments appear to have little effective control on the short-term performance of the economy. Sure, they can mess up the situation, with bad policies. But on the other hand, short of not messing up the situation, there is less and less that national governments can do to improve it.

The major forces that are now sustaining economic growth are not the stabilization policies of national governments, or their structural policies. Other factors matter more, making national governments less relevant. In particular, regions and cities play a more central role, specifically, by determining local growth conditions.

The growing economic irrelevancy of the traditional nation-state is sustained by two basic phenomena.[3] First, economic growth is fundamentally regionalized, centred mainly around the rich communication nodes of cities. In particular, the entrepreneurial renewal process described in Chapter Five, is a local process. Second, and more importantly, country-specific characteristics that influence economic growth are fading in importance relative to characteristics shared throughout the industrial world.

The most important economic characteristics of a country are to be found in the culture of its society and in its institutional framework. Cultural traits encompass the attitudes toward work, entrepreneurship and success, and shared beliefs and values germane to economic behaviour. For example, the Japanese are said to be more frugal, hard-working and team-oriented than the North Americans. The institutional framework encompasses the laws of the land as well as the economic institutions, from the unemployment insurance legislation and fiscal policies to the central bank and the exchange rate system it maintains.

But as globalization progresses, these cultural and institutional characteristics matter less in determining growth rates. Advances in communications and in transportation are slowly tilting the economic scales. What matters more is the wide dissemination of technologies. Not only are products universally available, but the ability to produce them is also widely distributed. Furthermore, the declining costs of transportation and the growing importance of machinery and equipment in the production of goods and services tend to homogenize production costs. At the same time, a global institutional framework is slowly superseding the national institutional framework. International economic regulations, such as GATT, are slowly emerging. Multinational corporations homogenize business practices throughout the advanced economies, slowly undermine the grip of national institutions.

Thus, we have on one side, culture and national institutional framework, and on the other side, technology and global institutions. The latter are gaining ground in shaping the future. National governments are on the losing side. Moreover, while culture matters, its influence is not great enough to reverse the tide.

CULTURE, VALUES AND ECONOMIC GROWTH

Are the Japanese better than us? They work hard, they are disciplined, they excel in teamwork, they value change and they are tough as nails when it comes to negotiation. James Fallows, a senior editor at The

Atlantic Monthly who doubles as an astute economic observer, recently examined this question in a controversial and somewhat misunderstood book, *More Like Us*. Fallows asks the popular question: are the cultural traits of the Japanese better attuned to higher productivity and economic growth than are North American values? The author makes a strong case that individuality and openness provide America with what it needs to maintain its place as the leading economy in the world. North America, he argues, must exploit the unique characteristics which in the past, have propelled its economy to the forefront.

As we have seen, economic growth rests entrepreneurial renewal and corporate innovativeness. There is no doubt that traditional North American virtues of individualism and openness favour entrepreneurship. These virtues are less appropriate for the production realm, where organizational effectiveness and the ability to adapt and to change the rules are paramount? Indeed, the Japanese virtues of selflessness, collegiality, obedience, and hard work, are more pertinent.

In the final analysis, international competitiveness depends on the ability to initiate and accept change. What is critical for a country is not to accept being an also ran. There are many ways of staying abreast. It is not always easy. Turning points are often missed. There is much room for error. The NUMMI example illustrates how an organization can err when the need for change is not immediately self-evident.[4]

For several decades, General Motors, the largest corporation in the world, got away with substandard productivity levels, a situation probably fostered by years of cohabitation with the same union leaders and the same competitors. But within its peer domain, GM had well-managed plants. In the late seventies, General Motors' competition in the mid-car market suddenly changed as the Japanese rushed in. At first, GM argued that the Japanese were unfair competitors, benefiting from lower labour costs. It convinced the U.S. government to impose quotas on the importation of Japanese cars. But its balloon burst when Toyota demonstrated its management skills at Fremont. Suddenly, General Motors was exposed, the largest corporation in the world, as a blatantly mediocre performer.

To be consistent with its own set of corporate values, General Motors had to meet these new industry standards. It was quite a challenge to change the biggest corporation in the world, and it took a decade to do it. GM also paid dearly for having been a laggard. A new division of the automobile market took place. GM's share of the North American automobile market fell from 45 per cent to less than 35 per cent, a drop of more than one million cars a year. General Motors shareholders and the communities and workers that depended on GM lost greatly because General Motors did not change rapidly enough, a heavy penalty that can be traced to the lack of foresight and leadership exercised by senior management and union leaders.

No government policy could have done much to prevent this slippage, which had to do with the corporate culture built over several generations of corporate leadership. It was not due to the inadequacy of the American value system. In fact, in retrospect, the "Not invented here" syndrome seemed to have played a big role: insular General Motors did it to itself. Big organizations often need a beating to adapt to changes. Indeed, the U.S. steel industry had a similar experience in the seventies.

GM's predicament over the past fifteen years is symptomatic of that of the whole U.S. economy: big, insular and slow to adapt to the new economic environment. The United States was not used to a turbulent environment. But the complacency will disappear, because the American value system does not accept "also-rans". Each industry will find its own way, adapting its structures, its technologies, and its practices to the new environment. Leaders will show the way. Experimentation will abound. There will be winners and losers.

This process of adaptation to the interdependencies of the Triad economy is to be found in all Triad countries. But some societies are better at adapting than others. Cultural and social values determine the ability of a society to adapt. For change displaces the present order and introduces uncertainty. It is mostly in this regard that values impact on economic growth. That Japanese or Germans work harder or longer than Americans or Canadians will not make their society significantly richer. After all, machines do most of the work in advanced economies. Whether they work smarter has a different impact. Whether they innovate, rapidly adapt the better ideas of their competitors, and keep up with the competition makes the difference.

James Fallows points to two conditions which must be met in a society for economic growth to be favoured. First, what he calls the "radius of trust", the "Us" which is found in any society, must be sufficiently broad. This bond of trust ensures that there is a common code of acceptable behaviour and the rule of law prevails. This "Us" has to be broad enough to allow for the development of a market economy, allowing for contracting between individuals and between organizations. The broader the radius of trust, the better organized an economy can be. But on the other hand, the set of shared values that defines "Us" must remain meaningful. "Us" is not mankind, at least not yet.

Second, people must believe that they have control over their future and can thus affect their destiny. The territory defined by "Us" has to be an island of sufficient tranquillity and of mutual trust. They can plan ahead, relying on the durability of the legal framework. This favours investments and long-term outlooks.

I will add a third condition, a collective willingness not to be left behind, the refusal to be an also-ran. Being able to do as well as "competitors" from abroad has to be a social norm. This creates the social drive that brings about change.

These conditions create an environment suitable for economic change and progress. Most societies find ways to achieve them, evening out the odds between societies with different cultures. This does not preclude particularities introduced by culture. The North American value system has numerous traits which favour growth, particularly entrepreneur-induced growth. The Japanese value system also encourages growth, albeit organizationally-induced growth. The two systems impact on growth potential from different angles. It is quite difficult to say which one is superior, and even whether one is superior.

Moreover, the whole debate about the relative contribution of each value system to economic growth turns out to be somewhat inconsequential. Other factors play more important roles in determining economic growth. Are economic policies among them?

INSTITUTIONALIZING GROWTH

There is no doubt that the Japanese government has done something right to foster economic growth. Nobody will deny that Japan has been pursuing policies that favour savings over consumption, and hard work over leisure. There is nothing wrong with such puritanical policies, and indeed, most governments are officially committed to them. The hitch is that Japan has been quite successful at it, for more than a generation. Japan produces more than it consumes and savings pile up. One consequence is a much lower cost for capital, the lowest in the world.

The Japanese also show a strong preference for Japanese products, which they hold to be better designed and more reliable. Short of significant price disadvantages, the Japanese favour goods made in Japan, from cars to rice. Most societies exhibit these streaks of chauvinism.

Europeans have long complained about implicit "buy American" attitudes in the U.S.. French-speaking Montrealers think that English- speaking Torontonians discriminate against their products, and vice-versa. But the Japanese appear to outdo everybody else at this game, a probable legacy of an insular tradition that discovered international trade only a few generations ago. Official policies condone this behaviour, reflecting its deep sociological roots.

The combination of austere macro-economic policies and chauvinism has sustained a chronic surplus in Japan's balance of trade. The huge domestic saving surplus spilled overseas, forcing the Japanese to gradually become the bankers to the world. They are slowly accumulating a tremendous amount of wealth abroad, much of it in financial assets denominated in foreign currencies. As a result, the rest of the world is getting worried. Not only is Radio City Music Hall a Japanese property, but so is E.T. and many of those Van Gogh paintings.

How is Japan's situation different from that of an individual who saves a high proportion of his revenues, piling up money at the bank and buying properties all over town? There are some similarities. Such a person will get rich and derive an increasing amount of his income just by cashing interest and dividend checks. Isn't that where "puritans" end up? Balzac and Dickens were writing about these old scrooges more than one hundred years ago. There are hints of Japan's story in their novels.

But we cannot carry the analogy too far. Countries are different from individuals. First of all, whereas old scrooges remain old scrooges until they die, countrymen and countrywomen do not. Individual citizens soften up as their country gets wealthier: most people do enjoy their new found wealth and the country loses its puritanical streaks. But also, countries have something that old scrooges do not have, which is their own currency. The inevitable rise in the value of the currency as the country get richer, is a pernicious virus that attacks and ultimately undermines all these puritanical economic policies. Japan is already feeling the sting of this virus that causes the Dutch disease.

As of 1991, the Japanese yen is significantly overvalued, by 25% relative to the U.S. dollar. This makes foreign assets much cheaper for Japanese buyers. Indeed, the Japanese have been on a purchasing spree, spending money on everything from real estate to impressionist paintings and old line companies. The high value of the yen has also affected the competitiveness of Japanese goods. Slowly but inevitably, corrections are appearing. This is already noticeable in the sharp increase of Japanese direct investments abroad, as Japanese manufacturers strive to remain competitive. Foreign goods are also much more competitive in Japan. It will take some time for foreign manufacturers to break through the Japanese distribution networks and gain the confidence of Japanese buyers. But it is only a matter of time: the Dutch virus will zoom in fatally on the production side of their economy, hiding behind the euphoria that an overvalued currency provides to bankers and consumers.

The Japanese are now discovering the pleasure of living more lavishly: bigger houses, bigger cars, longer holidays, better clothing. Their tourism sector is already deficitary, as they spend more abroad than foreign tourists spend in Japan. They also demand more efficiency from their local economy: more McDonald's, more K-Mart's, more Wall-Mart's, etc. All these changes will take time. But most people do not get more frugal as they get richer.

The direction of change is clear. The checks and balances are coming to play. Japan's wealth is generated in the export sector. But as the yen rises, it get spread to the domestic economy. The waiters in Osaka will join the automobile workers of Nagoya: they will not only upgrade their apartments, they will also discover Parisian chic and the sweetness of Australian sands.

Such developments slow down the march of any country toward greater wealth. The work ethic is assailed by temptations. The high-valued currency pushes manufacturing abroad. Indeed, fairly soon, we can expect books on the decline of Japan. The elements of the script will be familiar: over-consumption, a short-term outlook, growing resistance to change, myopic government policies, the greening of attitudes, the failure of the school system, the decline of the work ethic, and so on. Meanwhile, a new nemesis will emerge somewhere else to haunt the more mature advanced economies.

Economic policies, like cultural traits, are limited in what they can achieve in the long run in the advanced economies of the Triad. They can allow a country to rise slightly above the others. But it is most difficult for a country to escape the pull of international egalitarianism brought about by its own nouveaux riches. For some time a government can bias the economic framework, to favour producers at the expense of consumers. This is what Japan has done quite successfully. But a growing country cannot store its mushrooming wealth away from its consumers for a long period of time. Eventually, it reaches the consumers, which is after all, the whole purpose of the exercise. Given this new wealth, the consumers rearrange their priorities, between consumption and savings, between working and leisure, between expensive domestic goods and cheaper foreign goods. Consumers are not puritan, and the less puritan they are, the richer they get. This, more than anything else, sets limits on the pursuit of economic power.

THE END OF EMPIRES or THE LAST OF THE CENTURIES OWNED BY A COUNTRY

In a previous era when markets did not play their dominant role of today, economic power was bolstered by military power. This allowed countries to build empires and their kings to live in splendour with a retinue of aristocrats, as long as taxes could be levied throughout the empire. This world disappeared more than a hundred years ago, along with the empires. Modern economies rely upon their productivity, not on military might, to maintain their status.

A big economy facilitates having a big army. The converse does not hold, and indeed, escalating military expenditures doomed most empires. In 1987, a Harvard historian, Paul Kennedy, drew a parallel between several past "empires"— France, Spain, England— and contemporary U.S., allowing him to announce the end of the American century and to hail the coming of the Japanese century.[5] Such a metaphor may no longer be relevant. One can accept that the world has recently witnessed a period of American hegemony. Escaping the destruction of two World Wars allowed the U.S. economy to tower over that of any other country. Furthermore, the United States became chief banker to the world, and American corporations spread out beyond their domestic base with their technologies and know-how. Corn-Flakes appeared on the breakfast tables of the world, and Bonanza, on their TV sets. U.S. tourists flocked abroad, Van Goghs and Renoirs were bought by American collectors, and American investors purchased a big chunk of the Champs-Elysees. But that "hegemony" did not last long. As the economies of Europe and Japan were rebuilt, the checks and balances moved in the other direction. The American invasion faded into history.

The long domination of the U.S. economy is a contemporary aberration brought by the two world wars. No country is likely to ever own a century again. Moreover, the United States is likely to avoid the fate of Spain, France and Britain, coming out of its "century" in relatively good economic shape. It has managed to contain its military expenditures to 6%

of GNP, a significant levy, but not a crippling one, and which should not increase. Military force is slowly being replaced by the rules of law in governing the relations between countries, at least in the Triad economy.[6] If military might is withdrawn from Paul Kennedy's equation, it is difficult to foresee an approaching era of Japanese hegemony.

The twenty-first century, like the last part of the twentieth century, will most likely be inhospitable to the concentration of political might in the hands of the government of any single country. Moreover, it is most unlikely that any country will ever be able to build up the relative economic power that the U.S. held in the post World War II years. The age of empires is past. Technology is seeing to that.

TECHNOLOGY, THE GREAT LEVELLER

In an early chapter of this book, I mentioned that technology did not play a critical role in determining growth rate. Let us come back to this assertion. I wrote that technology was analogous to water in nature, an essential but abundant element. Furthermore, from a growth perspective, I mentioned that technological progress is market-driven, and not the other way. I alluded to a well-known demonstration of this phenomenon, the numbers of patents on horseshoes. As long as there was a large demand for horseshoes, patents were continually filed, reflecting steady improvements of that seemingly simple tool. When horses fell out of favour as a source of traction around 1920-1930, patent filing stopped abruptly.

The abundance and availability of technology does not make it unimportant. Indeed, more than anything else, it explains the emergence of the industrial world.[7] But technology is, by and large, a public good, a good whose usage by one individual does not imperil its usage by others.

The basic economic problem with public goods is the low value that markets assign them as they are available to all at no or little cost. Since they cannot be sold like a typical product, their production is not profitable. To correct this, conventions, such as copyrights and patents, have been developed to ensure that an idea is recognized as the property of someone for a certain period of time after its discovery. Those using the idea must pay royalties, creating an incentive to develop new ideas.

Not all ideas can be protected by such conventions. Basic research in the physical sciences yields know-how that is seldom directly applicable to a product. It only generates other ideas. For instance, several hundred billion dollars have been spent over the past thirty years on cancer research. Although we now know a lot more about cancer, cancer research has not yet generated many commercial products. Thus corporations concerned with profits tend to stay away from basic research. Most of their research is applied, targeted at commercial applications. They do basic research only if needed to stay abreast of future developments. Consequently, most of the basic research has to be funded by governments, and is done in universities and in not-for- profits institutions. The results are published in scientific journals, and easily made available to other researchers. Fame and not fortune drive the process.

There is no undisputed evidence that either basic or applied research is a limiting factor to economic growth. In industrial countries, they represent between 1.5% and 2.5% of economic activities. Spending more, such as 3% or 3.5% of GNP, is unlikely to accelerate economic growth. R & D is no longer (if it ever was) a bottleneck. The obstacle to growth is the integration of new know-how into products and production methods, and integrating these into the fabric of the economy. This demands change. The economy's ability to change is what determines its growth rate.

Difference in the ability to change explains why the level of economic activity differs so much throughout the world. The growth potential is associated with how the economy is organized to ensure that it is sufficiently dynamic and flexible, so that it can integrate the new ideas that at any given time, are floating around. The North American automobile industry illustrates the nature of the bottleneck. No other industry in North America spends as much as the automobile industry on R & D. And it spends much more than the Japanese and the European automobile industries do. But the major source of new economic value in the North American automobile industry in the coming years will be derived from its ability to incorporate superior design and production methods originating mostly from abroad.

I doubt that government can do much to ease these organizational bottlenecks, beyond ensuring a broad exposure to competition. Organizations are structured by a complex web of social arrangements. Competitive pressures may force them to adopt superior methods used elsewhere, but they will do it at their own rhythm.

It is in that regard that technology, in its broadest sense, is the great leveller. Technology is the application of human knowledge. Superior technological paths are easily identifiable in a competitive environment. Over time, these superior paths are incorporated in the economic production. The diffusion process takes place over a few decades at most. A backward country such as South Korea was able to master the technology of the automobile in less than twenty years. The Hyundai cars fabricated in Korea are as good as any other cars in North America, Japan and Europe. In fact, Koreans visualize the whole Triad economy as a cherry tree ready to be plucked for product ideas. There is no reason why Korea should not achieve the same level of economic activity per capita as the Triad economy within another one or two generations. The Korean government is able to accelerate the process with "puritan" policies that favour production over consumption. But the impact of these policies, beyond the obvious ones such as allowing the market economy to flourish, is relatively marginal compared to the contribution of technological assimilation.

This is demonstrated by the comparative performance of Taiwan and Korea. Both countries provide the basic conditions for the entrepreneurial process to flourish and for corporations to continually improve their competitiveness.[8] Nevertheless, each country pursued radically different economic development policies, allowing us to demonstrate that, beyond a certain level, policies make little difference.

In the mid-fifties, both South Korea and Taiwan had a GNP per capita of the order of $500, roughly about the same as their Communist counterparts, China and North Korea. Taiwan's economy took off first. Financial markets were deregulated. Interest rates went up, but capital was made widely available as savings were abundant. Small businesses thrived throughout the island. The government did little in terms of encouraging the transfer of technologies. Entrepreneurs and corporations did it by themselves. Over time, Taiwanese manufacturers succeeded in export markets. They developed alliances with foreign partners to access technology. This gave rise to a large number of small and medium size firms in technology advanced sectors. Even today, Taiwan does not have many large companies, but sheer numbers replace large size.

Korea started a few years later, in the early sixties, under the baton of General Park Chun Hee. The military influence permeated the country's economic development strategy. Although entrepreneurship was allowed to flourish, the government picked winners and encouraged those most likely to succeed through privileged access to credit. Interest rates were kept low, but capital allocation was controlled. Technologies were targeted. What emerged was a limited number of giant conglomerates, which now rank among the largest corporations in the world. Under the guidance of state planners, they entered in various "strategic" industries. Hyundai and Samsung are the best known of them. The top ten of them still account for half of Korean's GNP.

FIGURE 14.1
TWO COUNTRIES, TWO APPROACHES,
ONE GROWTH PATTERN

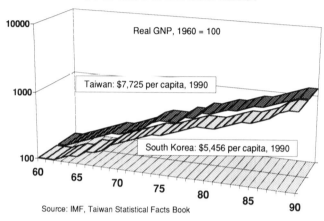

Source: IMF, Taiwan Statistical Facts Book

It is difficult to find two approaches so different, and yet for the past twenty years, both countries experienced very similar growth rates, slightly above 8% per year, on the average. Given its headstart, Taiwan is slightly better off, by about three years, and it has managed to maintain that lead for more than two decades. Korea's GNP per capita in 1991, is where Taiwan's was in 1988, about $7000. So much for superior economic development policies.

THE NEW INTERNATIONAL FRAMEWORK

The Common Market countries are bracing for that critical event, 1992, when the last impediments to the free flow of goods and services between them are removed. Most likely, 1992 will pass by with little fanfare and with few noticeable changes for the typical consumer. Yet, for individual governments, it will be a watershed year, as they will lose more of their ability to intervene directly in their economy. The 1992 agreement is another step in the direction of shackling the hands of national governments, preventing them from cheating by favouring their own domestic producers unduly. Producers will have to resort to innovation to improve their competitiveness, not on political clout.

Canada faced a similar passage in 1989, when the Free Trade Agreement with the United States took force. At the time, much attention was given to the elimination of tariffs, a highly visible measure. The dire predictions of the opponents of the Agreement did not materialize, nor did the exaggerated expectations of its most ebullient supporters. But in the long run, the treaty's constraining effects on government policies and its establishment of an international dispute arbitration mechanism will have by far a significant impact on the Canadian economy, as its production realm will have to compete solely on the basis of innovation and productivity.

Numerous international agreements already regulate the Triad economy from a global perspective. The General Agreement on Trade and Tariffs (GATT) is best known, probably because some of its terms are renegotiated every ten years. Last year, because of GATT, the price of French wine went down in Canada and California wine became more widely available. This is good not only for Canadian consumers, but also for the long term potential of the Canadian economy. The more intense price competition will force Canadian wine producers to improve the quality of their wine, increasing their chance of eventually exporting Canadian wine.

International tax treaties discipline governments. Local subsidiaries of foreign concerns must be treated as domestic firms. Royalties must be paid to foreigners as well as nationals. By and large, the framework which defines the business environment is fairly homogeneous throughout the Triad economy, and the trend is toward even more homogeneity.

A parallel trend is the homogenisation of trademarks, products, fads and behaviour throughout the Triad Economy. There are more similarities between the spending patterns of a French millionaire and an American millionaire than between the French millionaire and a French blue-collar employee. Fairly soon, the same statement will apply to a Japanese millionaire. Needs are converging, restraining national governments even further from pursuing independent tracks.

Governments still matter. The preceding three chapters illustrated the broad latitude of economic policies. Moreover, it is evident that governments can still do wrong. The demise of the Communist regimes of Eastern Europe can be seen as an interesting economic experience. By imposing a command economy, these governments had a tremendous perverse influence. But once these countries reverted to the rules of a market economy, their course of action became somewhat restricted. There are still critical choices to be made. For instance, it will be interesting to compare the long-term performance of what was Eastern Germany with that of Hungary, Poland and Czechoslovakia. The former will benefit from huge transfers from West Germany. However, like Atlantic Canada, it will suffer from sharing a strong currency. The other East European countries will benefit from weaker currencies, which will encourage production over consumption. In the long run, a healthier entrepreneurial process may turn out to be more useful than grants, subsidies and other largesse.

CANADA UNDER STRESS

Globalization, the process that led to the emergence of the Triad economy, also weakens the traditional nation-state government. At one end, international regulations and multinational firms become the norm, and escape direct control by nation-state governments. At the other end, global technologies and products pervade domestic economies, whether the government likes it or not. Dynamic cities matter more than governments, as they have more influence on the fertility of the entrepreneurial realm and on the innovativeness and flexibility of corporations.

What is happening to Canada points to the future of the nation-state. The traditional structures of the federal government, weakened by globalization, are assailed by pressures emerging from regional diversity. It is highly likely that, by the year 2000, the Canadian Federation will have been reduced to a much looser union of regions, as a result of pressures for greater autonomy in Quebec, Western Canada and by aboriginals. Nationalist sentiment was always strong in Quebec, the home of the six million descendants of 17th and 18th century settlers from France. Since the early sixties, it expresses itself in a growing demand for political autonomy. Montreal, where 50% of Quebecers are to be found, has become a hotbed of Quebecois entrepreneurship and now hosts several home-grown multinational firms. In 1991, a majority of Quebecers would like to bolt out of the present federal system. They want a sovereign Quebec associated economically with the rest of Canada. Whether this is realistic is a moot point, as the rest of Canada does not appear too keen on joining an economic union with a sovereign Quebec.

At the same time, residents of the two westernmost Provinces, Alberta and British Columbia, representing 22% of the population of Canada, are also grumbling about the federal government, which they see as controlled by central Canada. Their economies are growing strongly, led by two dynamic cities, Vancouver and Calgary, which are rapidly breeding their own international corporations. They are also demanding significant changes in the role of the Federal government.

Two regional parties, one in Quebec, one in Western Canada, have sprung up to defend these regional points of view. It is highly possible that in 1993, when the next Canadian elections will be held, Canada will end up with a coalition government, further weakening the federal structures.

The constitutional travails of Canadians bemuse most foreign observers. But in Canada, this is serious business, coming at a time when Canada can ill afford it. The public sector deficit is about 7% of GNP. Paradoxically, this structural deficit may turn out to save Canada, as no Province, and Quebec in particular, is able to break away and finance readily a deficit equal to 7% of its GNP. Indeed, locked together by their collective deficit, the Canadian provinces have few options. The search for constitutional peace will probably lead them to further decentralization.

The Canadian government is likely to see its economic role eroded significantly as the country's structures evolve toward those of the European Common Market. The central Common Market agency, the EEC Commission, control about 1% of the Common Market countries's GNP, yet wields enormous power. The Canadian government can be expected to see its fiscal bite reduced significantly, as spending responsibilities get progressively transferred to lower levels. The Federal government will still be responsible for the enforcement of a common economic framework, much of it constrained by international agreements. To this role would be added monetary policy and the coordination of the fiscal policies of the Provinces, the two most visible remnants of its former economic dominance. On maps, Canada will still be of the same colour and Canadians will be able to brag about their membership in the exclusive G-7 club, but the appearances will be deceiving. On the economic front, the Canadian regions and their dynamic cities will be very much on their own.

This marginalization of the traditional responsibilities of central governments reflects their diminishing relevance as national policy-making units. One does not need a strong central government to heed to international rules and regulations. But more interestingly, it is difficult to foresee, beyond the uncertainties and costs associated with the transition, how such fundamental changes would affect the daily life of Canadians, as public services, formerly financed by the federal government, would be provided by provincial and local governments.

The Canadian economy will likely be little affected by these changes. Will they impinge on the entrepreneurial fertility of the Canadian economy? Most likely, no. In fact, if such a decentralization results in a more efficient public sector, taxes could be lowered and one could argue that entrepreneurs would find a more hospitable environment. The same applies to corporations, which will most likely be unaffected in their ability to adapt to changing competitive situations and to innovation. Thus, the overall growth potential of the Canadian economy should be unaffected.

Canada has recently been held together by economic motives, particularly along its linguistic cleavage. But there is less and less an economic reason to be held together by a government. Market mechanisms are operating, Government does not hurt, but it does not help either. So other centripetal forces are more of influence in shaping the evolution of the country.

Similar pressures are also confronting the U.S.S.R. and Czechoslovakian federations. Their breakdown into a much looser union is also very likely. The economic impact of such changes will probably be marginal. To the extent that the resulting governments are more efficient, the net effect is most likely positive. As long as the rules of market economies prevail, the specific political structures matter less. The potential for economic growth depends on the ability of the emerging governments to create an economic environment conducive to entrepreneurship and to innovation in corporations, something that can be done as well, if not better, by smaller governments as by bigger ones.

The diminishing economic role of the nation state will be less apparent in the United States. Washington is the mecca of the raindancers: their chants will sustain the myth of the enlightened helmsman at the tiller. But more importantly, Washington is the biggest political souk in this world, where every year, a trillion dollar budget is carved and distributed by less than one thousand legislators and key officials. This function enshrines the power of Washington over the country. But meanwhile, elsewhere in the country, in cities such as Los Angeles, San Francisco, Boston, Atlanta, Miami, Dallas and Houston, without much guiding light from the raindancers in Washington, real growth occurs. There will come a time when the lack of connection will be evident.

ON BELONGING TO A COUNTRY

Future economic performance is likely to be tied to cities and their regions. Within the Triad economy, all countries and regions will be more or less in the same league, with the best performing regions doing about twice as well as the worst performing ones. Regions which fall behind should bounce back, more or less catching up with the pack. Technology flows and exchange rate movements will level the playing field.

Superior economic performance will transcend national boundaries. There will always be world-class corporations and institutions. These organizations will tend to be international, such as IBM and Harvard University. They will attract the best and the brightest from around the world. They will define the standards of performance. And they will be emulated. Great corporations can emerge anywhere in the Triad economy, and superior performance will allow them to become multinational rapidly, within a generation. In doing so, they will spread not only their products and technologies, but also their values and standards.

This diffusion process will impose a certain level of homogeneity. The IBM unit in Great Britain will try to do as well as IBM Canada. And Bull in France has to meet the standards set by IBM France if it is to compete. Thus, the same values will be spread throughout the Triad economy, and will even out productivity.

Nevertheless, at any given time, some regions will be ahead of others. Look for their cities. The entrepreneurial fertility that they sustain will determine in the long run their "portfolio" of economic activities. This is not sufficient. They also have to develop world-class corporations. But it starts with entrepreneurs, and it takes a generation or two.

What eventually makes a city perform better is the actual mix of activities implanted in its economic base. At any given time, some activities are more highly valued. Corporate governance, head offices and their ancillary activities stand out. Emerging industries, built around information, research and semi-conductors, such as we find around Boston can propel a city to the top. Governments have little direct influence on such a mix, although, in the long run, the cumulative impact of a series of coherent government decisions can be quite significant.

Moreover, the performance of cities will fluctuate as new industries spring up and others fade, altering their mixes of activities. Cities, and their regions, can live off their accumulated wealth only for a certain amount of time. If new activities are not generated, their fate is cruel.

Detroit, Cleveland, Montreal and Philadelphia were powerhouses less than one hundred years ago. They are all suffering from an aging economic base.

A short distance from Boston is the town of Lowell, which provides an effective lesson in the need not only to change, but also to be creative. About 150 years ago, Lowell was the "Silicon Valley" of the period, the textile capital of the world, as famous then as Silicon Valley is today. Politicians and officials from all over the United States and Europe visited it, not only to marvel at its factory system and its advanced technology, but also to learn what could be applied elsewhere.

The heyday of Lowell lasted less than 50 years. By the end of the nineteenth century, it was in a rapid decline. Lowell was not sufficiently creative to replace its industries of yesteryear with industries of tomorrow. The abandoned factories, which still abound in Lowell, are testimony to the dearth of entrepreneurship which characterized Lowell in subsequent years.

The miracle of Route 128 around Boston have recently, revitalized Lowell. In the early 1970's, a Boston entrepreneur, An Wang, decided to establish a minicomputer company in Lowell. Wang Computer went on to become one of the stellar performers of the computing industry. By the mid- eighties, Wang Computer employed over ten thousand employees in Lowell. Indeed, the whole city turned entrepreneurial, spurred by this potent model in its midst. Lowell even turned its old factories into a major tourist attraction.

But no amount of recent growth could mask the traces of the long decline which Lowell went through. It is a fate that I do not wish for any city. But Lowell may not have learned its lesson. One is greeted in today's Lowell by one of the biggest office building complexes I have ever seen in a town of this size, three 13-storey Wang headquarters towers. It reminds me very much of General Motors headquarters in Detroit, which was built in the 1950s, when Detroit was the Silicon Valley of the era. History often repeats itself. Will Lowell be cursed a second time?

Maintaining a fertile entrepreneurial realm is the best insurance against decline. It is also the best ticket to the top among the regions of the world. Out of the entrepreneurial ferment will emerge fast-track firms, which will develop the production realm of the region. The firms in the production realm will compete according to the standards of the Triad economy. It takes only a few generations for the best corporations to reach the top ranks. The cities that host their head offices will grow with them.

Such a process cannot be extensively influenced by national governments, making them marginal actors in the game of economic growth.

The economy is very much like a forest. The trees, the plants and the brush embody growth. The forest is slowly evolving. Over the years, the influence of the climate is paramount in determining whether a forest is barren or luxuriant. There is sufficient evidence at the moment to conclude that good policies can influence the rate of growth of the economy. The community and the regional level offer the greatest potential for intervention, providing a climate conducive to entrepreneurship. From higher level governments, what is demanded is the proper attitude rather than action per se. National governments are asked first and above most to define the rules of the game. Beyond that role, there is less and less to do that makes major differences in the economic realm, as the widely divergent policies of Korea and Taiwan or the inaction of the Italian government demonstrate. Governments that rely solely on the economy as their raison d'etre, will face growing challenges to their legitimacy, as their irrelevance will become increasingly evident.

As Leopold Kohr once remarked, nature does not need any outside interference for trees to stop growing at a certain height.[9] The same applies to the economic realm. In the not too distant future, what governments cannot do will be widely known. We will realize that national governments, those that are not responsible for operating the schools and cleaning the streets, are really no longer useful.

CHAPTER SIXTEEN

JUST A FEW HUNDRED YEARS

"200 years ago almost everywhere human beings were comparatively few, poor and at the mercy of the forces of nature, and 200 years from now, we expect, almost everywhere they will be numerous, rich and in control of the forces of nature"

Herman Kahn, 1975

T wo hundred and twenty-five years ago, on the eve of the Industrial Revolution, peasants constituted about two-thirds of the population of Western Europe. Life was not easy. Indeed, there is nothing today that compares, not even in the poorest of the poor countries. Peasants worked all day, 12 hours and more, especially in the summer. Mothers giving birth had only a few days off work. There was no medicine other than folk medicine. Peasants did not have machinery and only the rich had workhorses. Families, typically 5 to 10 persons, lived in small houses, a few hundred square feet divided into two or three rooms, and ate a lot of soup. The spectre of famine was always present. Peasants did not know how to read. They seldom had travelled beyond neighbouring villages. They were very superstitious. Physically, they were small, but strong. They lost most of their teeth by the age of 20, looked much older than their age and did not wash often. By the time they hit 35, life was over for most of them.

The Industrial Revolution changed all that. Suddenly, in less than ten generations, entrepreneurs seeded productive organizations which blossomed into large corporations, generating an unprecedented stream of goods and services. Material wealth sustained an explosion of the population. Figure 16.1 charts the evolution of the rate of growth of the world population, the best indicator of the cornucopia generated by economic growth.

FIGURE 16.1
THE POPULATION EXPLOSION

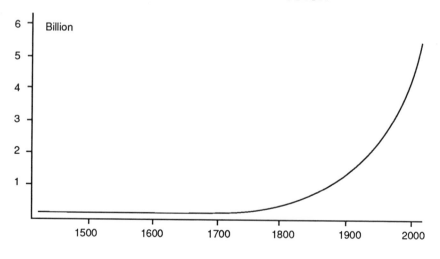

For thousands of years, population growth had been marginal throughout the world. By the mid-eighteenth century, the world population stood at about 500 million people, which is the present population of Western Europe. Then, life expectancy started to increase, as people were better fed and fewer children died. A population explosion ensued. The world population is now estimated to be between 5 billion and 6 billion.

Contemporary Cassandras warn us that economic growth contains the seeds of its own demise. Unchecked, the population explosion will precipitate a world catastrophe, as the resources of the earth become depleted. Overcrowding will lead to political crisis. Economic growth as we know it cannot last. The earth's resources will not allow it.

I do not share this apocalyptic view of the future. Humanity has adapted in the past and will continue to do so. Moreover, growth in the future will depend less and less on the volume of material resources. A new Industrial Revolution has already started, superseding the old one. Know how has replaced energy as the element which is being tamed.

The effects of the passage of the second Industrial Divide, as it was justly called, can already be seen. Since the mid-seventies, the rate of growth of the population of the world has peaked, and is now falling. As the less-developed countries improve their economic situation, family size will fall and population growth will slow down. Figure 16.2 presents the long view of the world population. The rate of growth of population should fall within the next two hundred years to a level which should more or less stabilize the world population, between 10 and 12 billion.

FIGURE 16.2
WORLD POPULATION : THE LONG VIEW

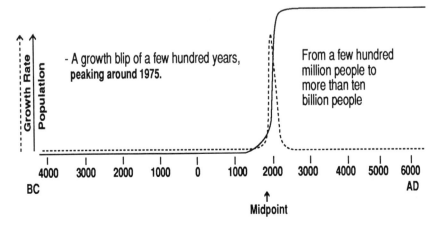

It is most remarkable that suddenly, a few hundred years ago, mankind has learned to expand its productive capacity. This allowed a fundamental adjustment in the world population, an adjustment which still has not run its course. But a divide has just been passed. World population should stabilize at between 10 billion and 12 billion inhabitants in the next two hundred years.

The progress in that short span of time will have been spectacular. For instance, for the first time in the history of mankind, food has ceased to be the central economic concern. Its production had remained close to the subsistence level since the origin of civilization. Only a few centuries ago did it start to increase to a significant point above that level and become more predictable, and its distribution more efficient.

Great famines where millions died were common from the early days of mankind. Within a period of two hundred years, they have slowly disappeared from the face of the earth. Even though it occurred less than fifty years ago, the world has forgotten that in 1943, four million people died in Eastern India, in the last of the great famines. Economic progress has relegated these catastrophes to history. In 1987, the Indian sub-continent suffered through the worst drought in this century, without the world noticing it, and without any famine. Only wars can now cause generalized food deprivation.

Where is the world heading? What will be our material situation 100 years from now? It's hard to tell. Entrepreneurs will keep on surprising us, bringing new products and new technology to the marketplace, fighting conventional wisdom, defying the establishment, rejecting the status quo.

The impact will be stupendous. Our collective memory is very dim. The past can assist us in assessing the magnitude of the changes to be expected. Figure 16.3 allows us to compare the world economic production of two hundred and of one hundred years ago with the present level of production. The grey area represents the world's annual economic output, whereas the per capita income is revealed by the height of the area. The productive capacity of the good ship Earth was relatively untapped until a few centuries ago. By taming energy with machines, man was able to produce much more than would have been imaginable before. Both output and population exploded. Now that we are taming information, where is the growth process leading the world economy?

One hundred years ago, in 1889, not even the most daring visionary of the period, Jules Verne, foresaw the existence of the automobile, the most influential product of the next hundred years. Indeed, it was nearly impossible to imagine the mechanically dependable automobile of today: silent ride; rubber wheels; stereo music; air conditioning; up to 100 miles an hour, a speed never attained at that period; a few hours to learn how to drive; etc. Millions of miles of paved highways and town streets were to be built, along with service stations, parking garages, etc. A car for every home, with the cheapest one costing the wages of a few months of work. The automobile is now passé, a commodity taken for granted, a low-tech machine. Detroit has lost its mystique. Indeed, automobiles are pests which pollute and congest. No poet would now write an ode to the car.

And then came the airplane, the computer, plastic, miracle drugs, heart transplant, insecticides, etc., products and technologies which were beyond the set of possibilities in 1889. What can we say about the next hundred years? Indeed, odes will be written to the many unforeseen products which will shape the coming century, and then, like the car, they will fall from grace. But entrepreneurs will keep ushering them in.

FIGURE 16.3
THE WORLD ANNUAL ECONOMIC PRODUCTION ($1985)

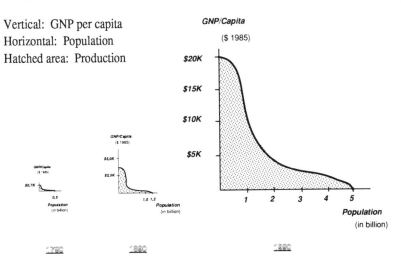

In fact, the next hundred years should change the world even more than the past hundred years. Population growth will slow down. But economic growth will continue its relentless march. The human genius will still be at work, entrepreneurs will keep trying, managers will rearrange production, and machinery will increase productivity. Economic prosperity will spread to the whole world.

The advanced economies will continue to grow. Let us assume conservatively that the growth rate of the most advanced economies for the next hundred years will be only of 1% a year per capita, half the historical average. (This should account for concerns for a prudent husbandry of nature's resources.) Nevertheless, such a paltry rate of growth, sustainable by technological progress only, will nearly triple the income level in one hundred years. A typical middle class household of the year 2100 will live on what today would be $150,000 a year, enjoy greatly improved products and live in a much improved natural environment.

The developing countries will catch up, growing at rates of 5 to 10 per cent a year. Most will join the Triad economy in the next hundred years. They will follow the route that is being traced at the moment by Spain, Turkey, Korea, Taiwan, etc.. Indeed, when China and India join, and it could take them only fifty years to do it (with an 8 per cent a year growth), most of the world will be characterized by an advanced production realm.

Figure 16.4 illustrates the magnitude of what will be achieved, how much will be done, with not many more resources than today. (The figure uses the same scale as figure 16.3)

Most of the growth will come from the diffusion of economic practices from leading industrial countries to the rest of the world. The Third World poverty problem will disappear, as the wealth curve will get inverted from a convex shape to a concave shape.

There will be challenges. The environment will remain a major concern. But we can expect to rise to the challenge. Other challenges will assail humanity: an aging population, North-South population imbalances, vegetarianism, etc. But the human genius will triumph.

Energy will fade as a constraint on development. A glass of water contains the energy equivalent of 100,000 gallons of gasoline. Sometime in the next hundred years, the human genius will crack the secret of that glass of water, and learn to fuse deuterium atoms in a controlled way. Energy will then disappear as a constraint, just like salt disappeared a few thousand years ago as an impediment to well-being. Furthermore, fusion energy, as opposed to fossil fuel such as oil and coal, does not generate greenhouse gases.

But let's not try to foresee the products and technologies of the next century. Like Jules Verne, we might miss the most important one. Moreover, we would appear as loony as somebody who, a hundred years

FIGURE 16.4
WORLD ECONOMIC PRODUCTION:
ONE HUNDRED YEARS FROM NOW

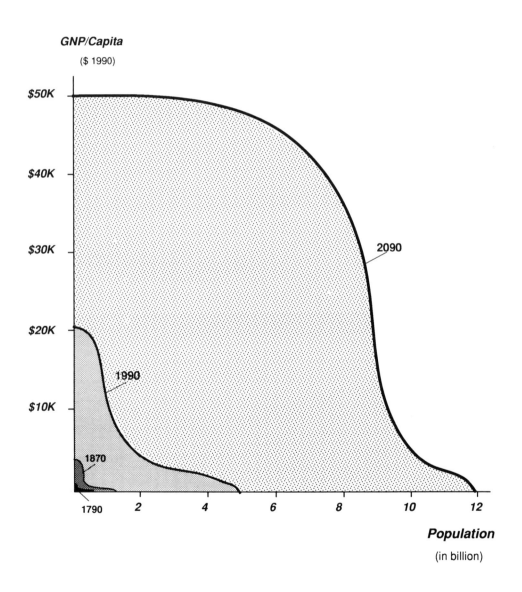

ago, would have speculated that one would eventually fly from Paris to New York in three hours in a "heavier than air" contraption, while enjoying a five-course meal and listening to the Berlin Symphony playing Beethoven. Crazy.

More interestingly, we know that we can influence growth, channel it the way we want. We know that the economy will not crash, that it is geared to grow. We also know enough about the growth process to manage it.

The economic garden began to grow luxuriantly sometime in the eighteenth century, as we learned to domesticate energy and to build productive organizations. At that time, Europeans already knew the rudiments of the market economy and how capital could best be allocated. The world economy is now exploring beyond energy, advancing into the information age. We are learning to use the microcosm, the manipulation of atoms, in a way that opens new vistas on the management of information. This will generate a new industrial revolution, and yield products and services which cannot even be imagined at this time. Economic growth, the process sustained by determined entrepreneurs and competitive organization, is continuing its relentless march. It is my hope that my gardener's musing has helped in the understanding of what is going on.

Acknowledgements

This book owes much to the assistance of numerous people. Jane Jacobs has always been an inspiration. Over the years, she encouraged me to put my thoughts and experiences into a book. Tom Axworthy was instrumental in getting me to spend four months at the Center for International Affairs, at Harvard University, in 1987. This is where the book was researched and a first version, drafted. Tom Haferd was a precious collaborator at Harvard, both as a research assistant and as a cognoscenti of the campus, making my short stay a very efficient one. The staff and colleagues at the Center provided a most supportive environment. On a Saturday night, out of the blue, I got a phone call from George Gilder, whose encouraging reactions to the first chapters, was a shot in the arm. His subsequent admonition to get the book published and "behind you" pushed me to wrap it up.

The manuscript benefited from readings by Mario Polèse, Caroline Pestiau, Roger Miller, Pierre Lortie, Daniel Denis, Pierre Lemieux, Reed Scowen and Léon Courville. Beyond providing sound editorial advice and numerous suggestions, Daniel Latouche, of L'Institut national de la recherche scientifique, and Larry Mone, of the Manhattan Institute, also spent countless hours assisting me in reaching publishers. Bruce Phillips, from the Office of Advocacy at the U.S. Small Business Administration, was most helpful in providing me with special data on job creation and the turbulent economy.

Honey Dresher was supportive from the start. She also turned out to be a wonderful editor and put me in touch with Ed Cowan, an important contribution. Tom Courchesne's interest in the book and his constant encouragements convinced me to finish the book. The financial support of the School of Policy Studies at Queen's University should not be left unmentioned. Ed Cowan and Howard Aster took upon themselves the responsibility of getting the book published. They provided solid encouragement, nudged me into finishing the manuscript and got the job done. Heather Wade of Mosaic Press was an efficient editor and Cam Mather of Axtext helped in the typesetting.

Many other people assisted me on the way. Donald Doyon reviewed the material on the Beauce. While I was in Ottawa, Nicole Guenette spent many evenings retyping, correcting and editing the manuscript. At Boston College, Richard Carroll Keeley organized a seminar on the work of Jane Jacobs at a critical time when I was developing my theories on entrepreneurship.

Finally, is should be stated that much of what is in this book reflects the unique working environment of Secor. It allowed me to work with entrepreneurs, with chief executive officers and with senior public officials, an unique blend of clients. My colleagues and the administrative staff were always supportive and it thanks to them that I was able to finish this book. And thanks also to Louise, who provided me with comfort and encouragement during these four years.

Marcel Coté
Montreal, August, 1991

ENDNOTES

Chapter Two

1. For a detailed analysis of the post-Plaza Hotel situation, see Funabashi, S., *Managing the Dollar: From the Plaza to the Louvres*, Institute for International Economics, Washington, 1988.

2. Among the doubters is Murray Feldstein who has argued specifically that the Plaza Agreement hasn't had any significant impact on the value of the U.S. dollar. See Feldstein, M.S., *New Evidence on the Effect of Foreign Exchange Intervention*, NBER Working Paper 2419, Cambridge, National Bureau of Economic Research, 1986.

3. For a review of the situation in theoritical macor-economic, see Mankiav, N. Gregory *"A Quick Refresher Course in Macroeconomies"*, Journal of Economic Literture, Vol 28, Dec. 1990, pp 1645-1660.

4. In the period 1854 to 1919, there were an average of 2.5 recessions per decade, and the average duration of a recession was 22 months. In the 37 years from 1945 to 1982, there 2.1 recessions per decade, but the duration of recessions averaged only 11 months. The average length of the business cycle went from 4.1 to 4.7 years. See Zarnowitz, Victor, *The Regularity of Business Cycles*, Working Paper 2381, National Bureau of Economic Research, Cambridge, Mass., 1987.

5. This comparison was given by Lester Throrow.

6. This broadside criticism of mainstream economic theory does not do justice to important contributions of well-known economists to the thesis developed in this book. Raymond Vernon's life-cycle hypothesis impregnates the vision of Jacobsville's economy. The life-cycle hypothesis says that new products are generated in advanced economies, usually in their

major cities. As the products mature, lower labour cost areas enter into production, competing with the advanced economies. The resulting pattern is often a shift of the production activities to these areas, while R & D remains in the advanced economies. A healthy regional economy must have a diversified economic base encompassing a well-balanced variety of young products and old products. Growth of the young products compensates for the slow growth and decline of the older products which face intense price competition from lower cost areas. Vernon's hypothesis is now found in all textbooks on international economics. The original argument is to be found in Vernon, Raymond, *International Investments and International Trade in the Product Cycle*, 1966, Quarterly Journal of Economics, Vol. 80, pp. 190-207.

CHAPTER THREE

1. Say's Law will hold provided that the producers' income is spent and that prices reflect demand and supply conditions.
2. For large metropolitan areas, with populations over one million, the percentage of basic employment to total employment can vary from a low of 15 per cent to a high of 30 per cent. (This excluded producers services sold locally.) For mid-size towns, the percentages typically vary between 20 per cent and 35 per cent. For isolated single industry towns with populations of more than 5,000, basic employment was never above 50 per cent of total employment in the several cases which I investigated in Canada.

CHAPTER FOUR

1. David Birch received a Ph.D. from Harvard Business School, where he taught marketing and became familiar with the Dun & Bradstreet's Dun Marketing Indicator. He then moved to M.I.T., to pursue his research. He built a computerized file which contained most of U.S. and Canadian business establishments, from the little hat store located on a sidestreet in Cheyenne, Missouri, to the General Motors headquarters in Detroit. For each establishment, the file contained general data such as the address, type of business, year of foundation, legal structure and number of employees, along with some financial information on their credit performance. Birch decided to trace, over time, the situation of individual establishments to see what happens to them. Under a research contract with the Small Business Administration, he looked at the evolution of the establishments in the years 1969, 1972 and 1974, and he later added 1976. The results were published in December 1979.

2.   There are numerous review articles that summarize Birch's findings. An article by Birch in the March 1981 issue of The Public Interest gives the main results of the original research. Birch published a synthesis of his finding in 1987. (Birch, David L. *Job Creation in America*, New York, The Free Press, 1987). The Office of the Chief Counsel for Advocacy, at the U.S. Small Business Administration published in June 1984 contains a good review article entitled "Job Generation". For a critical view of the respective roles of small and large businesses in job creation, see Brown, Charles, Hamilton, James and Medoff, James, *Employers Large and Small*, Cambridge, Harvard University Press, 1990. A good summary of the controversy can be found in Case, John, *The Disciples of David Birch*, Inc., January 1989, pp. 39-45. For an independent view of the whole area of research covered by Birch, see Johnson, Peter, *New Firms: An Economic Perspective*, London, Allen & Unwin, 1985. Finally, for an international perspective on the issue, see Sengenberger, Werner, Loveman, Gary and Piore, Michael, ed., *The Re-emergence of Small Enterprise: Industrial Restructuring in Industrial Economies*, Geneva, International Labour Organization, 1990.

 3.   See Averitt, Robert T., *The Dual Economy*, New York, Norton, 1968, for an explicit analysis of the respective role and importance of large and small business, as perceived by economists in the seventies.

4.   The Small Business Administration has built a national database for the American economy. The file is known as the United States Establishment and Enterprise Microdata (USEEM) file. Originally developed under contract by the Brookins Institution, it contains files for even-numbered years beginning in 1976 and ending in 1984. New files are added every two years, in conjunction with Dun & Bradstreet's updating cycles. For a general discussion of the microdata files which comprise the Small Business Data Base, see *"The Small Business Data Base: A User's Guide." (Washington, Government Printer Office, 1986.* For what seems to be the definitive compendium on the small business vs large business controversy, see Sengenberger, Loveman and Piore (op. cit.), who confirms, from an international perspective, the general thrusts of Birch's findings.

5.   In 1982, there were 105 million jobs in the U.S. economy, outside the Armed Forces. About 80 per cent of these jobs were in private organizations. The rest were accounted for by governments and by individual operators, such as a writer or an individual consultant. From 1982 to 1987, 12 million jobs were added in the U.S. economy, a gain of 12 per cent, or

an average of more than 2 per cent a year. In Canada, the growth rate was similar. In Europe, and in particular France, Germany and the U.K., practically no net new jobs were created, a few tenths of a percentage point per year. In Japan, from the trough of the business cycle in 1983, the annual rate of growth has been about 1 per cent, half of the North American rate.

Regional data also shows significant differences. Growing regions such as California have a growth rate in the order of 3 per cent and 5 per cent per year outside recession periods. On the other hand, declines in the number of jobs are sometimes encountered in "stalled" regional economies.

6. This statement is disputed by Brown, Hamilton and Medoff (ibid). They claim that large firms are gaining on small firms and thus are responsible for a larger share of the net new jobs. This is possible over a limited period. But, in a steady state situation, smaller firms must have a higher share of net new jobs. Furthermore, if technological change brings about a reduction in the average size of firms as one would suspect, then smaller firms should create more jobs than their proportion of total jobs in the economy.

7. David Birch has built a sophisticated model to explain the "flows" of jobs between business categories and how this translates itself to the growth performance of various size categories. In particular, the model demonstrates how small businesses always create more than their share of new jobs, and vice versa for large businesses. See Birch, David, *The Contribution of Small Enterprise to Growth and Employment*, in *New Opportunity for Entrepreneurship*, Herbert Giersch, ed., Tubingen, Morh, 1984.

8. The best source on the turbulence of the economy is Birch, David L., *Job Creation in America*, New York, Free Press, 1987.

9. I owe this reference to the invisible foot to Burton H. Klein, *The Slowdown in Productivity Advances: A Dynamic Explanation*, in *Technological Innovations for a Dynamic Economy*, Christopher T. Hill and James M. Utterback, ed., Center for Policy Alternatives, Cambridge, M.I.T., 1980

10. Michael E. Porter has written some of the best known works on the strategic behaviour of firms in competitive environment. See in particular *Competitive Strategy: Techniques for Analyzing Industries*, New York, The Free Press, 1980 and *The Competitive Advantage of Nations*, New York, The Free Press, 1990.

11. Jorgenson's seminal 1972 survey of econometric studies of investment behaviour established that the cost of capital was secondary to factors related to output and desired capacity utilization in investment decisions. Subsequent development in the study of investment decisions have introduced considerations about uncertainty, that is the risk at which the capital invested is subjected once it is dedicated to a specific use. This further reduces the role of the cost of capital as a determinant of investments. (Jorgenson, Dale W., *Econometric Studies of Investment Behaviour: A Survey*, Journal of Economic Literature, Dec. 1972, Vol. 9, pp. 1111-1147.)

12. Jorgenson, supra.

13. See Statistics Canada, *"Financial Statistics of Corporation"*, various issues.

14. Generally, corporations determine their level of capital investment based on their expected cash flow and their strategic needs. Then, capital budgeting, a tool where the internal rate of return and the cost of capital are used, is used to assist management in selecting between investment proposals.

15. One factor which lower the overall cost of doing business is the ability of Japanese corporations to leverage their financial structure, which allow them to benefit from the lower cost of fixed capital. On the other hand, the Japanese yen is overvalued relative to the U.S. dollar by about 25%. This disadvantage is much more significant than the advantages brought by the lower costs of capital.

16. But countries can abuse their borrowing privileges. This is presently the case of several developing countries, such as Brazil, Argentina, Mexico and Nigeria. Having borrowed too much from international lenders in the past, they must now face the music, as any overextended borrower must. A growing country, like a growing corporation, is a net capital borrower. But it usually can service its debt with the annual increase in savings generated by its rising income. The capital needed to finance a growth rate of 10 per cent a year, which is typical for fast growing countries, is significant, but largely within the borrowing capacity of most countries. A common capital-labour ratio of 3 implies that a country growing at 10 per cent a year would need the equivalent of 30 per cent of its GNP in terms of its yearly capital needs. Given the expected domestic savings, which are on the order of 20 per cent to 30 per cent of national income, such a rate of growth should not pose any serious financial problem.

The problems of the indebted countries of today are totally different. They borrowed to finance consumption needs (they all blame it on oil), and now are asked to curtail their present consumption in order to repay these debts, a politically difficult decision. In a sense, it has little to do with growth.

17. Jacob Schmookler studied the horseshoe industry patent life cycle and that of three other industries, building, chemicals, and paper. His seminal views on technological changes are as valid today as they were when he died 20 years ago. See Schmookler, Jacob, *Innovation and Economic Growth*, Cambridge, Harvard University Press, 1966 and *Patents, Invention and Economic Change: Data and Selected Essays*, Cambridge, Harvard University Press, 1972.

18. This is the major conclusion of Schmookler's lifetime work. Indeed, this whole section on the role of technology in economic growth relies on his thesis.

CHAPTER FIVE

1. I am indebted to Robert C. Ronstadt *"Entrepreneurship: Text, Cases and Notes."* Lord Publishing, 1984 for his historical notes. It is also an excellent book on entrepreneurship. A classic reference book on entrepreneurship and economic growth, Peter Kilby's *"Entrepreneurship and Economic Development"* (New York, the Free Press, 1971) deals more with developing countries. Another interesting reference book is Casson, M.C., *The Entrepreneur: An Economic Theory*, Oxford, Martin Robertson, 1982.

2. Schumpeter, Joseph A. *"The Theory of Economic Development"*, Cambridge, Mass, Harvard University Press, 1934. The German edition was first published in 1911.

3. "Creative Destruction" is often presented in a dialectical fashion, whereby waves of "newness" come and destroy the old. Schumpeter's theory of the business cycles encourages such a dialectical view. His business cycle theory postulated that an innovation is at the birth of a cycle. The economy expands as the innovation matures and spreads with imitators. But competition eliminates profits, investments fall, a recession develops. A new innovation starts the cycle again. This "tidal" view of creative destruction, necessarily associated with long waves, will most likely have the same fate as Schumpeter's theory on business cycle, a place in the history books. But creative destruction can also be seen as an ongoing small scale mechanism, whereby some new activities are im-

planted and some old activities become obsolete and fade away. This creative destruction is continually undergoing in any economy, the new replacing the old. Jane Jacobs in the *Economy of Cities* and George Gilder in *Wealth and Poverty* develop that vision.

4. Schumpeter, ibid, p. 91

5. Ronstadt (1984, Chap.2) offers a good defence of the generous view of entrepreneurs. However, he extends the concept of entrepreneurs to managers, a point of view which I do not share. In due time, the pendulum will swing back and proper recognition will be given to the role of the manager, who will become as revered as the entrepreneur is today.

6. For a good exposition of this view, see Robert C. Ronstadt, *"Entrepreneurship: Text, Cases and Notes"*, Lord Publishing, 1984, especially the first chapter, pp. 1-26.

7. For historical information on the IBM decision, see, Côté, Marcel, Allaire, Yvan, and Miller, IBM Canada, Ottawa, *Royal Commission on Corporate Concentration*, Government of Canada, 1976: Additional information on the industry comes from Augarten, Stan, *Bit by Bit: An Illustrated History of Computers*, New York, Ticknor & Field, 1984

8. These distinctions are encountered frequently in the economic literature, particularly in an attempt to reconciliate Schumpeter's restrictive definition of the entrepreneur with more generous views. For a discussion on these distinctions, see Liebenstein, Harvey, *"General X-Efficiency Theory and Economic Development"*, New York, Oxford University Press, 1978

9. By the most generous counts, high technology industries represent 15 per cent to 25 per cent of manufacturing jobs, which in turn represent 20 per cent of total employment. So making due allowance for all exceptions and other non-manufacturing high technology industries, and converting jobs into value added, one should safely arrive at less than 10 per cent of total demand.

10. George Gilder's *Spirit of Enterprise*, (New York, Basic Books, 1984) provides the best recent gallery of entrepreneurial portraits. However, like most authors, he concentrates on the great entrepreneurs, which does not necessarily give a good perspective on the whole entrepreneurial realm.

11. Stevenson, Howard H., *"A New Paradigm for Entrepreneurial Management"*, Cambridge, Harvard Business School, 1983. See also Stevenson, Howard H. and Gumpert, David E., *The Hearth of Entrepreneurship*, Harvard Business Review, March-April 1985, Vol. 63, Number 2, pp. 85-95.

12. At this point, we pass over an extensive body of scientific literature on entrepreneurial motivation. In particular, many theories associate the entrepreneurial drive with the resolution of a deep inner conflict between the entrepreneur and his father. The mother is also sometimes brought into the picture. But we heeded Stevenson's advice and have not ventured on such thin ice. For a discussion, see Ronstadt (op. cit.). There is also a less extensive body of literature which links the decision to start a business to overall business conditions, the paradox being that entrepreneurship is stimulated by the "invisible foot", which is a lot more active during bad times. However, the evidence does not present a clear-cut picture. See Brenner, Reuven and Courville, Léon *"Industrial Strategy: Inferring What It Really Is*, in McFetridge, Donald G., ed *"Economics Of Industrial Policy and Strategy"*, Research Studies, Volume V, Royal Commission on the Economic Union and on Development Prospects for Canada, Ottawa, Government of Canada, 1986

13. I have often observed the situational phenomenon that Stevenson speaks about in regions, cities and small towns where entrepreneurship has taken off with a remarkable effervescence that makes it easy to observe and analyze. Johnson (1984) presents interesting data that clearly demonstrate this point. Rate of formation in manufacturing in the UK varied by a factor of five between regions. The various factors accounting for such differences are discussed. A few years ago, I sat down with an old friend, Dr. Roger Miller, a professor of Business Strategy at the University of Quebec in Montreal, and a partner at Secor, who specializes in studies of high technology industries. We put our experience together to develop a "situational" model to explain the emergence of high technology clusters such as the Silicon Valley and Route 128 around Boston. The resulting model was first presented in an article published in the Harvard Business Review of July-August 1985. We later wrote a book about it. *"Growing the Next Silicon Valley"* (Lexington Press, 1987). The model is not specific to high technology and applies to all types of entrepreneurship.

14. The literature on the motivation of entrepreneurs is abundant. See Ronstadt (1984) for a survey.

15. This is known as the "push or pull" issue. For a discussion of the issue and a somewhat favourable treatment of the push factors, see Johnson, Peter, *"New Firms: An Economic Perspective"*, London, Allen & Unwin, 1984, pp. 69-83. Cooper, Arnold C. and Dunkelberg, William C.l, *Entrepreneurship and Path to Business Ownership*, (Strategic Manage-

ment Journal, 1986, Vol. 7, pp. 53-68) analyzed nearly 900 start-ups and found that pushes were involved in 22 per cent of the ventures. See also Brenner, Reuven and Courville, Leon *"Industrial Strategy: Inferring What It Really is"* in *"Economics of Industrial Policy and Strategy*, McFetridge, Donald G., ed., Royal Commission on the Economic Union and Development Prospects for Canada, University of Toronto Press, Toronto, 1985, for a discussion of this literature.

16. The literature on the conditions leading to a new venture is not that extensive. Cooper and Dunkelberg (op. cit.)provide a good review of the literature as of 1986 and of the main hypotheses on which the present consensus is based. They also present empirical results based on a survey of 890 start-ups. Only one result is somewhat at a variance with the thesis developed in the following chapter. They found that 25 per cent of the founders had moved when they started their business, a surprisingly high percentage. They do not comment on this result. Further research is warranted to know more about the specifics of the "move" involved and of the nature of the businesses. I would make the hypothesis that those entrepreneurs that moved prior to starting their businesses tended to be local copycat entrepreneurs and entrepreneurs that came back "home" to launch their ventures. Cooper, Arnold C. and Dunkelberg, William C., *"Entrepreneurship and Paths to Business"*, Strategic Management Journal, Vol. 7, pp. 53-68, 1986.

CHAPTER SIX

1. The earliest reference I found for the term incubator as I used it is M. Beesley *The Birth and Death of Industrial Establishments: Experience in the West Midlands Conurbation*, Journal of Industrial Economics, Vol. 4, No. 1, 1955, pp. 45-61.

2. Cooper and Dunkelberg (op. cit.) found that 36 per cent of their start-up entrepreneurs became "owners" at age 30 or less, 39 per cent between 31 and 40, and 25 per cent at 41 or more. Their paper does not distinguish between local and basic entrepreneurs and between innovative and copycat entrepreneurs.

3. Nevertheless, very few of these Cambridge high-technology firms have developed into medium-size and large-size firms. They are "soft" high-technology firms, more attuned to sub-contracting than to developing and marketing proprietary products on a world-wide basis. The original incubating organizations are major contributors to this particular orientation.

4. Managing the conditions which "loosen" this loose change is a highly strategic policy area. I have been involved in two major studies of the issue of supplying equity investments to start-ups and to small businesses. Given the nature of the investment decision, the number of such decisions which have to be made in a healthy economy, and the low performance of any diagnostic tool, I have become sceptical of any measure which is not broad-based and structured around investments by non-professional individual investors. Broad-based tax measures appear to be the most efficient approach, although I have yet to see a very efficient tax scheme. Measures to assist equity financing of small business have a way of ending up favouring real estate investments and other types of standard, safe investments where the market is already efficient. On the other hand, another well-publicized route, venture capital firms, is such a high cost route that it is not practical: it will never reach more than a small percentage of the new ventures. See *The Report of the Commission of Inquiry on the Financing of Small and Medium-Size Business*, Department of Industry and Commerce, Government of Quebec, 1984.

5. The term Beta-site seems to have originated in engineering. The first prototype is the Alpha model. The second one, which is the one first delivered to a client, is the Beta model. Thus, the first clients are associated with the Beta model. The term is generalized to the company who is the first client of a high-technology start-up.

6. Charles F. Sabel argues that a broad trend toward such attitudes is presently developing in U.S. manufacturing, in almost all sectors, particularly those which have been exposed to Japanese and European industrial practices.

7. St-Georges' main weakness is its technological base. The entrepreneurs have succeeded more on the basis of lower costs than technological innovation. Furthermore, its remoteness and relatively small size make St-Georges unattractive to immigrants. St-Georges' challenge is to enrich its technological base and open avenues to sources of new ideas.

8. The investment was made in 1957. Before it went public in 1966, the equity of Digital Equipment was valued at $26.5 million, or $750 a share. The stock was then split by 50, giving ARD 1,750,000 shares. The stock has split 18 more times to date. Value Line estimates the stock will vary in the $100 to $150 range in the nineties. It peaked at $160 in 1987. See also The Wall Street Journal, Aug. 8, 1966, p. 15.

9. See Small Business Administration, "The Informal Supply of Capital", Washington, 1988, which suggest that the amount of informal capital

is about ten times as improtant as the formal venture capital supplied by institutions.

10. See George Gilder, (1981) for a forceful defence of this general idea.

11. See Piore, Michael J. and Sabel, Charles F., *Italian Business: Lessons for U.S. Industrial Policy, in American Industry in International Competition*, J. Zysman and L. Tyson, eds., Ithaca, Cornell University Press, 1983.

CHAPTER VII

1. For more on what Chief Executive Officers of large corporations do, see the classic study by Henry Mintzberg, *The Nature of Managerial Work*, New York, Harper & Row, 1973.

2. An exact count is difficult to obtain, as difficulties are encountered in identifying the smallest businesses. Part of the problem is one of definition. Is a writer working at home a business? The mushrooming of autonomous workers has blurred significantly the frontiers between small businesses and autonomous workers, making somewhat meaningless any actual count of businesses. Another problem is the existence of several legal corporations operating from the same physical plant. Indeed, many small businesses operate under more than one corporate identity. Given the large number of small businesses, this makes it very difficult to get an accurate count. I estimate the number of "businesses" in the United States and Canada at 8 million with a 10% margin of error. At least a third of these businesses are entrepreneurial, intimately tied to one person, and belonging to the entrepreneurial realm. (One can also add to the entrepreneurial realm all the autonomous workers). This suggests that the production realm in North America is made up of 5 to 6 million businesses. Over 95% of these businesses are small businesses with a few employees.

3. There is an impressive body of scientific literature on management studies. Very seldom does it reach the general public. But there are also books which are addressed to the general public. In the early eighties, Tom Peters and Robert Waterman, two consultants at McKinsey & Co., wrote the international best-seller In Search of Excellence, which focused on the best-managed companies. But indirectly, it was a scathing indictment of large American corporations. (Peters, Tom and Waterman, Robert, *In Search of Excellence*, 1984, Simon & Schuster, New York.) The academic literature which is of interest to us deals with the productivity debate which has been going on for several years and is centered on whether U.S. productivity growth has entered a period of structural

decline. The majority view is that the United States (and Canada) faces a major productivity problem. For a typical view of this position, see William Ouchi, *The M-Form Society*, Addison-Wesley, Reading, 1984. The other school of thought is best illustrated by Lawrence, Robert "*Can America Compete?*", Brookings Institution, Washington, 1984, who argues that the U.S. competitiveness is not declining and that as soon as the effects of the revaluation of the yen are felt, it will become clear that the U.S. still has a productivity leadership. Finally, Porter (1990) takes a clinical view of the issue, focusing on the competitiveness of specific industries.

4.   There is a new field of "organizational economics" which is emerging in the literature, which aims at getting a better grasp of corporate behaviour. For an overview of this field, see Barney, Jay B. and Ouchi, William G., ed., *Organizational Economics*, San Francisco, Jossey-Bass, 1986. Gordon Donaldson and Jaw W. Lorsch, of the Harvard Business School, have probably best described the functioning of the large organization at the top, in *Decision Making at the Top: the Shaping of Strategic Decisions*, New York Basic Books, 1983. They emphasize the financial aspect of the decision making process. Milton Leontiades, in *Managing the Unmanageable*, (Addison-Wesley, Reading, MA, 1986), concentrates on the attitudes and strategic thinking of senior management. I made extensive use of the concept presented in these two books in this chapter and the following one.

5.   Michael E. Porter, *Competitive Strategy* (New York, Free Press, 1980) is generally considered the path-breaking work in modern corporate strategic analysis. One of my partners at Secor, Yvan Allaire and his wife, Mihaele Firserotu, have written extensively on strategy from the perspective of the CEO. See Allaire, Yvan and Firserotu, Mihaele E., *Strategic Plans as Contracts*, Long Range Planning, Vo. 23, No. 1, pp 102-115, 1990, for a good synthetic presentation of their approach.

6.   McGraw-Hill conducts an annual survey of R&D expenditures in large U.S. corporations. The highlights are published every June in Business Week. The above information is taken from these reports.

7.   See Allaire, Yvan and Firserotu, Mihaele E., *Theories of Organizational Culture*, Organizational Studies, 1984, Vol. 3, pp 193-226, for a survey of the various approaches to corporate culture.

8.   Generically, this modern management system, developed mostly in the United States, has been adopted throughout the world. Indeed, the American business schools, who contributed much to its development,

have been attracting the best students from all over the world and have served as models for the prestigious business schools in foreign countries.

9. Autonomous workers, who rely mostly on contractual work, now represent 15 per cent of the workforce, if Canadian data are extrapolated to all advanced economies.

10. Oliver Williamson argues that in a turbulent environment, large corporations will internalize peripheral activities to minimize the frequent transaction costs associated with them. In a placid corporate environment, these transactions are less frequent, and thus large organizations in placid environments should rely more on outside suppliers. Williamson has not given significant attention to the benefit of flexibility. Turbulent environments encourage the use of subcontractors, and placid environments encourage the use of internal operations, the opposite of what a strict analysis of transaction costs concludes. See Williamson, Oliver, *The Economic Institution of Capitalism*, Cambridge, Harvard University Press, 1984, pp.   .

11. Makino, Noboru, Decline and Prosperity: *Corporate Innovation in Japan,* New York, Kodansha International (Harper & Row), 1987.

12. See Nayak, P. Banganath and Ketteringham, John M. *Break-throughs!*, Rawson Associates, New York, 1986.

13. In the early seventies, in the heyday of the big corporation, they were running at the rate of 7,000 a year.

14. That a higher return would have been received if the money had been left in the bank is the usual conclusion of the editors of Fortune who conducted an annual survey of the largest "deals". Half of the businesses acquired in the seventies by large corporations had been sold off in the mid-eighties. For an overview, see *Corporate Takeovers: Causes and Consequences*, Edited by Aan Auerbach, Chicago, University of Chicago Press, 1987.

15. A study of 1,000 mergers in the U.S. of $10 million and more from 1948 to 1979 indicates that the stock price of the acquiring firm rises generally after an acquisition. See Lubalkin, Michael, *"Merger Strategies and Stockholder Value"*, Strategic Management Journal, Vol. 8, 1987, pp. 39-53.

16. See Lubalkin (1987) for a review of the literature.

17. For a review of this literature, see Lichtenberg, Frank R., *Industrial De- Diversification and its Consequences for Productivity*, National Bureau of Economic Research, Working Paper 3231, January 1990.

18. Reich, Robert B. *"The Next American Frontier"*, New York, Times

Book, 1983.

19. See in particular Shleifer, Andrei and Summers, Lawrence, *"Hostile Takeover as Breaches of Trust,"* working paper, NBER, 1987, for a summary of Lawrence Summer's position.

20. The evidence in the 1980's takeover wave suggests that the overall impact is positive, as inefficient management was pruned out. Over 20 percent of the Forture 500 firms were involved in mergers involving some sort of hostile innitiative. The net effect appears to have been a leaner more focus production realm. See Jensen, Michael, *"Takeover: their Causes and Consequences"*, Journal of Economic Perspectives, Vol 2, No 1, pp 21-48. and Jarrell, Gregg A., Brickley, James A. and Netter, Jeffry M., *"The Market for Corporate Control: the Emperical Evidence since 1980"*, Journal of Economic Perspectives, Vol 2, No. 1, pp 49-68.

21. About 40 per cent of the acquisitions and mergers involves a divestiture, according to Mergerstat Review, Merril Lynch Business Brokerage & Valuation (W.T. Grimm & Co.).

CHAPTER VIII

1. Most of the references to the automobile industry throughout the book can be traced back to research done through the Massachusetts Institute of Technology's International Motor Vehicle Program. Dr. Roger E. Miller, university associate at Secor, was a member of the research team and has provided most useful insights on the situation and challenges of the industry. The results of the program are condensed in Womack, James P., Jones, Daniel T. and Roos, Daniel, *The Machine that Changed the World*, Rawson Associated, NEW York, 1990.

2. Indeed, one person was asking tough questions. H. Ross Perrot joined the board of GM in 1984 after selling to GM the firm he had founded for $1.2 billion, making him the largest GM stock holder. He asked tough questions and soon feuded with GM's CEO. He was literally paid to leave GM's board two years later, in 1986. His brief but intense encounter with GM top brass is chronicled in an even-handed way by Doron P. Levin, in *"Irreconciable Differences: Ross Perot versus General Motors"*, Little Brown, Boston, 1989.

3. The Japanese way was developed mostly at Toyota, the leading Japanese manufacturer, and then adopted by all other Japanese manufacturers. Takashi Hono, a Toyota senior executive, is usually credited as the father of the system, which is characterized by three major features. First, quality is paramount, as the Japanese marketplace will not tolerate faulty

design or faulty workmanship. Thus, the whole line of production can be stopped to fix a small problem. Zero-defect is fundamental. Second, inventories are minimized. This is a Japanese fixation. An offshoot of that is a tightly-controlled production chain. Thirdly, flexibility is built into the system. With seven domestic manufacturers, the Japanese compete in the automobile market through product differentiation. This results in a highly segmented marketplace, which demand flexibility.

4. See Cohen, Stephen S. and Zysman, John, *"Why Manufacturing Matters: The Myth of the Post-Industrial Economy."*, New York, Basic Books, 1987.

5. The evidence indicates, however, that during the 1980s, U.S. manufacturing made significant gains, as a result of the corporate restructuring which took place and the lower dollar.

6. Hirshman, Albert O., *Exit, Voice and Loyalty*, Cambridge, Harvard University Press, 1970.

7. For a comparison between Japan and the U.S., see Lyman, John, *Governments, Markets and Growth*, Ithaca, Cornell University Press, 198x. For an analysis of the European situation, see Hall, Peter A., *Governing the Economy*, New York, Oxford University Press, 1986.

8. See Womack (op.cit.) for an extensive analysis of the Toyota system.

9. Porter (1990) provides a good summary of the competitive conditions in Japan.

10. American corporations argue, correctly, that they are frustrated in their attempt to penetrate the Japanese market, by a maze of legal restrictions and restrictive commercial practices. Only a few corporations managed to break into the Japanese market early. IBM entered Japan in the 1950s with a wholly-owned subsidiary, and got its usual dominant market share. McDonald's has also been in Japan for a long time. Their success proves that the Japanese are not supermen. Indeed, there are many inefficiencies in the Japanese economy. It is not surprising that U.S. firms have a larger share of the Japanese market than the Japanese have of the U.S. market. But U.S. firms manufacture in Japan, whereas the Japanese still export to the U.S., having not yet mastered the skills of managing multinational corporations operating in several countries.

11. In 1988, according to an analysis done by Secor on the comparative costs of car assembly in Japan and in Canada, the Japanese still had lower average labour costs than the North American producers, but the differences were fairly narrow. In 1991, the advantage had shifted toward North America. Peter Hooper and Karin Laren, economists at the Federal

Reserve in Washington, were quoted in the New York Times (4-21-1991) as estimating that unit costs in the United States were now 80% of those in Japan.

12. If a country becomes the banker to the world, it could prolong the duration of a chronic deficit. But this country will eventually learn one basic difference between a stock adjustment (the capital account) and a flow (the current account): the latter has a lot more stamina. Chronic international borrowers are also reminded of this simple truth by their bankers.

13. Some small countries are more able than other countries to avoid the crippling effect of a ballooning trade surplus. The Gulf emirates, Kuwait, and Saudi Arabia were able to run a sizable chronic surplus in their balances of trade in the past, by not repatriating their exports earnings. Nevertheless, a significant amount of their foreign earnings did enter their economy. Inevitably, these small countries went on unsurpassed import binges, which in less than 15 years radically transformed their economy. They were not able to immunize their economies from the necessary offsetting adjustments to the surge in the value of their exports.

14. Although these practices are often attributed to the Japanese, they started long before the present infatuation with Japanese management practices. Consider worker's involvement on the factory floor. In the late 1960s, the way the Swedish car manufacturer Volvo organized its shop floor, around small worker teams, was widely reported in business magazines. However, American manufacturing companies were not paying much attention to this issue until the Japanese success with high productivity using such a system became widely discussed in the 1980s. Workers' participation and decentralized management, also features of new management practices in manufacturing, were debated in business schools in the early seventies, where such models as those of Lincoln Manufacturing, who pioneered the practice of rewarding workers on the basis of the profitability of the company, and Linear Semiconductor, which developed worker participation, were routinely studied in the classroom. But these experiences were seen as somewhat deviant, until the productivity debate of the early 1980s.

15. Already in 1983, Abernathy, Clark and Cantrow were noticing a strong renaissance in industrial practices in the U.S. manufacturing industry, and in particular in the automobile industry. See Abernathy, William J., Clark, Kim B. and Cantrow, Alan M., *Industrial Renaissance:*

Producing a Competitive Future for America, New York, Basic Books, 1983.

CHAPTER NINE

1. Edgar S. Dunn is the scholar who has first developed this theory and who has introduced the distinction between managerial and development networks. See Dunn, E.S., *A Flow Network Image of Urban Structures*, Regional Studies, 1971, and Dunn, Edgar S., "The Development of the U.S. Urban System", Baltimore, Johns Hopkins University Press, Vol. I and Vol. II, 1980 and 1983. See also Noyelle, Thierry J. and Stanback, Thomas, *The Economic Transformation of American Cities*, Totowa, NJ, Rowman & Allanheld, 1983, who use Dunn's concept in their analysis of the post war evolution of the urban system. According to Thierry and Stanback, the concentration of producer services in some large cities, a result of their strong development networks, and the decentralization of production activities as managerial networks get more extensive, are the prime forces which reshape the urban structure in the United States.

2. Edgar S. Dunn, the scholar who developed the concept, put it this way: "Many of these creative activities, particularly the entrepreneurial functions, seek locations in the dominant centre and major sub-centres of the urban mega-system. The research, design and political functions are characterized by more intermittent transfers and can frequently be asymmetrical with respect to the topology of a central place hierarchy. In any case, the tendency is to create agglomerated communities of scholars, financiers, politicians, etc."

The passage was taken from Noyelle and Stanback, op. cit., p. 40., quoting Edgar S. Dunn Jr. Robert E. Lucas attributed the high price of office space in central business districts to the value added by the convergence of these networks and the advantages of physical proximity for doing business. See Lucas, Robert E., *On the Mechanics of Economic Development*, W.A. Mackintosh Lecture 1985, Discussion Paper no. 657, Queen's University, August 1986

3. These views were presented in Vernon, Raymond, *International Investment and International Trade in the Product Cycles*, Quarterly Journal of Economics, 1966. The model presented in this paper deals more specifically with an international environment, but it applies to regions as many applied it later on. Vernon himself used the concept in discussing the New York region in Vernon, Raymond, *Metropolis 1985*,

New York, Twenty Century Fund, 196?.

4. This is a well developed argument in regional economics. For an old reference, see Thompson, W.R., *A Preface to Industrial Economics*, Baltimore, John Hopkins University Press, 1965.

5. I am indebted to Peter Drucker for this point which he develops in an article in the Wall Street Journal, *"The Rise and Fall of the Blue-Collar Worker"*, (WSJ, April 22, 1987, p. 32).

6. Blue-collar workers in manufacturing are well paid. At the turn of the century, it took a blue-collar worker three years to earn the money to buy the cheapest car available at the time. A well-paid blue-collar worker today has a total annual compensation of the order of $50,000, seven to eight time the price of the cheapest cars available on the market. Korean blue-collar workers' annual earnings, on the other hand, are still below the price of a low-cost car.

7. Lester Thurow has documented these factors in a series of popular books. In particular, see Thurow, Lester C., *"The Zero-Sum Society,"* New York, Basic books, 1980, and *"Dangerous Currents"*, Random House, 1983, New York.

8. Waniski, Jude, *"How the Economy Works"*. Morristown, Polyconomics, 1978.

9. The following analysis is the traditional neo-classical analysis, which handles well the adaptation of a region to exogenous growth. What it does not do well is to explain growth.

10. Real per capita income is used to measure both economic well-being and the level of economic development. In neither case is it an accurate measure. But it is available, widely used and relatively sufficient for most purposes. Transfer payments, especially in poorer regions, introduce significant differences between earned income and total income. Earned income is a much better measure of the level of economic development. On the other hand, total income better reflects economic well-being. Economic growth can translate into lower rate of growth in total income, due to falling transfer payments.

11. Olson, Marcus, *"The Rise and Decline of Nations; Economic Growth, Stagflation and Social Rigidities"*, New Haven. Yale University Press, 1982.

CHAPTER TEN

1. See Mundell, Robert A., *"A Theory of Optimum Currency Area"*, American Economic Review, Vol. 51, September 1961, pp. 657-665

2.   Between 1979, at the inception of the European Monetary System, and 1987, the Danish Krone lost 26% of its value relative to the German Mark. Most of the changes were in step of 2% to 4%. It should also be known that most other EMS currencies depreciated by 20% or more against the Mark during the period.

3.   See Jacobs, Jane, *Cities and the Wealth of Nations*, Random House, New York, 1984. The Lao Tzu quotation at the beginning of the Chapter is also from the same source.

4.   A 1% cost on all international trade transaction amounts to a fraction of 1% of the GNP. If because the money is better valued, the economy grows faster, such costs will be absorbed by a few months of additional growth. The same applies to the cost of uncertainty. The costs borne by capital transactions are mostly irrelevant, for most of these transactions are triggered about by the existence of different currency areas, as speculators try to take advantage of different interest rates conditions. It is surprising how little research has been done on the "savings" of a common currency. The issue was somewhat debated among economists in the seventies, when the idea of a common European currency was first proposed. But the goals of the proponents of a common currency were lower inflation and fixed exchange rates. (For a good presentation of the arguments put forward see Magnifico, Giovani, *European Monetary Unification*, John Wiley and Sons, New York and Toronto, 1973.) The more recent attempt at a unified European currency pursues the same goal, price stability.   The care for a single currency is put forward in a publication of the European Economic Commission *"One Market, One Money"*, *European Economy*, "EEC, Brussels, Nov. 44, October 1990. It is a very deceptive analysis. There is no real attempt to assess the benefits of a properly valued currency.   Moreover, there is no analysis of the optimality of the Commerce market as a single currency area.   Given the low labour mobility between countries, it is definitely not an optimal area. Europe would pay a very dear price for price stability if it has to form a single currency area to get it.

5.   The Bank of Canada argues that in allowing the Canadian dollar to fall and then rise in the eighties, it spread the impact of changes in some sectors of the economy to the whole of the economy. See its Annual Report, 1990.

6.   For an analysis of the performance of the small European countries, see Katzenstein, Peter J., *"Small States in World Market"*, Cornell University Press, Ithaca and London, 1985

7.   Gilder also argue to the surge in the dollar in the early eighties was

caused by the strength of the U.S. computer sector and other export-related sectors. Gilder George, *American Technology at Fire-Sale Prices*, Forbes, January 22, 1990, Volume 145, No. 2, p. 60.

8. The analytical models used by economists rest on generalized sets of assumptions, some of which become inapplicable in specific situations. The response of mainstream economists to the effects of currency devaluation is a case in point. The standard position of economists on devaluation is that it seldom works because it generates its own off-setting inflation. The decrease in the exchange rate brings about a reduction in real wages, but workers bid back their wages to their previous level as the market conditions for their services are unchanged. If prices go up, their wage demands go up. Such an argument misses two points. First, it does not take into account the reaction of the tradeable sector of the economy, the exporters and the import- substitutors. As the value of the currency falls they face a significant improvement in their price conditions, three to four time as high as the unfavourable inflationary impact face by labour as a whole. Thus the economic base get a significant break, allowing for a change in output which then generate its own multiplier effect. Second, economic models do not generally take into account the relative speed of adjustments of the economic base to the better price environment, compare to that of the overall factor markets to the higher price level. When devaluation is not a chronic situation, the evidence suggests that the tradeable production sector adjust much more rapidly. As a consequence devaluation and revaluation can have real impact on the economy.

9. See Maddison, Angus, *Phases of Capitalist Development*, Oxford University Press, Oxford, 1982. See also Maddison, Angus, *The World Economy in the 20th Century*, OECB, Paris, 1989, for the latest years.

10. Despite the wide availability of PPS, some people still cling to exchange rate to national convert economic data. This is often the case of proponents of the these of the decline of the United States. For example, see Kennedy, Paul, *Fin-de-Siècle America*, The New York Review of Books, June 28, 1990, p. 37, for a sleight-of-hand rejection of PPS.

11. For a review of the recent research on Purchasing Power Parity, see Blades, Derek, and Roberts, David, *Note sur les nouvelles parités de pouvoir d' achat de référence de l' OCDE pour 1985*, Revue Économique de l'OCDE, Paris, Automne 1987.

CHAPTER ELEVEN

1. The figures are in equivalent U.S. dollars using purchasing power

standards developed by the O.E.C.D.

2. For a typical treatment, which runs nearly 250 pages and addresses only the rate of change of productivity, see Litan, Robert E., Lawrence, Robert Z. and Schultze, Charles L.," *American Living Standards: Threats and Challenges*", The Brookins Institution, Washington, 1988.

3. The OECD publishes regular analyses of the economic policies of its member countries. On the whole, these small countries are not held as models of good economic management, the exception being Switzerland, widely admired for its monetary policy.

4. The term was coined by the influential Japanese economist Kenichi Ohmae.

5. The Triad countries missing from Table 10.1 are Luxembourg, Ireland, Spain, Portugal, Greece and Israel. All of them, save Luxembourg, had a 1985 GNP per capita in the $5,000 to $8,000 range, a much lower level than other Triad countries.

6. According to U.S. Commerce Department data, Massachusetts per capita income is 21 per cent above the U.S. average in 1986. The richest state, Connecticut, has a per capita income 33 per cent above the U.S. average. According to the U.S. Annual Statistical Yearbook, Switzerland in 1985 had a income per capita 20 per cent above the United States average.

7. For a detailed comparative analysis of labour required to assemble a car, see Womack (op. cit.).

8. Mancur Olson and Christopher Lasch are two well-known representative of that school of thought.

CHAPTER TWELVE

1. David N. Allen and Victor Levine (*Nurturing Advanced Technology Enterprises*, New York, Praeger, 1986) are also somewhat critical of incubators. Based in Penn State, these two authors had the opportunity to observe incubators in Pennsylvania, one of the areas where they are most common. Roger Miller and I are more critical in *Growing the Next Silicon Valley*.

2. See Malone, Michael, *The Big Score*, New York, Double Day, 1985.

3. I am all in favour of these real estate operations and have designed numerous strategies to this effect. Suburbs in large metropolitan areas should have an "industrial strategy", an expedient misnomer to describe a coherent approach to optimize its industrial and commercial mix.

4. Several propositions were floated in the early 1980s to rebuild the

infrastructure of America, as part of an industrial strategy. If new infrastructures are needed, then this is justified. But if it is done solely on the basis of providing a stimuli to the economy, strong reservations can be expressed. While rebuilding a community's infrastructures makes sense if the federal government pays for it, it is a zero-sum game for the whole country, as these expenditures are not very productive in a dynamic sense.

5. There are few better testimonials to the lucidity of capitalism than Barron's, a weekly paper that covers publicly-owned companies. In the March 30, 1987 issue, a review of the main corporations in the semiconductor industry was presented, separating the mostly good apples, from a few large rotten ones.

6. This anecdote was told by Eastern Asia specialist at a Harvard seminar in 1987.

7. George Gilder documents some of the targeting problems that Japanese entrepreneurs had with MITI. The errors and shortsightedness documented leave no doubt about the inefficiencies of targeting. See George Gilder, *The Spirit of Enterprise*, New York, Simon & Schuster, 1984. For other reviews on Japan see Krugman, Paul R., *"Targeted Industrial Policies: Theories and Evidence"*, in *Industrial Change in Public Policy,* The Federal Reserve Bank of Kansas City, 1984. For France, another ambitious targeter, see De Will, Francois, *"French Industrial Policy From 1945-1981: An Assessment"*, in Adams, F. Gerard and Klein, Lawrence, R., ed., *Industrial Policy for Growth and Competitiveness*, Lexington, Mass., D.C. Heath, 1983.

8. In 1984, Hufbauer and Rosen estimated that protectionism in the six major sectors cost the U.S. consumers $49.9 billion, or 1 per cent of personal income. Textiles accounted for half of the costs. Quoted in Fortune, *Protectionism can't protect jobs*, May 11, 1987.

9. This description of the adjustment process supposes that the various elements of the balance of payments are independent of each others, except through the effects of the exchange rates.

10. Reich, Robert and Donohue, John D., *New Deals: The Chrysler Revival and the American System*, New York Times Books, 1985.

11. There is a rethinking underway among economists of the traditional trade theory, on which opposition to protectionism is founded. The "new international economics", often associated with the MIT professor Paul Krugman, takes into account the fact that the economic advantages of nations are now based mostly on their "business" endowment, that is their production realm, and the know- how, the people, the facilities and the

strategies which are associated with this endowment. Policies which make their production realm more competitive should be pursued. That has led some economists to promote selective "trade policies". But that leads us to the other objections raised in this Chapter. See Krugman, Paul R., *Rethinking International Trade,* MIT Press, Cambridge, 1990.

CHAPTER THIRTEEN

1.   Smithburg is a composite of many towns which I have analyzed in the past 15 years in Quebec, northern Ontario and New Brunswick. I have seen wild grass multiplying and sprouts appearing in these towns. Indeed, wild grass grows everywhere. The objective of a strategy is to build on that initial development to seed activities with higher potential.

2.   Indeed, this is the rationale for the Chrysler bailout which is solidly defended by Robert Reich and John D. Donahue in *"New Deals: The Chrysler Revival and the American System,* New York, Times Books, 1985

3.   The program is managed by the Ontario Department of Revenue and is known as the Small Business Development Corporation program. As soon as an investor or a group of investors registered their SBDC, 25 per cent of the capital has to be put into a trust. They can invest the rest in eligible investments. A few weeks after the registration is entered at the Department of Revenue, grants equal to the 25 per cent are given to the investors. "The cheque is in the mail" is a powerful motivator in the program. The Department subsequently audits the investments and release the 25 per cent in trust, which is free from any further restriction. (Incidentally, giving a grant of 25 per cent is an imaginative application of a consumption tax approach. Savings invested in small business equity are untaxed).

4.   Denis, Daniel, **Le Programme REA**, Montréal, Bourse de Montréal, 1988.

5.   Defining what is an establishment is a major problem at the low end, those that have only a few employees and which are relatively new. Susan Briley has tackled this problem. (Briley, Susan, *Finding the New Firm,* in Proceeding of the Academy of Management, Pierce, John A. and Robinson, Richard, etc., Boston, Academy of Management, 1984). For monitoring purposes, I use a simple rule, a cut-off at four employees or less. I assume that these firms are not in the economic base. Since these firms collectively are not large employers, it does not make much of a difference on the job count. Moreover, exceptions are allowed whenever it is warranted.

I found this rule satisfactory except on one count, dating the birth of a new firm. It is a minor drawback when the survey is done for the purpose of clinical interventions.

6. Every year, Rand-McNally publishes a detailed analysis of the major American cities on various criteria. A startling conclusion which is evident by merely looking at the list, is that the best North American cities to live in are all slow growth, such as Buffalo and Pittsburgh, etc. The fast-growing cities have all sorts of growing pains which make living there rather unpleasant.

7. Local taxes do not play a big role in economic development, at least within the range commonly encountered, as many studies have demonstrated.

8. Unfortunately, developers are often the most visible element of the business community. Developers are passive elements in the growth process. Office development and improvement of commercial neighbourhoods are induced by the development of the economic base and not vice versa. Stories that corporation XYZ is not coming to this city because it could not find space are mostly apocryphal developer hype. Indeed, in terms of commercial and office space, most cities are overbuilt. This tendency to overbuild, that is putting up oversized buildings, can slowly destroy a downtown area. Too many developers build to clean the market for the next few years. The resulting fifty- and sixty-story tall buildings create monstrous urban problems which are passed to taxpayers. Minneapolis is a charming city, a city that works well and where the entrepreneurial spirit is strong. The downtown business centre houses some of the best architecturally designed buildings in North America. Yet, the downtown area is also an urban disaster, dominated by a few giant phallic symbols planted in a desert of parking lots. A limited number of monster buildings, 50 stories and more, have sucked up so much demand for space that the downtown core does not have this multitude of good sized office towers which ensure that the variety spreads around the downtown core. Naturally, speculators hold onto parking lots and low-level buildings hoping that an obsessed CEO will lay his eyes on a site to plant his flagpole. New affirmative buildings can be important as morale boosters in depressed cities. This happened in Detroit in the mid-seventies and in Cleveland in the early eighties. But now that all large cities are overbuilt, business should be wary of developers. In the pursuit of their deals, they often give a bad image to the whole business community.

9. A good overview of what is being done is provided by an annual

survey by The Corporation for Economic Development, *Making the Grade: The Annual Development Report Card for the States"*, The Corporation for Enterprise Development, 1725 K Street, Washington, D.C.

10. **George Gilder**, *"Microcosm: the Quantum Revolution in Economics and Technology*, Simon & Schuster, New York, 1989

CHAPTER FOURTEEN

1. The MacDonald Commission, as it was generally known, published its report in 1985. Royal Commission on the Economic Union and Development Prospects for Canada, The Report, Government of Canada, Ottawa, 1985.

2. The U.S. counterpart is President Reagan's President's Commission on Industrial Competitiveness, which also published its report in 1985.

3. See Dertouzos, Michael L., Lester, Richard K, and Solow, Robert M., *Made in America: Regaining the Productive Edge*; the MIT Commission on Industrial Productivity, The MIT Press, Cambridge.

4. Porter (1989).

5. For a good book from the seventies on the supply-side revolution, see the third edition (1989) of Jude Wanniski's *"The Way The World Works"*, and in particular Robert L. Bartley's introduction. For an assessment, see Lindsay, Lawrence B., *The Growth Experiment*, Basic Books, New York, 1990.

6. Many explanations have been advanced to explain the greater stability of the economy. Better information systems, which allow corporations to avoid huge inventory imbalances, a more service-oriented economy, which adjusts more readily to demand conditions and the bulkier presence of governments in the economy are the three most common explanations. Edward Yardini, of Prudential-Bache, is the economist most strongly associated with the position that recessions, other than those caused by central banks, are things of the past.

7. The whole issue of aggregate demand management is beyond the scope of this book. Suffice it to say that a significant proportion of economists are far from convinced that governments are not more responsible for causing recessions than for curing them. But whatever the cause, the situation is improving.

8. George Gilder and other supply-side economists offer a different explanation. The U.S. exchange rate increased in value under the

pressures of surging exports of computer-related products.

9. The Plaza Accord and the Louvre Accord were attempts to stabilize the value of the U.S. dollar. Many economists have argued that they were not effective at all. Martin Felstein, a noted American economist who was President Reagan's first economic adviser in 1984, has expressed such a view in The Economist, January 1989.

10. Many economists are calling for a return to fixed exchange rates, an improved version of the gold standard and of the Bretton Wood arrangement. See McKinnon, Ronald I., *"Monetary and Exchange Rate Policies for International Financial Stability: A Proposal"*, Journal of Economic Perspectives, Vo. 2, No. 1, Winter 1988, pp 83-103.

11. Privatization also encompasses the devolution to the private sector of activities done in the public sector. But the common discussion of privatization concerns mostly the selling of government-owned assets. I restrict the use of the term to this latter definition.

12. A study by the consulting firm Mackinsey, reported that not only did restructuring increase the net value to shareholders, but that 80 per cent of the benefits were due to improvements in operations and only 20 per cent to the new financial structure. See Bergsma, Ennius, *Do-it-yourself Takeover Curbs*, Wall Street Journal, February 12, 1988.

13. See Drucker, Peter F, "Reckoning with the Pension Fund Revolution", Harvard Business Review, March April 1991. For evidence of activism, see Fromson, Brett Duval, *The Big Owners Roar*, Fortune, Vol. 122, No. 3, July 30, 1990, pp. 66-78. A related article in the same issue suggests that senior management is ready to accept more active institutional shareholders "Paré, Terence P., *Two Cheers for Pushy Investors*, pp. 95-98.

14. On this matter, I disagree with Michael Porter's prescription, which is a strict enforcement of antitrust laws, to the point of forbidding most cooperating ventures between competitors.

15. The argument is advanced in its most pungent form in the case of Japan in the late nineteenth century. The take-off of industrialization is credited partly to the modernization of the educational system undertaken in the later part of the nineteenth century. Whether there were simultaneous events or there was a causal link will never be clearly established. But there are sufficient counter examples to demonstrate that education does not necessarily precede economic growth, and often is a consequence of economic growth, to dispute the causal effect. Edward Denison's work on economic growth is also advanced to bolster the case of education as

an economic lever. What is forgotten is that Denison labelled the residual component of the equation that explains economic growth as the contribution of education and of the general increase in knowledge. (See Denison, E., *The Sources of Economic Growth in the United States and the Alternatives Before Us*, London, Allen and Unwin, 1962). That residual label could also have been labelled the contribution of the ingenuity of entrepreneurs and managers who have found better ways of making better products and services.

16. For a summary of the evidence, see Constantatos, Christos and West, Edwin G.: *"Measuring Returns from Education: Some Neglected Factors"* Canadian Public Policy, Vol. 17, No 2., June 1991, pp 127-138.

17. The data on R&D was taken from Roark, Anne C.: *Research Emphasis is Military*, Los Angeles Times, Sunday April 12, 1987.

18. Furthermore, there is evidence that the relationship between R&D intensity and productivity gains is tenuous at best. Capital investments, as opposed to R&D, seem to drive productivity. See Griliches, Z. and Mairesse, J., *R&D and Productivity Growth: Comparing Japanese and U.S. Manufacturing Firms*, NBER Working Paper 1778, Cambridge, National Bureau of Economic Research, 1985.

CHAPTER FIFTEEN

1. Ohmae, Kenichi, *"The Borderless World"*, Harper Business, New York, 1990.

2. Courchesne, Thomas J., *"Global Competitiveness and the Canadian Federation"*, School of Policies Studies, Queen's University, Kingston, Ont., 1990.

3. Predictions about the demise of the nation-state are old hat and indeed, hard to defend. Nationalism is thriving throughout the world, sustaining the nation-state. What we are discussing in this chapter is the decling economic role of the nation-state. Indeed, nation-states which were glued together for economic reasons, as many multi-ethnic nation-states, are becoming much more fragile.

4. This can be set up as an external-internal validity issue. Management strategies and practices can insure internal validity. But external validity is not guaranteed. In rapidly changing environments, internal validity is insufficient to cope with industry challenges, as new, unpredictable, significant elements are continuously integrated into the relevant performance assessment set.

5. Kennedy, Paul, *The Rise and Fall of Great Powers*, New York,

Random House, 1987.

6. One may argue that the First World War, the Second World War and the simmering Cold War do not suggest that military power is falling into disuse to settle conflicts among the most advanced economies. Paul Keegan, the noted military historian, draws our attention to a sensible explanation for these military adventures which has temporarily over-shadowed the relentless progress of the rule of law to resolve conflicts between advanced economies. Since the latter part of the nineteenth century, the growing economic capacity of industrial economies has allowed their military and political establishments to build military arsenals of a size unimaginable a few centuries ago. That these arsenals would get out of control and be put to use was not unexpected. So we had the Two World Wars. Lessons were learned, this was demonstrated by the Cold War. Indeed, military solutions have disappeared as relevant solutions to international conflicts among industrial countries. The arsenals should gradually fade in relative importance, as they get less and less used and countries experiment with other conflict resolution mechanisms.

7. This argument is best laid out by Rosenberg, Nathan and Burdzell, L. E. *How the West Grew Rich*, Basic Books, New York, 1986. For a cogent summary of their argument, see Rosenberg, Nathan and Birdzell, L.E. Jr., *Science, Technology and the Western Miracle*, Scientific American, Vol. 263, No. 5, November 1990, pp. 42- 55.

8. Surprisingly, most "developing countries" do not offer such conditions. Consumers, which have more political clout than producers, are unduly favoured by subsidies and price controls. The basic industries are state-owned, imports are severely controlled, the financial sector is atrophied or nationalized, prices are distorted by controls, tariffs and quotas, and entrepreneurship is discouraged by taxation, corruption and bureaucratic shenanigans. Their poor economic performance is easy to understand.

9. Kohr, Leopold, *"The Breakdown of Nations"*, Dutton, New York, 1978.

CHAPTER SIXTEEN

1. The projection assumes a 1 per cent growth rate per capita for the most advanced economy and superior catch-up rates of 5 per cent for the rest of the world. I consider 1 per cent per capital to be a very conservative estimate, and it should be easily attained provided that there is no cataclysmic war. A more probable estimate of the growth rate per capital

would be 1.5 per cent, yielding a 4.4 x rise in per capita income over the century. Even a 2 per cent growth is within the possibilities. The population of the earth is estimated to reach 12 billion in 2087, a somewhat generous projection. There is no doubt that mankind can produce the food to nourish adequately such a population. Providing 4 to 6 times the present level of food is well within the range of estimates for potential food production. The energy needed implies that new sources are tapped, namely fusion power and solar power. No material shortages are foreseen, as even modest increases in price would bring a significant amount of exploitation of low yield deposits and more recycling. Indeed, the problem of the 2087 society will not be associated with material discomfort but with managing the social neurosis of a well-to-do society. For an analysis of the material possibilities, see Simon, Julian, and Kahn, Herman, eds, *The Resourceful Earth*, Oxford, Baric Blackwell, 1984. See also Singer, Max, *Passage to a Human World*, Indianapolis, Hudson Institute, 1987

Index

Index

Index